D0277073

HARRY REDKNAPP

THE BIOGRAPHY

LES ROOPANARINE

JOHN BLAKE

Published by John Blake Publishing Ltd,
3 Bramber Court, 2 Bramber Road,
London W14 9PB, England

www.johnblakepublishing.co.uk

First published in hardback in 2010

ISBN: 978-1-84454-806-4

British Library Cataloguing-in-Publication Data:

A catalogue record for this book is available from the British Library.

Design by www.envydesign.co.uk

Printed in Great Britain by CPI William Clowes, Beccles, NR34 7TL

1 3 5 7 9 10 8 6 4 2

Papers used by John Blake Publishing are natural, recyclable
products made from wood grown in sustainable forests. The
manufacturing processes conform to the environmental
regulations of the country of origin.

To Elizabeth McFarland – still, always – and to

my mother, Joan Roopanarine.

Contents

Acknowledgements

A huge debt of gratitude is owed to the friends, former team-mates and other professional associates of Harry Redknapp who gave freely of their time to be interviewed for this book, including: Kenny Allen, John Best, Richard Cooke, Leon Crouch, Tommy Docherty, Jimmy Gabriel, Trevor Hartley, Bobby Howe, Alan Hudson, Peter Jeffs, Rupert Lowe, Milan Mandaric, Rodney Marsh, Alvin Martin, Jim McAlister, Wilf McGuinness, Dejan Stefanovic, Ian Thompson and John Williams.

Thanks are due also to Nick Callow, who got the ball rolling, and Allie Collins of John Blake, who was patient and supportive throughout. Nicola Benn, Paul Edwards, Stephen Farmer, Wendy Hardy, Dick Hookway, Howard Nurse, Joanna Olszowska, Nick Pitt and Paul Vanes all provided much appreciated help in terms of contacts or research material. Particular thanks to Frank MacDonald of Seattle Sounders for his invaluable assistance in helping me to track down various contacts Stateside.

Several written resources were helpful in terms of research and reference. They include: *My Autobiography*, by Harry Redknapp (with Derek McGovern); *The West Ham United Football Book*, by Dennis Irving; *NASL: A Complete Record of the North American Soccer League*, by Colin Jose; *Sleeping Giant Awakes* and *Stay Up Pompey!* by Pat Symes; *Bonzo*, by Billy Bonds; goalseattle.com; and the 1974 and 1978 editions of the *Seattle Sounders Media Guide*. A wider debt is owed to the exhaustive chronicling of Harry's life and times by friends and colleagues in the national and regional press.

I would like to thank several people who have had a shaping influence on my career to date: at the *Observer*, Brian Oliver and Roger Alton; Peter Mitchell and Jim Bruce-Ball of the *Sunday Telegraph*; and everyone on the guardian.co.uk sports desk. Particular thanks also to Jon Henderson for numerous kindnesses.

Of the many others whose generous assistance contributed either directly or indirectly to this book, three deserve special mention. Tim Haynes put me back on the road to journalism after a lengthy spell pursuing alternative interests, for which I shall always be grateful. Andrew Truscott has been an unfailingly stimulating source of debate on all things sporting. Above all, without the love, support and encouragement of Elizabeth McFarland, this book would still be in extra-time.

Introduction

Bournemouth had made a so-so start to the 1982/83 season. By the time the conkers bounced, Dave Webb's side were already occupying the mid-table area in which they would remain for the rest of the campaign. Now it is October and Harry Redknapp, Webb's number two at Dean Court, is driving back to the club's West Parley training ground after watching a reserve game at Southampton. Still a couple of months away from his first foray into management, he is mulling over the players he has just seen, wondering if any might do a job for Bournemouth. Redknapp is approaching the Eastleigh turn-off when he notices that the car behind is flashing him. 'At first I thought it was the Old Bill,' he would say later. 'When I saw it wasn't I kept driving, but the geezer stayed behind me.' They reach some traffic lights, and the car draws up alongside Redknapp. 'Pull over,' says the driver, 'I want to have a word with you.' They stop at the next lay-by. As the man gets out and starts walking in his direction, Redknapp winds down his window.

'How much do you want for your number plate?' asks the stranger.

'What?' stammers Redknapp.

'Yeah, how much? It's my initials.'

'Harry sold his number plate to him for about three hundred quid,' recalls Kenny Allen, Bournemouth's goalkeeper at the time. 'It could only happen to Harry. He obviously didn't have the wealth then that he's got now. That was him, always had an eye for a bargain. Now he does it with players, and turns them into decent players.'

Fast-forward to the last Sunday of October, 2008. Much has changed. Football is awash with unprecedented wealth and Redknapp, his Third Division days long since consigned to sepia, has established a reputation as one of the finest English managers of his generation. He is not the only one whose circumstances have changed. Ten weeks into the new season, Tottenham – a club that finished the 1982/83 campaign fourth in the old First Division – are bottom of the table with two points from eight games. Only two sides have ever retained their Premier League status from a similar position. Crucially for Spurs, however, one thing remains unaltered: Redknapp's relationship with the unexpected. The day before, he had been the manager of Portsmouth. Now, after a whirlwind sequence of events – and with a league game against Bolton minutes from kick-off – he is about to be presented to White Hart Lane as the successor to Juande Ramos, the Spaniard given his marching orders late the previous evening. At £5 million, the sum Tottenham have paid Portsmouth in compensation for his services, Redknapp has become – overnight – Britain's most expensive manager.

Driving one minute, dealing the next; Portsmouth manager on Saturday, in charge at Tottenham come Sunday. Such are the natural rhythms of life for one of football's most whimsical characters. And to think that for the best part of two decades Redknapp took charge of just two clubs, Bournemouth and West Ham.

Suit-and-tie dapper, Redknapp emerges from the tunnel to the inquisitive glare of a battery of flash-bulbs and the sonorous roar of a capacity crowd. Briefly, he stands by the touchline, arms raised, returning the warm applause of the crowd. If this was politics or showbiz, you would swear the scene had been choreographed. Yet Redknapp's demeanour – the head-bowed entrance, the awkward half-smile – hints at anxiety. Within twenty seconds, he turns on his heel and disappears into the bowels of the West Stand.

'I didn't sleep much,' Redknapp would reveal afterwards, 'I was very nervous.' No wonder. Only twenty-four hours earlier, he had been overseeing training at the Wellington Ground in Eastleigh, preparing Portsmouth for a visit from Fulham. Thereafter events had moved with such speed that uncertainty swirled even within his own, famously tight-knit family. 'We didn't know anything about it,' Mark Redknapp, the older of Harry's two sons, told friends. 'He just came home on Saturday and told mum he was off. He's always fancied a go at one of the big clubs; all of a sudden it was bang, "I'm off to Spurs." You know what dad's like.'

Of course they knew. It could only happen to Harry.

The surreal nature of the weekend is underlined by

events on the pitch. Within seventeen minutes, a Tottenham side previously brittle of confidence and blunt of edge has taken the lead against Bolton through Roman Pavlyuchenko. That in itself is remarkable. Having failed to score in the Premier League following his summer arrival from Spartak Moscow, the Russian had been branded an expensive flop. Now, skilfully fed by David Bentley – another costly but hitherto anonymous newcomer – he is belatedly displaying the predatory instincts befitting of a £13.8 million striker. The biggest revelation is Luka Modric, the little Croatian who, revelling in the freedom afforded by Redknapp's decision to play him in a more advanced role, suddenly looks like a player with magic in his boots rather than concrete.

That is more than can be said for the Spurs goalkeeper, Heurelho Gomes. More than any other player, Gomes has epitomised Tottenham's season-long travails. Today is no exception; colliding with Ledley King, flapping at corners and clearing ineffectually, Gomes looks about as reliable as an MP's expenses form. No matter. Bolton fail to capitalise on the Brazilian's blundering, and when Gavin McCann is dismissed shortly after the interval, you begin to sense that it will be Tottenham's day. So it proves, Darren Bent winning and converting a penalty within minutes of replacing Pavlyuchenko. Spurs have their first victory of the campaign; Redknapp has achieved within hours what Ramos could not in over two months.

This, of course, is a major part of what Harry Redknapp does: goes into struggling clubs, lifts confidence, turns things around. He has always had the qualities that underpin this victory, the tactical intelligence, the gift for squeezing maximum benefit from the resources at his disposal, the commitment to expressive football. Even so, this game is different. Special. It is an instant and emphatic response to a question that no chairman of a leading club has previously thought to ask: to wit, what might Redknapp achieve given the opportunity to work with top players in their prime? That it has taken until now to start finding out is and isn't a surprise. Dyed-in-the-wool football men have always recognised Redknapp's talent. But those who do the hiring and firing are never dyed-in-the-wool football men. It is a curious footnote to Redknapp's career that he was fifty-seven by the time he was first appointed as a manager from without, rather than promoted from within. That was at Southampton – and even there he arrived contrary to the wishes of the club chairman, Rupert Lowe. It is fair to say that a man who conquered Manchester United as Bournemouth manager, led West Ham into Europe and won the FA Cup with Portsmouth has not always been properly appreciated.

After a lengthy round of handshakes, a triumphant Redknapp heads for the tunnel. Many months have passed since the Lane was last in such good voice. But while the Tottenham fans have spent much of the afternoon urging their new manager to give them a wave – ever the populist, he does not disappoint – down on the south coast they are singing a different refrain. 'Who the fuck is Harry Redknapp?' Fratton Park demands to know after Peter Crouch has temporarily given Portsmouth the lead against Fulham. For several of Redknapp's former charges, the more pertinent question is: where.

'Some players came to the ground and only heard Harry had left when they arrived,' reveals the Portsmouth defender Sylvain Distin after a 1-1 draw. 'I only found out on the internet in the morning of the game, but that was quite a surprise. It happened so late on Saturday night that most of us had gone to bed preparing for the game. Some people bought a newspaper on the way to the game, but others just came to the ground and found out when they were told. That might seem strange, but that's the way football works.'

It is certainly the way Redknapp works. Those who know him of old have come to expect the unexpected; the switch to Spurs, and the turnaround that followed, were nothing out of the ordinary. 'If it had been someone else, I'd have been surprised,' says Trevor Hartley, who played alongside Redknapp at West Ham and Bournemouth and later went on to become Tottenham's assistant manager. 'But it was Harry. It's just him. If people take Harry, they probably expect something to happen – and it did.'

No one was less taken aback than Dejan Stefanovic, the former Portsmouth captain. 'I knew that, in private, he wanted to manage Tottenham one day,' says Stefanovic. 'We had a bit of a chat three or four years ago, we were in his office. He said: "The only [other] club I want to manage is Spurs." I asked him why and he just said it was because it was a good club and he grew up in London, that kind of stuff. You can see what's happened with Tottenham in the last year. They were bottom of the league, but as soon as he came into the club he turned it around and Tottenham nearly played

European football again. He's done some magical things at every club he's been at.'

For all his thaumaturgy, Redknapp – unlike the game that has been life – has never forgotten where he came from. As football has become increasingly money-obsessed, its participants ever more remote from the people who pay to watch them, Redknapp has remained – resolutely, unwaveringly – the archetypal East Ender. Plain old 'Arry. He has the common touch, and that quality – allied with an irrepressible wit – has made him popular throughout the football world. Unlike other managers, Redknapp speaks the language of the man in the stands. Rafael Benitez or Arsène Wenger would never send on a substitute with the immortal instruction to 'fucking run around a bit', as Redknapp did with Pavlyuchenko when Tottenham beat Liverpool shortly after his arrival, but in the cheap seats such exhortations are a stock-in-trade.

As Rodney Marsh, who has known Redknapp since they were both teenagers, puts it: 'Even today, with all the accolades and success that he's had, Harry is a real person. He talks the same way now as he did when he was nineteen, he's still got the same self-deprecating manner. It's rare in today's football. He'd be the first person to say "That was a cock up, I shouldn't have made that substitution." Equally, as a player, if he hit a cross behind the goal he wouldn't look at the pitch as though it was the ground's fault, he would be more like, "What a wally, I've just missed a cross." In today's football, everybody is looking for a way out, nobody wants to take any responsibility. But Harry is the type that looks you in the face and tells you it how it is.'

A Tuesday afternoon at the Guildhall in Portsmouth. Nothing is ever routine in the life of Harry Redknapp, and today is no exception. Forty-eight hours have passed since the Bolton game, and Redknapp is back on the south coast to receive the Freedom of the City after bringing the FA Cup back to Portsmouth for the first time since 1939. The timing is unfortunate, to say the least. Redknapp shifts awkwardly in his seat on the auditorium stage as the assembled councillors joke about his spell at Southampton, the rival Hampshire club to which he defected after leaving Portsmouth first time round. Directly in front of him is the squad of players that he left behind three days earlier. He eyes them intently, as a racehorse trainer might peruse a stable of thoroughbreds. In time, Jermain Defoe, Peter Crouch and Niko Kranjcar will join him at White Hart Lane. For now, the pomp-and-circumstance preliminaries finally at an end, it is time for Redknapp to speak. For the second time in as many days, he must satisfy the demands of an expectant crowd. The potential for a hostile reception is clear; he has already been barracked on the way into the building. No one quite knows how the next couple of minutes will unfold.

'Mr Mayor, ladies and gentlemen,' Redknapp begins, 'my timing has never been very good and certainly this week it couldn't have been worse, I realise that.' There is a ripple of gentle laughter; so far, so good. He is greatly honoured, he says. Only part of a team. Had fantastic support. The club has fantastic fans, an amazing football team. Redknapp is heckled a couple of times, but it is a polished performance. He returns to his seat to the sound of thunderous applause. The old boy has done it again.

'Harry is like that,' says Stefanovic. 'He keeps things simple but he's an exciting person – for the media, for players, and for supporters. He's totally different to other managers in England.'

Totally different: that, in a nutshell, is Harry Redknapp. Ordinary bloke. Extraordinary life.

Chapter One

Bill Nicholson fixed his gaze on the scrawny, slightly breathless eleven-year-old. The young trialist had been up early that morning, excited at the prospect of parading his skills before Nicholson, the recently appointed Tottenham manager. Now, having done so, he looked up at the stern, slightly intimidating Yorkshireman with a mixture of awe and unease. Nicholson, a one-club man, was well known for his view that any player coming to Spurs, whether a major signing or just a ground-staff lad, 'must be dedicated to the game and to the club.' The youngster qualified on the first front – how could he not? His father, Harry, was a football obsessive, and so it followed naturally that his own upbringing had been steeped in the game and its traditions. But Nicholson's second stipulation left him on shakier ground. The boy shared his dad's passion for Arsenal, idolised Gunners midfielder Jimmy Bloomfield and was a regular at Highbury, where he would arrive early to claim his favourite spot – on top of a raised manhole cover – on the North Bank. Hardly the ideal credentials for a career at White Hart Lane. As for other clubs, if any had a place in his affections it was West Ham, whose Upton Park ground was a stone's throw from the East London council estate where he lived. Could he seriously look Nicholson in the eye and proclaim his undying devotion to Spurs?

'What's your name, son?' asked Nicholson.

'Harry, Mr Nicholson.'

'OK, Harry. I see you're a winger. Score a lot of goals, do you?'

'Not really, sir.'

'Well, the only winger who doesn't score goals is Stanley Matthews. And I don't think you're another Stanley Matthews, are you Harry?'

Fifty years have elapsed since that conversation took place and, as with most things football, Nicholson was proved right. Harry Redknapp didn't become another Stanley Matthews. He was never dubbed 'the wizard of the dribble' or voted European Footballer of the Year. Yet Dickie Walker, Tottenham's chief scout, showed sound judgement when he approached Redknapp's father after watching young Harry star for East London Schoolboys against Wandsworth Boys at the Old Den. Five years later, when Redknapp became old enough to put pen to paper on schoolboy forms, every top club in London was after his signature. Nicholson, who invited Redknapp to train with the Spurs youth team following his trial, was among those suitors, as were the Arsenal boss George Swindin and Tommy Docherty, the Chelsea manager. Docherty, who had been alerted to young

CHAPTER ONE

Harry's potential by Chelsea scout Jimmy Thompson, even made a personal visit to the Redknapps' home in Poplar in an effort to persuade them that their son's future lay at Stamford Bridge. 'I wanted Harry to sign for Chelsea,' recalls Docherty, whose unexpected appearance on the doorstep left the teenage Redknapp agog. 'In those days you used to speak to the parents. You wouldn't speak to the boy because, in fairness, he was just overawed by big clubs wanting to sign him. Harry's parents were very pleasant and hospitable. At the end they said: "The decision will be Harry's." We had a few Eastenders at Chelsea already, people like Jimmy Greaves and Terry Venables, and we were hoping to tap into that link because they had great character. But we also had Peter Brabrook at Chelsea at the time, who was a good player, a winger, and Harry probably thought "I'm going to have to wait a bit of time before I get my opportunity in the first team".'

The decisive factor in Redknapp's eventual decision to join West Ham was his mother, Violet. While she did not share her husband's passion for the game, Violet instinctively perceived that the Hammers, under the shrewd stewardship of Ron Greenwood, embodied principles that would benefit her son's development not just as a footballer but also as a man. West Ham was a family club, an East End institution forged on the anvil of a local businessman's conviction that the borough, though poverty-stricken, was 'rich in its population'. Arnold Hills, the businessman in question, had once owned the Thames Ironworks, a nearby shipbuilding firm that provided numerous locals with employment at the Victoria and Albert Docks where Redknapp's father worked. Hills died in 1927, but Thames Ironworks Football Club – formed in 1895 at the suggestion of Dave Taylor, a shipyard foreman, and reconstituted five years later as West Ham United Football Club – lived on. A pivotal factor in Hills' support for the project was his belief that sport was conducive to good morals and good morale. As a modern ambassador for those typically Victorian ideals, Greenwood – dubbed 'Reverend Ron' by his players – was perfect. To Violet Redknapp, though, such details were secondary; to her, the club simply had a family feel that inspired comfort and confidence in equal measure.

Greenwood invited the Redknapps to attend West Ham youth games, and by the time a decision needed to be taken about Harry's footballing future, there was little doubt where the teenager was headed. 'They were Hammers through and through,' remembers Docherty, who had little reason to suspect the Redknapps' Arsenal affiliation. 'Harry was an East End lad and he was a Hammers lad. He was a terrific kid and an outstanding player, an out-and-out outside right or attacking winger. I always said that, when Harry finished playing football, he would become a manager, because he loves the game and he loves his players to love the game. He loves his players to go out and entertain the people that pay his salary, the supporters. And that's why Harry has always produced good players and good teams. To this day, when I see Harry looking for a player, I know he's looking for a player with a lot of flair and imagination. It's always been a characteristic of his and he's never lost that.'

It is a characteristic of which the late Bill Nicholson

doubtless approved. 'No matter how football changes,' Nicholson once said, 'the fundamentals will always apply. Nothing can be achieved without individual ability.' As the architect of the dazzling Spurs side that in 1961 became the first modern Double winners, Nicholson was the ultimate football purist. 'It's no use winning,' he would tell his bemused players, 'we've got to win well.' Today, in an era when football is ruled by money, few managers outside the elite can afford such high-minded principles. Redknapp comes closer than most. His reign as West Ham manager was notable for its embodiment of the belief that losing with style is better than winning without it. Had Nicholson lived to see Redknapp's ascent to the White Hart Lane throne, he might have recognised in the former trialist, if not exactly a kindred spirit, then at least a man noteworthy for his determination to marry attacking football with the more pragmatic aspects of the modern game.

Then again, Nicholson could no more have imagined that the young boy he first met that winter's morning in 1958 would one day be his successor than Redknapp could have envisaged that, half a century on, he would make the best start to a managerial reign at White Hart Lane for one hundred and ten years. 'I'm certainly not the best boss in a hundred and ten years for Tottenham,' said Redknapp on achieving that milestone. 'I couldn't lace Bill Nicholson's boots.' Maybe not, but Redknapp's initial impact at White Hart Lane was hardly less dramatic that that of the man who marked his first match as manager by leading a team flirting with relegation to a celebrated 10-4 win against Everton. The

Bolton win was followed by a 4-4 draw at Arsenal, Redknapp's first official game in charge, which had the *Guardian*'s David Lacey recalling 'the unfettered football Spurs produced in Nicholson's first season as manager.' The same cavalier spirit was evident throughout the six-game unbeaten run that got Redknapp's tenure underway; with five wins, and eighteen goals scored, few doubted that Nicholson's legacy was in good hands.

It will do little harm to Redknapp's standing among Tottenham fans that he also possesses certain other qualities redolent of Nicholson. Most notably, he has something of the great man's celebrated ability to build teams amounting to more than the sum of their individual parts. Like his illustrious predecessor, Redknapp is universally recognised – within the game, if not always outside it – as a shrewd judge of players and their abilities. 'Harry has a wonderful eye for talent and a wonderful eye for seeing how that talent would fit into his existing squad of players,' says Bobby Howe, who signed professional forms at Upton Park a few months before Redknapp's arrival in 1963 and subsequently worked alongside him, as a player and coach, for over fifteen years. The powers of appraisal identified by Howe are partly the legacy of the countless hours Redknapp spent watching football as a child. If he was not kicking a ball around with friends outside the family's Barchester Street home, he was usually on the touchline cheering on his dad, a talented local-league player, as he demonstrated his skills at inside forward.

Redknapp also witnessed at first hand the value of

hard graft. Harry Snr's dockyard income was supplemented by his mother's work in a cake factory and as a daybreak office cleaner. Their zeal instilled in Redknapp a work ethic that provides another point of contact with Nicholson, whose early starts and burning of the midnight oil are the stuff of White Hart Lane legend. Redknapp, who resides on the exclusive Sandbanks peninsula in Dorset, regularly leaves home for Tottenham's Chigwell-based training ground at half past five in the morning, prefacing the day's toil with a tedious trawl around the M25. 'Beneath that laid back, cheeky exterior there's a man that works very, very hard,' says Howe. 'For me, that's the most important aspect of Harry's success, because he's always looking for the next step, always looking ahead and trying to gain an advantage. And he was like that from day one.'

In other respects, Redknapp, with his sharp wit and natural exuberance, could hardly be more dissimilar to his relatively strait-laced predecessor. Nicholson, who grew up during the Great Depression as the second youngest of nine children, was an inherently austere character. Conversely, Redknapp is an only child and a congenital gambler. The latter quality has served him well throughout his football career. As John Williams, the imposing centre-half who later became a mainstay of Redknapp's Bournemouth side, explains: 'If you're getting beaten or it's nil-nil and they're having a right go at you and you can't get out defensively, Harry's more likely to turn it the other way round and put a forward or a winger on and try and get out of it that way. He won't put a sweeper on and try to defend. That's not the way he is. He's a very offensive manager, and that's why

I think, if you look at his record, he tends to win or lose rather than draw.'

Harry Redknapp was born in Poplar, East London, on March 2, 1947, when post-war Britain was in the grip of a snow-swept, bitterly cold winter and a national power crisis. Neither of his parents were betting people and it was Maggie Brown, his maternal grandmother, who implanted the gambling gene in the young Harry's DNA. A bookies' runner, she would welcome her grandson home from school – both Harry Snr and Violet were out working – with a hot meal and a copy of the lunchtime paper. Never mind that Redknapp was too young to read: he would make his random selections with a pin, and they would later be collected by Cyril, the septuagenarian paper boy who doubled as an illegal bookmaker. It was the ideal preparation for the West Ham dressing room, where gambling – be it on dogs, cards or horses – was a way of life.

Trevor Hartley, who played alongside Redknapp in his early days at West Ham, soon came to recognise the depth of his team-mate's love for the turf. 'We played in a Metropolitan League match at Chadwell Heath one afternoon in 1965,' recalls Hartley. 'It was the day of the Grand National. I was playing up front, and I was waiting for Harry to come down flying down the right wing. After fifteen minutes, I hadn't even seen him. "What's Harry doing?" I asked someone. I looked round, and he was hanging about by the halfway line listening to someone's radio, trying to find out where his horse was placed. In the dressing room at half-time, he was up. One of the lads said to him: "How'd your horse get on?" Harry said: "It won, it won!" He bombed on

CHAPTER ONE

for the rest of the game.' Billy Bonds, the overlapping full-back whose right-wing partnership with Redknapp became an important weapon in West Ham's armoury, remembers his former team-mate as the wiliest member of the club's card school. 'Harry was always a slippery customer – so much so, in fact, that we called him The Fox,' wrote Bonds in his 1988 autobiography, *Bonzo*. In the same volume Bonds also recalls Redknapp's dismay at the implementation of a spot-check system designed to weed out the school's more inventive players. 'If you won't take my word for it I'm not cheating,' stormed Redknapp on the train journey back from an away match, 'I'll sling the cards out of the window.' Pressed by fellow youth product Peter Bennett, Redknapp soon proved that he was in earnest. 'That was Harry in those days,' muses Hartley.

Despite such antics, Redknapp soon established himself as a real prospect. The West Ham youth set-up he joined at sixteen was among the best in the country. It had been established a little over a decade earlier by former manager Ted Fenton, who recognised that the club's inability to compete with the major players in the transfer market necessitated a greater emphasis on homegrown talent. Within months of Redknapp's arrival, the youngsters gave further lustre to West Ham's reputation as one of the game's foremost talent factories by winning the FA Youth Cup. It looked an unlikely outcome when, having suffered a 3-1 defeat to Liverpool in the first leg of the final, the Hammers found themselves 2-1 down by half-time in the second. But a four-goal salvo from Martin Britt, who reaped the benefits of a skilled supply line led by Redknapp and fellow winger Johnny Sissons, left Greenwood 'over the moon' and the young Harry in possession of his first medal. Two days later he collected a second as West Ham's youngsters claimed Chelsea's scalp in the final of the London Minor Cup. 'We had a fantastic first year, and to win the FA Youth Cup at the end of it was great,' recalls Howe. 'We had an excellent youth team with good balance and some really good players, including Harry. For me, Harry was a typical right winger. He wasn't a wide right midfield player by any stretch of the imagination, he was an out and out winger, with much more attacking flair than defensive prowess. One of his greatest assets was his ability to cross the ball. I would say that, in his prime, he was one of the best crossers of the ball in England, from the right side. His left foot needed a bit of work, but with a right foot like that he didn't really need to use his left too much. I would say that you'd have to compare Harry to [David] Beckham when it came to crossing.'

It was around that time that Rodney Marsh, then of Queens Park Rangers, first met Redknapp at The Two Puddings, a pub in Stratford. He remembers his new pal as 'a skinny right-winger, a bit of a flying machine. If you threw someone a live hand grenade and asked them to run with it, that's the way Harry played. He went on the outside a lot and he was very fast. But it was all so quick and scatterbrainish. That was his way of playing – it wasn't about control and getting the ball down, it was a case of running with it, all scurry, scurry.'

Redknapp's dynamism may sometimes have erred on the side of over-enthusiasm, but Wilf McGuinness, who managed Redknapp and his England team-mates to victory in the 1964 Junior World Cup in Holland, paints an alternative picture of the seventeen-year-old. 'He was gifted, the lad,' says McGuinness. 'Harry was our tricky winger. He's still tricky, but he's not a winger! He was very talented, tremendous on the ball, and he was a good outlet. You could say that he was one of the star players. We won the competition – which they used to call the Little World Cup, because the South Americans hadn't really joined in then – and he played every game. I was fortunate to be around Harry when he was growing up, because I saw the fun side of him. He's still like that now, of course, but he's got more serious because the job calls for him to be serious at times.'

While the teenage Redknapp was embellishing his CV in Amsterdam, his senior counterparts were dining out on the most significant result in West Ham's history.   A 3-2 win over Preston North End in the FA Cup final gave Greenwood's men the club's first major trophy and a place in Upton Park folklore. The roll of honour included Peter Brabrook, the very player whose presence at Stamford Bridge had, in Tommy Docherty's view, contributed to Redknapp's decision to turn down Chelsea. The England winger was a significant obstacle. Having lost out to Chelsea in the race for Brabrook's signature nearly a decade earlier, West Ham lavished £35,000 to bring the East Ender home in 1962. Consequently, while Johnny Sissons, who played on the opposite flank to Redknapp in the Youth Cup triumph of 1963, progressed so rapidly that twelve months later he became the youngest-ever scorer in a senior final, Redknapp – who was eighteen months younger – had to bide his time. Another season passed – during which West Ham claimed more silverware, beating TSV Munich to lift the European Cup-Winners' Cup – before Redknapp made his long-awaited senior debut. In the interim, he won the best player award at the Augsberg International Youth Tournament in West Germany, where the Hammers kept the trophy after winning the event for the third successive season. Now eighteen, Redknapp was closing on a first-team call up.

His chance finally came on August 23, 1965. With Sunderland the visitors to the Boleyn Ground and the forward trio of Brian Dear, Johnny Byrne and Alan Sealey all ruled out by injury, Greenwood handed Redknapp his first league start. He took the opportunity with trademark alacrity. With just four minutes gone, Redknapp floated a corner onto the forehead of Martin Peters, who nodded home to draw first blood in a 1-1 draw. Five days later, Redknapp hit the woodwork as title contenders Leeds were beaten 2-1 at Upton Park. Appearances against Sunderland, Leicester and Nottingham Forest followed before Redknapp was again demoted to the sidelines.

History repeated itself the following April, an injury crisis again handing Redknapp a crack at the first team. He once more made the most of his chance, setting up West Ham's only goal in another 1-1 draw, this time against Burnley, before cementing his growing popularity with the West Ham support by scoring his first goal for the club in a 4-1 away win at White Hart

Lane. Redknapp returned to the bench for the remainder of the campaign, but Greenwood knew he had a player on his hands. Indeed, he had several. West Ham were beaten in the League Cup final by West Bromwich Albion, but four first-team regulars – Byrne, Peters, Geoff Hurst and Bobby Moore – were selected for Alf Ramsey's England World Cup squad. All but Byrne played in the final against West Germany on July 30. Hurst famously became the first player ever to score a hat-trick in a World Cup final, with two of his goals set up by Moore, the captain. Peters also made the scoresheet, rattling home the second in a historic 4-2 victory. England were world champions, and some of the key figures in the win were men with whom Redknapp brushed shoulders daily.

As Moore raised the Jules Rimet trophy skywards, he completed an extraordinary Wembley treble. In successive seasons, the twin towers had stood sentinel as he lifted the FA Cup, Cup-Winners' Cup and World Cup. Back in Stepney, Redknapp, who did not have a ticket for the final, was watching on television alongside his parents, a rapt observer bursting with pride. It wasn't just that West Ham had won the World Cup, as Alf Garnett never tired of reminding us afterwards. Moore was a close friend of Redknapp's, and would later have a defining influence on his career. Redknapp still regards the iconic image of Moore holding the Word Cup while being borne aloft by Hurst, Peters and Ray Wilson as sport's greatest image. Even then, long before he began routinely referring to the boy from Barking as 'God', Redknapp regarded Moore as football royalty. Their friendship began the day Redknapp set foot in Upton

Park and lasted until Moore's death in 1993. As was his way, Moore took the new recruit under his wing and – despite their obvious disparity in status – did everything possible to make him feel welcome at the club. That included inviting him to his house parties, where Redknapp's inherent vibrancy struck a natural chord with the gregarious company favoured by Moore.

A regular at such gatherings was Rodney Marsh, who witnessed the camaraderie between Moore and Redknapp at first hand. 'They were very close,' recalls Marsh. 'Harry had all the time in the world for Bobby and thought that he was the greatest defender, if not the greatest player, of all time. I would concur with that. I always had the utmost admiration for Bobby Moore. Bobby was a gentleman in football and a gentleman in life. He was what I call inclusive. If Bobby was in the company of a dozen people, and one of them was the president of the United States and another was a cleaner at Upton Park, Bobby would treat them equally. We were round at his house many times, and there were always people there from all walks of life, some very colourful characters. It was a good time: we drunk a lot and we ate a lot and we laughed a lot, and Harry was at the forefront of all that.' The last detail is telling. Redknapp has long maintained that self-confidence is a prerequisite for success; that he was able to hold court in such distinguished company while still a teenager points to an intrinsic self-assurance.

'He's always had great belief in his ability, whatever he's done,' says Marsh. 'The best compliment I could pay Harry Redknapp is that he was one of the chaps. He was always up for having a drink and a laugh, and he'd talk football non-stop.' The impression of a chirpy, larger-than-life character is confirmed by McGuinness. 'He was very chatty,' says McGuinness. 'Coming from the north of England, I would call him a likable cockney. He was buzzy and we always encouraged that, because we felt it helped to create good team spirit.'

Bobby Howe, who likewise remembers Redknapp as the life and soul of the dressing room, believes that his former team-mate's natural charisma – allied with an innate football intelligence – has been central to his success as a manager. 'Harry was a real product of the East End,' says Howe. 'His wit and his story-telling were fantastic. He was also a prankster and incredibly street smart. He's maintained all those characteristics throughout his playing and managerial career, and undoubtedly the smarts that he brought to the game and has applied to his management career have really served him well.'

Of more immediate use to Redknapp were his on-field skills. He returned to the first eleven on December 3, 1966 and immediately picked up where he had left off, scoring the opening goal as West Bromwich Albion were beaten 3-0 at the Boleyn Ground. He did not feature again until the following February, but his return marked the beginning of an extended run in the side. A regular at number seven for most of the 1967/68 season, Redknapp notched up twenty-eight appearances, almost trebling his previous year's tally. The only hiccup came in late October, when Greenwood, exasperated by his side's defensive deficiencies, ditched Redknapp and Sissons and switched to a 4-3-3 system. 'They were both good attacking players,' recalls McGuinness, whose

England youth team also included Sissons, 'but the pair of them weren't known as great defenders.' Nevertheless, by mid-November both Redknapp and Sissons were back in West Ham's starting line-up, and it wasn't long before Greenwood was estimating the combined worth of his two wide boys at £150,000.

Whatever Redknapp's transfer value, he had certainly earned a special place in the fans' affections. 'Redknapp has been the idol of the Upton Park terraces since he was a boy,' wrote Dennis Irving in *The West Ham United Football Book* in 1968. 'Maybe it is because he is a local and can shift, maybe it is because his Dad works in the docks – anyway Harry Redknapp has that certain something for the West Ham crowd.' Marsh has no doubt about the reason for Redknapp's popularity. 'He was one of their own,' he observes, 'an East End boy playing in the East End.' That helped, but only up to a point. Later in Redknapp's West Ham career, when his form and confidence dipped, the fans' affections likewise waned. Ability, not background, was what counted most at the Boleyn Ground – not least in the eyes of Greenwood, who longed to see the Hammers' cup form translated into an improvement in their mid-table league status.

Redknapp's place in the team rested above all on his crossing expertise. Greenwood, a devoted admirer of the great Hungary team coached by Gusztav Sebes and captained by Ferenc Puskas, was a fascinated spectator at Wembley in November 1953 when the Mighty Magyars infamously inflicted a humiliating 6-3 defeat on England. He absorbed various lessons that day, not least the art of the near-post cross, a tactic he worked tirelessly to perfect at West Ham's Chadwell Heath training ground. Two posts were placed in large, concrete-filled paint tins and positioned out on the flanks. Time and again, Redknapp and his team-mates would be encouraged to bend the ball around these artificial markers and into the near-post area of the six yard box. 'Harry could hit it great near post,' recalls Howe. 'It was a less used tactic then. Everybody knows now the danger of playing balls in at the near post. Players know they've got to gamble and get in there, but we were doing it a little bit before our time. We did it a lot in training and we scored a great many goals from it. You had people like Geoff Hurst going in at the near post, and I think we were probably as good as – if not better than – any team in the country at hitting those balls. Harry was one of the best exponents of it.'

Redknapp's attacking brio and pinpoint delivery from the right wing placed him among the early upholders of what would become a proud playing tradition. 'In the fifties and early sixties West Ham developed a way of playing that has been their trademark ever since,' says Marsh, who had a brief spell at the club as a fifteen-year-old before the recruitment of a young rival named Hurst led to his departure for Fulham. 'Malcolm Musgrove, Phil Woosnam, Malcolm Allison, Ken Brown and others developed a certain way of playing; they wanted to play football. When Ron Greenwood took over that was carried through, and Harry was part of that. When you're involved in something like that, along with three World Cup winners in Bobby Moore, Martin Peters and Geoff Hurst, it rubs off. Being part of that system is a major part of what Harry Redknapp is today.'

Whether it is obscured by his natural ebullience – or by the popular perception of him as 'onest 'Arry, the East End wheeler-dealer making his way in a world of foreign sophisticates – Redknapp is too rarely given credit for this technical and tactical pedigree. When Greenwood died in February 2006, he was widely and rightly lauded as one of the game's great thinkers, a coaching visionary who brought flair and imagination to the game. Those qualities did not die with him. Redknapp is merely the most high-profile beneficiary of a legacy that has kept many of Greenwood's former charges in gainful employment. 'We all inherited certain qualities from Ron,' says Howe, who went on to become director of coaching for the United States Soccer Federation. 'He used to have an expression: simplicity is genius. Anybody who played for Ron would understand what that means: play the game simply and efficiently, play to your strengths. While he encouraged us to try to improve our performance in training and to expand our repertoire, he wouldn't encourage us to do that in games, he'd just want us to play to our strengths. I think that's the basis on which West Ham grew at that time. A lot of clubs back then concentrated on running. The ball was kept away from the players, with the theory being that it would make them hungry for the ball at the weekend. But Ron got us to do a lot of work with the ball, and so practices were always interesting. We did a tremendous amount of technical stuff in training, and I think that anybody who played through that era and went on to coach believed in that philosophy as well.'

Equally, Redknapp learned from Greenwood what not

to do. The memory of how Moore once complained to him of Greenwood's reluctance to offer praise or encouragement has become one of Redknapp's most frequently-recounted vignettes. 'The most important thing anyone ever said to me in football was what Bobby Moore said one day,' recalls Redknapp. 'He said he had sixteen years at West Ham under Ron Greenwood, the best coach I have seen without a doubt, but never in sixteen years did he give him a pat on the back and say well done. Mooro said to me: "Harry, we all need that." And that is a lesson I learned.' Small wonder, then, that an ability to lift players, to instil confidence and belief, has been so central to Redknapp's success. Results don't lie. Redknapp has masterminded Cup shocks against Manchester United with three different teams. He transformed Portsmouth from Championship strugglers to Premiership stayers. He wrought an instant upturn in the fortunes of a Tottenham side that had gone eight games without victory. It is a CV of genuine substance.

John Williams believes that Redknapp's empathetic handling of players has been central to these achievements. 'Harry was never one for the big Churchillian speech,' says Williams. 'He might speak collectively about how the team would play, but he was very keen after that to get stuck in to individuals. He would go round the changing room and have a quiet word with everyone individually. Once he'd spoken to you, you were concentrating and you didn't look up. But I'd imagine that after he'd gone from myself, he was whispering words of wisdom in somebody else's ear. So it was more a one-to-one thing than massive speeches, and I've heard that he still does that to this day.'

While Redknapp's ability to inspire is an aspect of his coaching acumen that owes little to Greenwood, it would be an injustice to suggest that he learned nothing about pastoral care from his mentor. Redknapp recalls an episode early in his West Ham career when a club official, eager to lock the gates, called time on an impromptu kickaround in the club car park involving himself, Bobby Moore and Frank Lampard Snr. Greenwood was not amused when he learned that his players had been turfed out. 'He told me that from then on, if we wanted to kick a ball around until midnight in that car park, that was fine,' recounted Redknapp in the *Mirror*. 'He said even if we finished playing in the middle of the night, he'd make sure there was someone there to lock the gates. He didn't want to do anything to stop us playing football. He loved the game and he loved seeing people who wanted to learn.'

Greenwood was similarly keen to see that the knowledge he imparted to his protégés was passed on to the next generation. To that end, he actively encouraged his players to obtain their coaching badges and to work at local schools. 'I went to West Ham in 1964, and in 1965 I took my preliminary badge with Bobby Howe,' recalls Trevor Hartley, who had acquired his full badge by the age of twenty-one and later became the Football League's youngest manager when he took over at Bournemouth. 'Ron used to encourage Bobby and I, instead of going to play golf in the afternoons, to coach at local schools. We ended up at the Holloway School in Islington with Bob Wilson from Arsenal and Mike England from Spurs. Ron thought that Bobby and myself would be the type to become coaches, and that helped us out because we grew in confidence while teaching the kids.' Redknapp benefited in similar fashion from the culture of learning established by Greenwood. 'Harry was one of the players that we took on the preliminary badge when John Lyall was coaching at West Ham under the auspices of Ron,' recounts Bobby Howe. 'I would have to say that Harry was one of the better coaches, even then – and it was a very long time ago.'

Having taken the first step along his future career path, Redknapp wasted no time in putting his new-found skills to use. Along with Frank Lampard Snr and John Bond, his future manager at Bournemouth, he spent four afternoons a week taking coaching sessions at a nearby school. 'When we had finished training,' recalls Redknapp, 'me and Frank Lampard [Snr] used to go to a place in Canning Town called Pretoria School. It was a tough place but it was Frank's old school and they had a lovely sports master called Dave Jones. We used to teach the kids and play a game of football in the gym. We loved it and as we were only on six pounds a week, two pounds fifty for the afternoon didn't half come in handy.' The experience instilled in Redknapp a commitment to youth development that has never left him. The legacy bore its richest fruit at West Ham, where Joe Cole, Rio Ferdinand, Frank Lampard and Michael Carrick all reaped the benefits of Redknapp's experience, progressing through West Ham's youth ranks en route to achieving international recognition and league titles. Lampard describes in his autobiography, *Totally Frank*, how Redknapp, together with Lampard Snr, 'nurtured young talent, encouraged it and then gave players a platform on which to develop', in the process ensuring that 'parents whose kids were coming through trusted the club to help their sons make the grade.'

While Greenwood no doubt applauded the efforts made by his former charge to restore West Ham's reputation as the Academy of Football, he was rather less appreciative of Redknapp's contribution to the cause on October 12, 1968. Half an hour into a league clash at Elland Road, Redknapp became involved in a contretemps with Billy Bremner, Leeds United's fearsomely competitive captain. Bremner turned up the temperature on a heated exchange by skimming Redknapp's shins with his studs, Redknapp retaliated, and Bremner went down as if shot by the proverbial sniper. 'It was a joke,' remembers Bonds in his autobiography. 'H never stuck one on anyone in his life – and if he tried his hardest could not have flattened Bremner the way the Leeds star dropped.' As the referee scribbled down his name, an incensed Redknapp could not hold his tongue. The result was a second yellow card, this time for dissent, and with it the dubious distinction of becoming only the second player dismissed during Greenwood's tenure. 'Obviously the club are upset about it,' said Greenwood after a 2-0 defeat. 'We have a proud record for behaviour on the field. You cannot go seven years without a player being sent off unless discipline is of a high standard. I am not forgiving Redknapp, but a young player does not kick out like that unless something has happened to him.'

The following week Redknapp bounced back in style, supplying the ammunition for Hurst to complete a double hat-trick as West Ham trounced Sunderland 8-0 to equal the biggest league win in their history. Hurst's third of the afternoon came from a Redknapp cross off Billy Bonds' short corner, while the England forward later swept home his sixth from a typically inviting Redknapp centre. A fortnight later, Redknapp completed his redemption in emphatic fashion. 'We played against QPR at Upton Park and Harry won it for us, 4-3, with a tremendous volley,' recalls Hartley. Redknapp reverted to his more customary role of provider either side of the New Year, winning a penalty at Southampton on Boxing Day before setting up Peters for a blistering half-volley as Newcastle were beaten 3-1 at the Boleyn Ground. By the season's end, he had racked up thirty-six performances in a side that finished eighth in the First Division.

Nonetheless, Redknapp's best result of the campaign – as his son, Jamie, has never been slow to remind him – came in pre-season. On June 30, 1968 Redknapp married Sandra Harris, an eighteen-year-old hairdresser from Essex, at St Margaret's Church, Barking. A staunch ally throughout the numerous highs and lows of her husband's career, Sandra is the unsung hero of the Harry Redknapp story. 'I think Sandra is the fortress behind Harry, to be honest,' says Milan Mandaric, the business tycoon whose takeover of Portsmouth would later have such significant implications for Redknapp. 'Sandra is tremendous for him, she's a pillar.'

Best man at the Redknapps' wedding was Frank Lampard Snr, who presided over the occasion on crutches after breaking his right leg against Sheffield Wednesday toward the season's end. Lampard proved an apt choice, for he later married Sandra's sister, the late Pat Harris. The couple had met four years earlier, shortly after Harry and Sandra began dating, and their marriage completed the foundation of a distinguished football dynasty. A serious ankle injury prematurely curtailed the development of Mark, the older of the two Redknapp boys. But Jamie, a cultured midfielder who signed for Tottenham as a teenager before deciding that he would be better off playing under his dad at Bournemouth, went on to reach the highest level. Jamie's Dean Court career was just thirteen league appearances old when Kenny Dalglish took him to Liverpool, where he would spend eleven years and become captain – as well as winning seventeen England caps – before seeing out his playing days at Spurs and Southampton. Jamie's cousin, Frank Lampard Jnr, boasts a still more impressive CV. After a difficult start to his career at West Ham, where a management team consisting of Uncle Harry and his father led to scurrilous accusations of nepotism, Lampard joined Chelsea, where he has amassed league and Cup silverware as well as a substantial increase on the two England caps won by his father.

That football runs in the family blood is something Redknapp never doubted. Convinced that his son would learn more valuable life lessons in the dressing room than the classroom, he regularly drove young Jamie to the Bournemouth training ground rather than dropping him off at school. The fourteen-year-old's skills made an abiding impression on John Williams, who could see even then that the youngster was destined for the top. 'I can remember Jamie joining in five-a-sides, and he was like third pick,' says Williams. 'The rest of us were just left on the side. It was an absolute cert that he was going to go on. He was a great kid. Mark's a lovely lad, too, although he doesn't get mentioned a lot. They're just a great family. They make you ever so welcome when you're in their home or in their company and it was an absolute pleasure to work with them. Just being around someone like Harry, who's been a manager in the game for over twenty-five years, has been really inspiring. Everything I've done in the game is down to him.'

Chapter Two

In the summer of 1972, £31,000 would have bought you four houses, a small fleet of cars or a flying winger named Harry Redknapp. The preference of John Bond, the Bournemouth manager, was never in doubt. With his E-type Jaguar, penchant for bling and preposterously large cigars, Bond had a flamboyance which made you suspect that houses and cars were to him mere trinkets. Of greater value to the man who seemingly had everything was a winger capable of providing Ted MacDougall, the club's talismanic goal poacher, with the precise service on which he would thrive. So it was that Redknapp was lured two tiers down the football pyramid, to the Third Division club recently renamed AFC Bournemouth because Bond felt that the club's original moniker, Bournemouth and Boscombe Athletic, was 'too old-fashioned.'

Rarely had the club spent so lavishly on one player, but the sense that Bournemouth were going places was strong. Bond had taken over at Dean Court two years earlier after a disastrous relegation campaign under his predecessor, Freddie Cox. It was the first time in history that the club had gone down, and the jaunty new boss was not a Division Four kind of guy. Bond had an instant impact, leading the Cherries out of the Football League's lowest tier at the first time of asking before narrowly failing to mastermind a second successive promotion. 'The idea was to try and turn us into a continental football club,' says Bond, 'so we changed the shirts [to red-and-black stripes reminiscent of Milan] and lots of other things. The players responded tremendously and the fans loved it as well. The crowds went from three thousand up to twenty thousand. It was unheard of.'

A key element in Bournemouth's success was the lethal marksmanship of MacDougall, a future Scotland international. The November before Redknapp's arrival, MacDougall earned himself a place in the record books by scoring nine goals against Margate in a first round FA Cup game. At a time when the difference in standard between the lower divisions and the top-flight was nowhere near as great as it is today, Bond knew that providing MacDougall with an effective supply-line could take Bournemouth far. Bond's last appearance for West Ham had preceded Redknapp's debut by four months, but he had trained alongside him often enough to recognise that the Redknapp-MacDougall axis had the potential to reap dividends.

'John Bond knew Harry and knew what a quality winger he was, so he brought him into the team to provide service to Ted from the right side of the field,' recalls Bobby Howe, whom Bond had recruited from West Ham the previous January. 'Harry was a wonderful crosser of the ball – he could take people on, make little angles for himself and get great little balls in, and I think that's what John wanted at that time. Anytime players like Harry were available, he did his best to get them. Bournemouth at that time was a pretty competitive team.'

In the event, Redknapp supplied the ammunition for MacDougall all too briefly. With seventy-seven goals in his previous two seasons, MacDougall was a wanted man long before a spectacular diving header against Aston Villa in February 1972 earned him rave reviews on *Match of the Day*. Bournemouth had rebuffed interest from a number of top-flight suitors by the time Manchester United came calling seven months later, but an offer of £200,000, a Third Division record, was too good to decline. With Redknapp's Dean Court career less than two months old, MacDougall left for Old Trafford.

If the loss of such a prolific goal-scorer was a blow, the fact that Bournemouth were capable of smoothing the edges on a player of Manchester United calibre only reinforced the club's status as an emergent power. Consequently, Bond's ability to attract players of pedigree – not least from his old Upton Park stamping ground – remained undiminished. In MacDougall's absence, Redknapp's fortunes would be influenced by another Scot. Bond's summer recruits included Jimmy Gabriel, a defensive midfielder signed from Southampton whose career had taken in league and Cup triumphs with Harry Catterick's Everton. 'Jimmy was a tremendous force in the game, a wonderful player,' recalls Howe, who was part of a claret-and-blue coterie that also included Keith Miller, the adaptable midfielder whom Bond made club captain, and Trevor Hartley, Howe's brother-in-law. 'John brought Jimmy in because of his tremendous experience. Jimmy was very aggressive, a great motivator on the field and someone who really made you feel good. He was a driving spirit.'

As Gabriel's leadership qualities impressed Howe, so the technical excellence of the cadre of Greenwood graduates stirred respect in Gabriel. From his central midfield station, the former Scotland international was well placed to appreciate Redknapp's marauding right-wing runs. 'Harry could dance down that wing, he really had the skills,' recalls Gabriel. 'He was the best crosser of a ball I've seen. He could drop it on a sixpence and he could do it all the different ways: bending it, high in the air, driving it across – he was always very, very accurate. I'm sure that's why West Ham hired him in the first place. He was very fast, too, he could cut behind the defender and whip the ball in. It was hard for a defender to play against Harry, because he could whip it in in front of you and if you went to make a tackle he could get behind you.'

Professional respect aside, Redknapp and Gabriel also hit it off on a personal level, their friendship cemented by a combination of coincidence and shared aspiration. 'Amazingly enough, the day I went up to sign for Bournemouth Harry was there too,' recalls Gabriel. 'He was signing from West Ham and I was signing from Southampton. Frank Lampard [Snr] was there, because Frank's related to Harry through their wives. They took a photograph and it had the three of us in it, even though Frank wasn't signing, so it was funny.' Funny in a different sense was Redknapp's decision to purchase a house in Mudeford, a small fishing village just outside Christchurch. By chance, he suddenly found himself living within a hundred yards of both Gabriel and Howe. 'Harry bought a house across the road from me, so we were obviously destined to become friends,' muses Gabriel. 'Bobby lived just around the corner, and we all used to share a car into training. We were always talking about soccer, and we made a pact that whoever got a job first as a head coach or manager would bring the other two with them.'

That pact was to have a shaping influence on the future of Bournemouth's three wise men. United by their passion for the game and by a shared desire to become coaches, their exchange of tactical and technical insights harked back to the days when Bond, Noel Cantwell and Malcolm Allison held court before West Ham's younger players at Cassettari's, an Italian café close to the Boleyn Ground. In his book *1966 And All That*, Geoff Hurst, frequently a rapt attendee at such gatherings, recalled how salt and pepper pots became the 'essential props in long discussions on tactics and strategies.' A similar process was now enacted on the south coast, albeit in more colourful surroundings.

'We would talk to each other about football on the way to training as well as after games, when we regularly had a post-mortem at our local,' recalls Howe. 'There was a little pub around the corner, within walking distance for all three of us, called The Ship in Distress. We'd go in there and we'd use whatever glasses were on the table and talk about the game. We spent so much time in there that we renamed it the QE2! But those are the times that football strategy and [methods of] analysis are formed.

When John Bond was playing with Malcolm Allison and Malcolm Musgrove and all those guys at West Ham, they went round to a local coffee shop near Upton Park and did something similar. That sort of thing forms the basis of how the game moves forward, and we had lots of those discussions because we lived so close to each other.'

On one such occasion, their efforts to move the game forward almost came to an abrupt halt. With Redknapp at the wheel, the trio were locked in conversation as they drove along the winding country lanes from Christchurch to Bournemouth's West Parley training ground. All seemed well until a tractor appeared in the road ahead. 'We were chatting away when suddenly Harry decides he's fed up of driving behind this tractor,' recounts Gabriel. 'It wasn't going too fast, so he decided to overtake.' To the horror of his two team-mates, Redknapp swung out directly into the path of an oncoming car. 'Look out!' cried Howe. Too late; Redknapp was committed. 'I couldn't even speak,' says Gabriel, 'I was petrified. It was certain death – we were goners.' As the pair braced themselves, the shrill screech of torn metal reverberated around them. 'It was James Bond stuff, unbelievable,' says Gabriel. Somehow, Redknapp – his steering evidently no less accurate than his crossing – charted a route between the two vehicles before bringing the car to an abrupt standstill. For interminable moments, a stunned silence prevailed. 'I thought we were dead,' Gabriel finally stammered. Redknapp had more pressing issues on his mind. 'Geez,' he muttered with exasperation, 'I've scratched my car.'

It was not the only occasion on which Redknapp left Gabriel with his heart in his mouth. One day they were returning to the south coast from London, where Redknapp had started a business. 'It was a shop – just ordinary clothes, stuff like that, and it wasn't going too well' recalls Gabriel. 'It was my car, but Harry loved to get behind the wheel so I said "You can drive, Harry." We were driving along a cliff-side in Bournemouth and Harry says: "You know what, Jim, I just feel like turning this car over." And he went to do it! I said "No, no, keep it on the road, it's my car!" I'm sure he was just joking, but he got my attention, I can tell you. He can be so funny, Harry. You're never short of a laugh with him.'

For the first few months of Redknapp's Bournemouth career there was just as much to smile about on the pitch. Despite MacDougall's departure nine games into the season – his swansong came with a 4-0 mauling of Port Vale in which Redknapp scored his first goal for the club – defeats were rare. Looking every inch potential champions, Bond's side began the new year with a victory over Watford that hauled them to the league summit. Promotion to Division Two for the first time in history was becoming a genuine possibility. 'It was just like playing at West Ham, but on the south coast,' says Howe. 'John had a similar philosophy to Ron Greenwood, with a tremendous amount of ball work in training and very interesting, enjoyable sessions.' Howe believes that Bond's tutelage, allied with a lengthy Upton Park apprenticeship, furnished the framework around which both he and Redknapp subsequently built their respective coaching careers. 'The experience of working with Ron and then with John Bond really helped us to form our own opinions,' says Howe. 'Beyond that, your own style is brought out by your own personality. I think that's what Harry has added since: he's added his own personality to the information that he received from two very good coaches.'

More immediately, the most important addition to Redknapp's reservoir of football knowledge was a salutary lesson about the importance of maintaining momentum. Having claimed pole position in the title race, Bond's side managed just five more wins all season. A modest haul of seventeen points from the last forty saw Bournemouth stagger across the finish line a disappointing seventh. The club's abrupt change of fortune was exacerbated by speculation linking Bond with a move to Norwich City. Conjecture finally became reality in November 1973, when Bond, no longer able to resist the allure of First Division football, took over at Carrow Road following the departure of Ron Saunders. To Redknapp, who had only ever known the rock-solid stability of Upton Park – Greenwood, under whom he played for almost a decade, was only the fourth manager in West Ham's history – such upheaval was alien.

Bond nevertheless left Bournemouth in good shape. Flying high in fourth place, four points off the league leaders Bristol Rovers, the club looked poised for another promotion push. But Bournemouth's apparent good health was an illusion. 'Money wasn't available and the chairman [Harold Walker] wanted to get out, I think, so John took the opportunity to go to Norwich,' recalls Trevor Hartley, who was subsequently promoted from reserve-team coach to manager. 'It was a difficult time at the club and John had ambitions of managing in the First Division. I think he thought "If I turn down Norwich then I may not get anything else".'

CHAPTER TWO

Bond's departure spelt trouble for Bournemouth in more ways than one. Supporters who once crowed with delight as Bond poached players from his former clubs now watched in dismay as Fred Davies, John Benson and Mel Machin, all key defensive personnel, departed for Carrow Road. They were later followed by Phil Boyer, MacDougall's former strike partner and a future England international. 'We had players who wanted to go and play in the top division, which was understandable,' says Hartley. 'But it was hard, because I was the youngest manager in the Football League – I took that [record] from Graham Taylor, who was at Lincoln at that stage – and the chairman wanted to cut back financially.'

Redknapp too was on Bond's hit list. He had started the season well, scoring against Bristol Rovers, Aldershot and Tranmere. With Bond gone and Bournemouth reluctant to spend, a return to the top flight would have been both timely and welcome. But the move was thwarted by a knee injury that would ultimately bring the curtain down on Redknapp's domestic playing career. Once courted by some of the biggest clubs in the country, Redknapp would never again play Division One football. He was twenty-six. What prevented him from fulfilling the promise he had shown as a youth player? 'That's a good question,' says Howe. 'At that time there were some pretty dangerous left full-backs around, and they left their scars on him. I think that may have had something to do with it. I'm not saying that he was necessarily injured, but he got tackled fairly heavily. If you played left-back and you were up against a right winger who was very effective, in any sort of fifty-fifty situation you'd make sure that they landed up on the track. In an era when yellow cards weren't shown around as much as they are now, I think Harry may have been a victim of some of that. When he was at Bournemouth he missed a lot of playing time with a sore knee.'

The rudimentary medical support of the day did little to allay Redknapp's injury problems. 'The trouble then was that you didn't have to have fully-qualified physiotherapists,' says Hartley. 'I think a lot of the injuries that people had in those days, including Harry's, could have been cured. It took the FA one hundred years to get qualified physiotherapists in football clubs. All we had was the sponge and the water bucket.'

Injuries aside, there is a school of thought which says that the lucky breaks that have peppered Redknapp's managerial career were more elusive in his playing days. One subscriber is Jimmy Gabriel. 'I don't know why Harry never made it big time with West Ham or with another big club,' says Gabriel, 'because he certainly had the skills. Sometimes you need a break, and I'm not sure he got too many breaks. I think he played for the England youth team, but I don't know for sure because Harry never boasted about anything like that.'

Wilf McGuinness, the manager of that all-conquering team of England tyros, was equally puzzled by the fading of Redknapp's star. 'It surprised me in some ways,' says McGuinness, 'because if you win something as good as the Little World Cup, you expect those players to come on – and some did. John Sissons also did well for a time, but then he faded a bit and ended up at Sheffield Wednesday. Some players just need that break. I would have thought Harry could have played at a higher level than he did at the end, as he had done for most of his career.'

CHAPTER TWO

Injury and opportunity may have conspired against Redknapp's top-flight ambitions, but the early weeks of Hartley's Dean Court tenure at least promised hope of a tilt at the Second Division. Festive fixtures against Wrexham, Cambridge, Huddersfield and Hereford yielded a maximum return, leaving Bournemouth in second place, just three points behind Bristol Rovers. But a 2-1 defeat at Chesterfield, notable for Redknapp's fifth and final goal of the season, proved a turning point. 'I still remember that game,' says Hartley. 'Harry scored but we lost, and all I could do afterwards was go and shake hands with all the players because we played great.' With Hartley's efforts to replenish his depleted squad thwarted by the chairman's desire to adopt a continental set-up – 'if we wanted to buy players,' he recalls, 'there was a four-man committee and I would quite often get out-voted by three to one' – wins became increasingly elusive. The slump culminated with an eleventh-place finish. Another year of Third Division slog beckoned.

Hartley's managerial ambitions were dealt a further blow at the outset of the new season when Redknapp's ongoing knee injury worsened. A three-month spell in plaster left Redknapp sidelined for twenty-five games. By the time he returned, Bournemouth, hovering a point above the drop zone, were facing a relegation scrap. 'When players of Harry's enthusiasm and ability aren't in the team, you miss out,' says Hartley, who finally parted company with the club in January 1975. 'Although Harry wasn't old, when other players left for Norwich he became one of the senior players. Harry was a good footballer, always a crowd favourite, whether at West Ham or Bournemouth. He was exciting to watch. When Harry got the ball you always expected something to happen – even if it wasn't always what everyone wished!'

Redknapp's return to fitness coincided with the appointment of John Benson, who was lured back to Dean Court in a player-manager role. Confronted by the same obstacles as his predecessor, Benson was unable to stave off relegation. By the time Redknapp played the final game of his first spell at the club, on January 17, 1976, Bournemouth were eleven points adrift of top-placed Lincoln. Six years later he would return, just in time to see the Cherries finally escape Division Four. In the meantime, though, there were bills to pay and mouths to feed. The legacy of the Bournemouth experience was an enduring love affair with the south coast but little by way of cold, hard cash. Jamie, born on June 25, 1973, was approaching his third birthday and Sandra had been working as a mobile hairdresser in an effort to help cover the mortgage on the Redknapps' £6,000 home in Christchurch. It was, Redknapp later recalled in an interview with the *Sunday Mirror*, a trying time: 'When I finished playing I didn't have a penny to my name. We could barely afford to pay the mortgage and I had absolutely no idea what I was going to do. I was trying to save up enough money to buy a taxi and started to read up about doing The Knowledge.'

As Redknapp laboured to make ends meet, Gabriel and Howe were taking their first steps in the world of coaching. Gabriel had left the south coast two years earlier, moving on to Brentford before heading off to the United States to work in the North American Soccer

League. Howe, meanwhile, who was Bournemouth's assistant manager during Hartley's reign, had taken up a role as the youth-team coach at Plymouth. Before long, the paths of all three would once again converge.

Chapter Three

'We need a winger,' said Jimmy Gabriel. 'Harry Redknapp can play wing, he'd be excellent if we can get him.' John Best, the Seattle Sounders head coach, was in receptive mood. Best had guided the Sounders to second spot in the Pacific Division the previous year, but the need for reinforcements was clear. Portland Timbers had bettered his side both regionally and in the national play-offs. More ominously, the New York Cosmos had enticed Pelé out of semi-retirement with a three-year deal worth almost five million dollars. The Sounders could not match that kind of financial firepower, but they could make the most of Gabriel's English connections. If Gabriel thought Redknapp could cut it against Pelé and co, Best was not going to argue. 'OK,' he replied, 'let's do it.'

It was March 1976, and the North American Soccer League (NASL) was on the cusp of an unprecedented period of growth. Formed in 1968 when the United

States Soccer Association merged with the maverick National Professional Soccer League, the NASL struggled during its formative years. But Pelé's arrival gave the fledgling competition a previously unimagined profile and credibility, encouraging owners to release the purse strings and players to relinquish their preconceptions. Gripes about the artificial turf became less frequent and suddenly it no longer mattered that the native distaste for a draw meant every game was concluded with extra-time and penalties. If the NASL was good enough for Pelé, it was good enough for anyone. The league's newfound magnetism attracted a bewildering array of ageing but class acts, household names such as Eusebio, Franz Beckenbauer, George Best, Johan Cruyff and Gordon Banks. It had taken time, deep pockets and a major marketing push but, belatedly, American league football had arrived.

Against this background, Jimmy Gabriel's decision to join the Sounders as a player-coach two years earlier smacked of foresight. Having arrived in Seattle armed with a wealth of experience and strong coaching beliefs, the former Everton man became a valued and popular figure, acquiring an influence at the club that would prove central to Redknapp's transition from player to manager. Gabriel charmed the locals with his reflections on the literary merits of John Steinbeck ('a very fine writer [who] puts people before money') and Ernest Hemingway (a 'more reportorial style, very down to earth'), and claimed an equally prominent position in the affections of John Best, whose admiration for Gabriel's initiative and determination was unswerving. 'He's our leader, both on and off the field,' said Best.

'Whatever success we attain, Jim Gabriel will have played a key role.'

It would be misleading to portray Best as a mere bystander in the Sounders' recruitment of Redknapp and the other British players who followed him to Seattle. Best, who was born in wartime Liverpool and went on to play for Tranmere Rovers before moving to the United States in his mid-twenties, had first-hand knowledge of the English game. Importantly, he bowed to no man in his admiration for the verve and technical proficiency of Ron Greenwood's West Ham side. That much became evident when Redknapp's arrival was closely followed by that of Geoff Hurst. The duo, who were already familiar with several of the NASL grounds from their visits to the United States with the Hammers a decade earlier, brought a dash of Upton Park derring-do to a formidable British contingent. Among them were Tom Jenkins, the former Southampton winger, Eric Skeels, the left-back dubbed 'Mr Dependable' during his lengthy Stoke career, and fellow full-back John McLaughlin, who had left Everton the previous December. They were joined by Mike England – the doughty Welsh centre-half who helped Spurs to the 1967 FA Cup, and whom Redknapp knew from his occasional visits to London's Rhinegold Club while at West Ham – and Gordon Wallace, the Lanark-born striker whose injury-blighted Liverpool career had been played out in the shadow of Roger Hunt and Ian St John.

Best recalls the influence of the Academy of Football brains trust chaired by Gabriel and Redknapp with particular affection. 'The group of players that Ron Greenwood had at West Ham all had a well-rounded knowledge of the game and played in an attractive way,' says Best, who perceived in the twenty-nine-year-old Redknapp a vibrant blend of affability and intelligence. 'Harry was a real character, always has been, but he also had a great mind for the game. His vision on the field was tremendous. He'd always find space wide, so he was very dangerous, although he was quiet in a way – his style of play was not that flamboyant, so it contrasted with his personality. But it was very effective. We liked "H" a lot.'

The feeling was mutual. While Redknapp's knees could no longer withstand the rigours of the English game, the NASL, with its AstroTurf pitches and less exacting physical demands, gave him a new lease of life. He was able to continue making a living from the game while travelling to some of America's most glamorous locations. He could also renew old friendships with the likes of Gabriel and Hurst, who lived nearby. It was footballing and social nirvana. 'It was a wonderful time for me,' Redknapp later recounted to the *Sun*'s Andrew Dillon. 'The setup was so different. If we played Miami we would fly down and play the game but stay in Florida for four or five days and then play Tampa. You could be away from home for eight or nine days. Fans would turn up at these great stadiums hours before kick off and have "tailgate parties". Barbecues, beers and wine would be flowing and a great festival atmosphere prevailed.'

Scarcely had Redknapp finished unpacking before he was making his Sounders debut. He could not have picked a more auspicious occasion. To mark the opening of the new King County Domed Stadium, or Kingdome, the Sounders arranged a high-profile exhibition match against the New York Cosmos.

CHAPTER THREE

Redknapp's last appearance on a football pitch had been for Bournemouth at Newport County before a meagre crowd of mid-winter die-hards. Now he was rubbing shoulders with Pelé in front of a sell-out audience of 58,128 – a record at the time for a football match in the United States. The Redknapp gob was well and truly smacked.

At thirty-six Pelé was past his prime, but age had not diminished the legendary Brazilian's dead-ball prowess. The maestro scored with a deflected free-kick inside three minutes to give the Cosmos an advantage that was almost immediately doubled by Dave Clements, the former Northern Ireland manager. Yet Best and Gabriel found grounds for touch-line optimism in the lurking menace of Hurst. 'I remember Geoff was playing in that game, and we wanted Harry and the other players to run off him,' says Best. 'We figured that the opposition would be intent on him, so we wanted our players to time their runs and be a fraction behind Geoff. We were dangerous on crosses, most of our game was built on that, and Harry was a great crosser of the ball.'

With an hour gone and the Sounders still trailing, Gabriel – who had retired at the end of the previous season – was itching to get on. 'It was a huge game, because we were sold out, Pelé was playing and they had a fantastic team. We were getting beat two-nil and I stripped myself down, because I could still play at that time. I thought I'd give it a go, and I went on and I scored a goal, the first in the Kingdome for the Sounders, which lifted the crowd and put us back in the game. Pelé then scored another one, so we got beaten 3-1, but it was a big occasion for all of us because that was our home playing field from that time on. To play against Pelé in front of a sold-out stadium was unbelievable.'

For Redknapp, the only downside was a minor recurrence of the knee injury that had forced his retirement from the English game. The problem would ultimately restrict his involvement to fifteen of the twenty-four games comprising the Sounders' league programme. Nonetheless, his influence on the season was significant. After missing the opening three matches, Redknapp made his competitive debut in a 1-0 win against San Diego on May 7, 1976, helping the team to a record-equalling third successive clean sheet. Redknapp then matched another Sounders landmark – if one may talk of records in relation to a club that had been in existence less than three years – by setting up three goals in a 4-3 defeat to the Los Angeles Aztecs at the Murdock Stadium. George Best's match-winning contribution for the Aztecs stole the headlines, but Redknapp's credentials as the Sounders' creative fulcrum had been established.

Within a fortnight of his star turn, Redknapp was once again watching from the stands. This time, though, injury was not the culprit. To mark the two-hundredth anniversary of the Declaration of Independence, the United States Soccer Federation organised a four-team tournament that brought together some of the world's most celebrated players. A Team America side composed of various NASL stars and captained by Bobby Moore, who had joined San Antonio Thunder for the season, was pitted against Brazil, England and Italy, the latter two having failed to qualify for the European Championships. Moore's role in Team America's clash with England, which took place in Seattle on May 31, made an indelible impression on Redknapp, and not just for the novelty of watching a man synonymous with the Three Lions take to the field against his own country.

'When the game finished I was sat in the stand with Bobby's wife Tina, my wife Sandra, and my boys Jamie and Mark,' recalls Redknapp. 'I saw this fella in the Team America side called Keith Eddy, who'd played for Watford and somehow ended up at New York Cosmos, go up to Rivelino and start taking his shirt off to swap it with him. But Rivelino shook his head, and sprinted to catch up with Bobby, who was ninety yards away from him on the other side of the pitch. Rivelino, who was a superstar himself, wanted Bobby's shirt. I can still see it now.'

While that moment reinforced Redknapp's appreciation of Moore's colossal standing in the game, back on the pitch his regard for the talents of Hurst and Gordon Wallace, the Sounders' strike partnership, was growing daily. Twice in the weeks ahead Redknapp laid on late winners for the forward duo, first when he set up Hurst in the dying moments against Dallas Tornado, then when he released Wallace late on against an overbearingly physical Philadelphia Atoms side. Nor had he left his own shooting boots at home. When the Sounders defence succeeded in keeping the LA Aztecs at bay for ninety minutes despite another swashbuckling display by George Best, it was Redknapp who drove home the decisive shoot-out penalty. And when Hartford visited the Kingdome with the season nearing an end, Redknapp came within a whisker of scoring his first Sounders goal in open play, a solid effort cannoning off the post before falling to Hurst, who turned in the rebound.

'Harry was a good player for the Sounders,' remembers Best. 'Both he and Geoff Hurst brought intelligence and thought to the game, which was very good for our young players. He was an entertaining player, too, the crowd liked him.'

The Sounders finished the campaign second in the Western Division of the Pacific Conference, earning a first round play-off tie with Vancouver Whitecaps. At the season's outset the Vancouver head coach, Eckhard Krautzun, had dismissed the thirty-four-year-old Hurst, the Sounders' marquee signing, as 'over the hill'. Now the former England hero repaid that slight with the goal which saw Redknapp and his team-mates through to a Division Championship showdown at the Minnesota Kicks' Metropolitan Stadium.

Best was confident. The Sounders had beaten Minnesota home and away during the regular season and were in good form on their travels. 'We have developed a plan that has kept us in good stead on the road,' declared Best. But it was not to be. Minnesota fired in three first-half goals, effectively bringing the curtain down on the Sounders' season long before Mike England's late dismissal rendered the result a formality. Even so, it had been a successful year for the fledgling side. The English players had been seamlessly assimilated into the team, the average gate at the Kingdome was almost twenty-five thousand and the Sounders had reached the play-offs for the second time in their three-year existence.

Significantly, Redknapp's contribution ranged beyond the first team. Mindful of his old pal's training-ground nous, Gabriel encouraged Redknapp to play a role in coaching the Sounders' reserves. Such was his impact that when Gabriel was promoted to head coach after Best made a close-season move to Vancouver, his first act was to hand Redknapp full control of the second string. 'I became the head coach,' recalls Gabriel, 'and I got him to play and to coach the reserve team, because Harry's a great coach. We know that now, but in those days you had to make a decision on it. I always liked what he said about the game, how he wanted to get the kids to play better, so I said "Right, he's for me".'

Redknapp, whose Stateside sojourn did not provide employment all year round, was hopeful that Gabriel would not be the only manager to utter those words. The American season spanned only six months, starting with pre-season friendlies in March and ending with the championship-deciding Soccer Bowl in August. For the remainder of the year, the players fended for themselves. Accordingly, while Gabriel began planning for the next season, Redknapp, his knees much improved, returned to England in search of a short-term deal. He was eventually offered a temporary contract by John Docherty, the manager of Fourth Division Brentford. At sixty pounds per week – barely enough to fuel Redknapp's beaten-up Morris Marina for the daily one-hundred-and-seventy-mile round trip from Christchurch – it was hardly the road to riches. But it was a job.

Redknapp's flirtation with Griffin Park was to prove ill-fated. At half-time during a reserve team run-out intended as a prelude to Redknapp's full debut, Docherty informed a stunned dressing room that he had been dismissed. Worse was to come when Redknapp made his first and only Brentford appearance a few days later. Named in the starting line-up for a trip to the Recreation

Ground on Friday September 10, 1976, he lasted just twenty-five minutes before a hefty challenge from an Aldershot defender left him nursing three broken ribs.

Nothing if not resilient, Redknapp soon resurfaced. Three years earlier Jimmy Knox, the former Coventry City striker, had been appointed manager of non-league side AP Leamington. Knox, a plain-speaking football man who, having spent much of his career with Rugby Town, knew the non-league world backwards, can hardly have imagined then that he would one day wake to the headline 'Ex-Hammers star signs'. That it should happen with Leamington rooted to the foot of the Southern League Premier Division beggared belief. But circumstances contrived to bring about a move that Knox at one point described as having "a cat in hell's chance" of coming to fruition. After rejecting offers from Brighton and Peterborough that would involve uprooting from Bournemouth, Redknapp was close to accepting an approach from Yeovil. However, the ambitious Glovers expected him to train with them three nights week. It was a level of commitment that Redknapp – who would later be the subject of another audacious but ultimately unsuccessful plan to lure him to Huish Park, this time as manager – was reluctant to make.

Knox was more accommodating. With points on the board paramount, he agreed to let Redknapp train with Bournemouth. Knox's only proviso was that Redknapp make himself available for one training session a week. 'Redknapp has assured me that he will do our side a power of good,' Knox told the *Leamington Spa Courier*. 'Providing he produces the goods, there will be no need for him to come once a week. Sometimes you can make allowances like this and this bloke falls into this category. He's just the bloke we need. He has plenty of class and experience and has every attribute a good winger should have. [His signing] will show the people of Leamington that we're not taking this bottom-of-the-table situation lying down.'

So it was that Redknapp made his AP Leamington debut against Maidstone United on Saturday October 23, 1976. It soon became apparent to the modest gathering of home fans why Knox, in his programme notes, had declared himself 'absolutely delighted to find a player of [Redknapp's] calibre at the club.' In a move that echoed the defining moment of his West Ham debut eleven years earlier, Redknapp planted a second-half corner onto the forehead of the Leamington striker Adrian Stewart to create the opening goal. It was the catalyst for a victory that lifted the Warwickshire club off the foot of the table.

Though injury limited Redknapp's subsequent involvement to a handful of games, one episode lingers in the memory of locals. On a Saturday afternoon in mid-December, Leamington were scheduled to host Gravesend at their Windmill Ground home. Redknapp, however, succumbed to injury in the build-up to the game, prompting him to decline his wages. As the club programme noted, it was – even then – 'a remarkable gesture. Harry said he did not want it because he hadn't earned it. He insisted on handed [sic] it back – A nice gesture Harry.'

On Monday 28 February, 1977, Redknapp and family arrived in Seattle in preparation for a second season with the Sounders. The tedium of the ten-hour flight from London was mitigated by the welcome presence of Bobby

Howe, whom Gabriel – honouring the terms of the pact made by the trio in their Bournemouth days – had recruited as assistant coach during the close season. By ten o'clock the next morning it was just like old times, the three men supervising first-team training on a drizzly winter day redolent of countless similar occasions at the Bournemouth training ground.

'When Jimmy took over as the head coach and invited me to come over as a coach, I felt that it was a wonderful opportunity and I've been here ever since' says Howe, now the Director of Coaching at Emerald City FC, a Seattle-based club specialising in youth development. 'Jimmy and I were coaching the first team – along with Harry for home games – and then Jimmy and I went to the away games while Harry stayed behind and worked with the young players at the club. We had a local scout at that time called Jimmy Johnson, a friend of Jimmy Gabriel's, who brought in some local college players. Harry's job was to work with those players, and he did a great job with them. Harry had a terrific rapport with the youngsters. He was a gambler and he used gambling terminology; he came out with some unforgettable sayings that really kept the young kids entertained. We had a reserve team programme – we played against the Vancouver Whitecaps reserves and some senior amateur teams from British Columbia and the Seattle area – and it was a very good experience for those young players. Harry helped them to move forward, although the gap between the young American player at that time and the players that were imported to play was quite large, so it was hard for the young players to break into the first team.'

CHAPTER THREE

Nonetheless, it did not take Redknapp long to work his alchemy. A summer-long reserve programme against local teams from Oregon, Washington and Canada produced twelve wins in fifteen games. More importantly, it yielded several players who would go on to bolster the native-American presence in the Sounders first team. Among them was Jimmy McAlister, a twenty-year-old graduate of Seattle's JFK High School, who made his full debut against Vancouver in the final game of the regular season and was named NASL Rookie of the Year the following year.

'Harry was the most fun guy I've ever worked under,' says McAlister, an overlapping left-back who, like fellow reserve Bruce Rudroff, went on to become a United States international. 'He is a very shrewd coach. Harry can see talent from a mile away and he tends to be able to see who can put up with the pressures of the [professional] game and who can't. He did a phenomenal job. Pretty much every side had a reserve team, but they weren't funded much. Harry was really trying to be part-time right wing, part-time coach. That was the way the NASL was, there wasn't a big reserve team like you'd have in England. He was always engaging, always up to something and he was very skilled on the ball. He told me about [Kenny] Sansom, the England left-back, and about how good the English players were. At training, he always had time for the young boys who wanted to stay on afterwards. He would work with anybody who wanted to work on his game. He did a good job with a lot of young kids.'

That Redknapp's earliest foray into coaching produced future internationals says much about his natural aptitude for the job. More of a tracksuit manager than the suited-and-booted modern incarnation would perhaps suggest, his relish for the nuts and bolts of management was evident even in his earliest musings on the subject. 'When you do get the boys to come in and play on the first team it's very satisfying,' said Redknapp back in 1977. 'It's a boost for me to see them coming in after working with them. [A reserve team] is a very important thing for a club to have. There's nothing like playing games to learn the sport. If they don't play, they don't learn.' The sincerity of Redknapp's belief in the primacy of youth development would later be borne out by his readiness to blood the clutch of West Ham youngsters who went on to form the nucleus of the current England team.

Redknapp offered a further hint that his coaching philosophy was already beginning to calcify when he remarked of the Sounders' reserves: 'If they don't feel confident, they're always going to feel second best. And if you feel that way in life, you're never going to be the best, are you?' Three decades on, the sentiment remains a cornerstone of his management creed. As Redknapp put it after Tottenham defied the laws of probability by twice retrieving a two-goal deficit in his first official game as manager: 'I've tried to make them believe in themselves; everything in life comes down to confidence.'

Another stock-in-trade to which early beneficiaries of Redknapp's idiosyncratic methods were exposed was humour. For Alan Hudson, the former Chelsea and England midfielder who later joined the Sounders from Arsenal, Redknapp's training-ground banter remains indelibly etched in the memory. 'Harry and I would go to a racecourse called Longacres after training,' recounts Hudson. 'He would go in the next day and the young Americans he was training would try to take the piss out of him. They would say to him, "How did you get on at the races yesterday, Harry?" And he'd say, "We won a few quid, me and Al, but there's two horses to look out for, they'll win for a cert." So they all ran to the locker room to get their pen and paper. Harry said: "One of them is called Loose Button, it's never come off. The other one's called Dusty Carpet, it's never been beat." Every day we'd go into training and these daft Americans would say, "When are those horses running, Harry?" And he'd say, "They'll be running, don't you worry." We got so much mileage out of that one it was unbelievable. It's a lovely memory, because he still takes that humour into the dressing room and it relaxes players.'

Once underway, however, Redknapp's coaching sessions were no laughing matter. 'When it came down to the actual training itself, it was full of business, very serious and of high quality,' says Howe. That defeats were few and far between bears testimony to Howe's appraisal. Come match day, Redknapp's ability to motivate and inspire his charges – a perennial theme of his later career – ensured that tactics and techniques honed on the training ground were played out to maximum effect. It left Gabriel in no doubt that a successful future lay ahead for his former Bournemouth buddy. 'Harry was great at getting the players to play for him,' remembers Gabriel. 'They would go out there and give their best. Like all really good managers, Harry can get the most from his players – and he did that right from the start, right from when he was coaching young kids in

Seattle. He'd make them feel that they wanted to be the best, and he'd bring that out of them. That's a talent. So I always thought Harry was destined to go far in the managerial sense.'

Best had reached a similar conclusion. 'It was pretty clear that Harry would do well if he stayed in the game and went into management,' says Best, who was at Vancouver by the time Redknapp's work with the reserves began in earnest. 'He had a very good eye for players, for spotting what they could do and identifying their talents.' Redknapp was already beginning to confound the expectations of Wilf McGuinness, his former England youth team manager. 'I wouldn't have thought of him as a manager in those days,' says McGuinness, 'although I thought he might become a comedian!'

Gabriel's plan for the forthcoming campaign had been to deploy Redknapp and Howe purely as coaches, but the latter stages of the English season impinged on the early weeks of the NASL, necessitating a rethink. 'I didn't come over with any intention of playing,' says Howe, 'but we were called into service because there was an overlap between the English and American seasons of about three weeks to a month. So until the players were available to come over from England, we played in a few games.'

Happily, the Sounders' first fixture was against Team Hawaii, the renamed San Antonio Thunder team, at their Honolulu-based Aloha Stadium. 'We went there two or three days in advance and it was amazing, like going on holiday to prepare for your first match,' recalls Howe. Bolstered by the experience of Redknapp and Howe, an under-strength Sounders side held their hosts to a goalless draw only to lose on a tiebreak, the new system whereby a lone attacker, dribbling goalwards from the thirty-five-yard line, was given five seconds to beat the keeper. Nor were the former West Ham team-mates able to avert a second defeat, against Minnesota eight days later. Even when Redknapp set up Mickey Cave for a second-minute opener against the Washington Diplomats, the Sounders left the RFK Stadium on the wrong end of a 3-2 verdict. In fact, in the five games in which Redknapp featured that season, the Sounders tasted victory just once, when he came on as a substitute in an early-May victory over St Louis at the Kingdome.

It was an inauspicious start to what would prove an unforgettable campaign. The Sounders lost ground in the Pacific Conference pecking order, eventually finishing third in the Western Division behind John Best's Vancouver Whitecaps and traditional rivals Minnesota. However, an increase in the number of play-off spots, from twelve to eighteen, ensured post-season qualification, and the Sounders did not waste the reprieve gifted to them by the rule makers. A 2-0 victory over Vancouver, their first in three years at the Whitecaps' Empire Stadium, tied up the Division Championship before home and away wins against Minnesota secured west coast bragging rights.

Standing between the Sounders and a historic first Soccer Bowl appearance were George Best's LA Aztecs. In the injury-induced absence of Steve David, their prolific marksman, the Aztecs' hopes were pinned firmly on Best. While it had been a chequered year for the former Manchester United man, whose season was scarred by various personal problems, a tally of eleven goals and eighteen assists provided all the evidence required of his enduring class. Yet destiny decreed that the Sounders would contest Soccer Bowl '77. Best was marked out of both legs by Adrian Webster, a utility player whose only previous claim to fame was a losing appearance in the FA Trophy final for Hillingdon Borough. A 3-1 win at the Los Angeles Coliseum was followed by a 1-0 second-leg triumph at the Kingdome. Against the odds, the Sounders were one match away from being crowned NASL champions.

If it was a triumph for the collective coaching nous of Gabriel, Redknapp and Howe, it was also a run touched by magic. The press acknowledged as much, dubbing the Sounders a 'Cinderella' side possessed of a witchcraft that conjured win after win. 'It was a fairytale year and Harry was instrumental in that achievement,' recalls Howe, 'because he participated in a lot of the first-team practices and his influence was huge. We were zero and three at the beginning of the season, and then we were four and seven after eleven games, wondering how we were going to turn it round. We worked hard at it and ended the season having won fourteen games and lost twelve. We were wining games towards the end of the regular season, so we had some momentum going into the playoffs and got to the final against the New York Cosmos.'

The Sounders' heroics notwithstanding, the central protagonist in the season's story – beyond Seattle, at least – was Pelé. By now in his final season with the New York Cosmos, the Brazilian was bidding for his first NASL championship in what would be his last competitive match. In working its way from an unpromising start to a potentially glorious denouement, the Cosmos' season was a mirror image of the Sounders'. Frustrated by the New York club's failure to assemble a side worthy of his talents, Pelé failed to report for pre-season and frequently looked disinterested during the initial stages of a campaign marred by in-fighting. But the arrival in late May of Franz Beckenbauer, which was closely followed by a run of five successive wins, combined with the late-season recruitment of Carlos Alberto, the flamboyant defender who captained Brazil to the 1970 World Cup, had a galvanizing effect. By the time the Cosmos arrived in Portland's Civic Stadium for the season finale, a rejuvenated Pelé had bagged four play-off goals. The sense of theatre surrounding the occasion was unprecedented in the American game.

Drama quickly turned to farce, however. There was no obvious sign of danger when Tony Chursky, the Sounders goalkeeper, beat the Cosmos forward Steve Hunt to a loose ball. But Hurst, deaf in one ear, failed to hear the warning cries from his team-mates as he subsequently rolled the ball out of the area with Hunt, now back on his feet, stealing in from behind. Chursky was dispossessed, and a comical goalward scramble with Hunt culminated with the Cosmos taking the lead. Tommy Ord, a recent acquisition from Vancouver, levelled five minutes later, but a late strike from Giorgio Chinaglia, the volatile Italian striker whose goals carried Lazio to the 1974 scudetto, left Pelé purring: 'God has been kind to me. Three World Cups and now a championship in America.' 'It was a wonderful game,' recalls Howe, 'a fabulous occasion that is remembered as one of the most entertaining NASL finals.'

It was also a notable staging post on Redknapp's path into management. Thrown in at the deep end, he had been part of a backroom team tasked with thwarting the collective talents of a trio of former World Cup winners. Not a bad addition to the CV of a thirty-year-old, even if the Cosmos' stars were past their prime. 'I'm sure Harry learned a lot, both good and bad, because he's applied those skills as he's moved forward,' says Howe. 'He had some good success from very early on and as a result he's grown in stature, confidence and style over the years. But his development was a gradual process. When you're in your early thirties you're learning the trade. There's no such thing as an expert in the game; when you think you're an expert, it comes back to bite you. You're always learning and you're always keeping an open mind, and that's what Harry did.'

The following April brought another handful of early-season appearances for Redknapp, who featured in games against Toronto (where he scored the first goal in a 4-2 tiebreak shoot-out victory), Tulsa and San Jose. By now, however, Redknapp's ability as a coach was beginning to attract as much attention as his ability on the pitch. Jimmy McAlister's success, in particular, fuelled the growing perception of Redknapp as more than just a decent player. 'I've had coaches of other clubs come up to me and say [about McAlister] "That's a good player you've got there",' said Mike England. Unsurprisingly, indirect praise of this kind soon had Redknapp re-evaluating his priorities. 'I'd like to play for this club,' he said, 'but I also enjoy coaching as well.'

That enjoyment was increasingly reflected in the make-up of the first team. Bruce Rudroff became a mainstay of the Sounders' back four that season, while the defender Ed Kreuger also broke into the first team. But for all Redknapp's success with the reserves, Gabriel's side struggled to scale the heights of the previous year. Third place in the Western Division of the National Conference was sufficient to secure a play-off berth, but there would be no repeat of the previous year's heroics. Despite completing the regular season with a run of three successive wins and acquiring Bobby Moore from Herning, the Danish Third Division club where the former England man was briefly a player-coach, the Sounders slumped to a 5-2 defeat against the New York Cosmos in the first round of the play-offs.

For Redknapp, it was the cue for another busy close season. 'Whenever Harry went back to England he always did a lot of scouting for the Sounders,' recalls Howe. 'He did a really good job, because we got some terrific players for Seattle over a period of time, many of whom Harry had chatted to and negotiated with.' On this occasion, however, Redknapp was outshone in the recruitment stakes by Gabriel, who pulled off the unlikely signing of Alan Hudson. A prodigiously gifted playmaker, Hudson was the creative heartbeat of the great Chelsea side that defeated Real Madrid to win the European Cup-Winners' Cup in 1971. He later inspired Stoke to a fifth-place finish in Division One before returning to the capital with Arsenal, where things went sour after eighteen months when he fell out with the manager, Terry Neill, following the Gunners' 1978 Cup final loss to Ipswich.

Reluctant to return to Highbury after the contretemps, Hudson was in a box at Stamford Bridge one October afternoon when he bumped into Bobby Moore. 'What are you doing sitting in a box?' enquired Moore. 'You're sat here watching when you should be playing. Jimmy Gabriel's out in the restaurant having lunch. I've been to Seattle, Al, it's a lovely place, why don't you try it?' When Hudson approached Gabriel, the Scot was incredulous: 'Are you really serious, Alan – you would actually come to Seattle?' Hudson confirmed that he would, and by Monday lunchtime a £100,000 deal had been agreed. Still only twenty-seven, Hudson bucked the NASL trend for attracting veterans seeking a final big pay-day. Gabriel could scarcely believe his luck.

Redknapp first learned of the midfield maverick's impending arrival when Gabriel called him at his Bournemouth home on the evening the deal was concluded. He could still recall the exchange when Hudson arrived in Seattle five months later. 'The last conversation I had with Jimmy,' Redknapp told Hudson, 'he could hardly talk. He was just mumbling about signing Alan Hudson for a hundred grand, saying he'd had lunch with you and that you'd been for a drink together to celebrate.'

Hudson's signing marked the beginning of an enduring friendship with Redknapp. Both men were later involved in serious road accidents, horrific experiences which strengthened their mutual warmth, but Hudson also attributes their closeness to a similar upbringing. 'Although he was from the East End and I was from south-west London we were both pretty much brought up with the same background,' says Hudson. 'We both had a hard time of it all and he'd been on the dole queue by the time he got to Seattle. He was only the youth team coach there, so to think that he's got where he's got is quite phenomenal.'

Unlike Best and Gabriel, Hudson did not detect signs of a managerial heavyweight in the making. 'I don't think Harry is a particularly good coach,' says Hudson with trademark candour. 'I think he would probably agree with that. He's not a Don Howe or a Jose Mourinho by any stretch of the imagination. I think he's a man manager, he's one of those that can get the best out of players. And he knows a good player. So I see him as a manger, not a coach. Coaches are there to be shot at by the players, whereas he walked into the Tottenham job and the players who weren't playing for Ramos are playing for him. It's something you see in every walk of life: if, in your job, you can get the best out of the staff that work for you, then that puts you in a stronger position. I think Harry knows that. His big talent is that he can spot a good player – and if you've played with Bobby Moore, then you should be able to.'

In Hudson's case, Redknapp's powers of judgement were not required. 'Alan was a fabulous player,' says Howe of the midfielder whose meagre haul of two England caps is widely regarded as a travesty. 'Probably, player for player, in the seven years that I was at the Sounders, I think Alan Hudson was the best they ever had.'

Hudson quickly acclimatised to the American game, setting up eleven goals and scoring a further two, but it was an otherwise frustrating season for the Sounders, who failed to qualify for the play-offs after finishing third in the Western Division of the National Conference. Howe pins much of the blame for the team's travails on a player strike in the opening month of the season. The boycott stemmed from the NASL's refusal to recognise a players' association headed by Ed Garvey, whose background as the chief executive of the National Football League provoked deep misgivings among administrators struggling to establish soccer alongside American football, baseball and basketball. In the short term only the April 14 fixtures were affected, but in Seattle the shock waves were felt for months.

'There was a players' union developing and many players on our team were very strong union people,' recalls Howe. 'They went on strike for one game, and I think we had nine first-team players out. It was early in the season and Jimmy, Harry and I all played.' The game, against a virtually full strength Dallas Tornado side, was played in the Ownby Stadium on what Howe recalls as 'a very, very hot night.' Under the circumstances a 1-0 defeat was a creditable effort. But while the damage to the Sounders' league standing was limited, the injury to team morale was not. 'There were some existing senior players at the club who decided not to go on strike,' remembers Howe. 'That created an incredible management problem. Many of the senior players went on strike simply because they didn't want to let their mates down, but others didn't go on strike because they thought the conditions were good enough. Once the strike was over, those coming back into the team were playing alongside those who didn't go on strike, and that created a very difficult management problem for us within the club. In terms of player personnel, we had some good players within the club, but I think the strike created a sort of rift. It made team spirit a little less than it should have been. All these things had gone on and, even though the players were trying, when you're in a situation like that team spirit is key. As a consequence, we didn't make the play-offs, which was a tragedy given some of the players we had on our team.'

For Redknapp it was another lesson learned, an early reminder that in football the sum of the whole exceeds that of the parts. He had scarcely had time to absorb the situation, however, before another of the game's realities hit home. Unhappy at the way the season had gone, the Sounders board decided that it was time for Gabriel and Redknapp to move on. 'When Harry and Jim got the sack in Seattle I was in London, in a restaurant,' recalls Hudson. 'I phoned Seattle and I said to Jimmy: "Cancel my contract, I'm not going to play for the Sounders if that's the way they've treated you." But Jimmy said: "Do yourself a favour, don't throw your career away again. Give Alan Hinton [Gabriel's successor] a chance, he deserves it."' Hudson eventually relented, and went on to captain the Sounders to Soccer Bowl '82, where they were once again thwarted by the New York Cosmos.

Redknapp, meanwhile, agreed to join Gabriel at Phoenix Fire, a fledgling club with aspirations of joining the NASL after demonstrating its viability in the hinterlands of the lower league. 'I was the head coach and I got Harry to come over as my assistant coach,' Gabriel recounts. 'Before we'd even started, someone on the board ran off with the money. It was a behind-the-scenes thing; just before we were getting ready to play, the club folded. I'd got Harry to get me some players, and there were a lot of players over there. Of course, the guys were scrambling a bit financially to get themselves home, although they all made it. It was out of the blue – somebody, somewhere, took the money out of the club and we were just left hanging there. It was a shock and a let-down because we'd put together some good players. It was just one of those things.'

In the wake of the fiasco Redknapp briefly lived in a house provided by Tom Sidero, a property developer who was one of the principal investors in the thwarted enterprise. Sidero hoped to get the team up and running again, but his efforts came to nought and Redknapp's American adventure ended on a sour note.

In Hudson's view, bouncing back from the experience ranks among Redknapp's finest achievements. 'When Harry was in Seattle coaching kids, I just couldn't see how he was going to become a manager at all,' says Hudson. 'I couldn't see where he was going – you get the sack from Seattle Sounders in the North American Soccer League, and there's only one way, isn't there? It's not a great thing to have on your CV. But he went back to Bournemouth and resurrected his career.'

Chapter Four

Harry Redknapp's managerial debut had not gone to plan. As the ball eluded Kenny Allen's despairing grasp for the ninth time, Redknapp's pre-match rallying call echoed afresh in his memory: 'Okay lads, it's tin hats on, fix bayonets.' Not two hours had passed since Redknapp uttered those words, but to the Bournemouth keeper it felt like a lifetime. Allen had known from the outset that it would be a long afternoon, and not simply because Colin Murphy had his pace-setting Lincoln side playing the best football in the Third Division. Equipped only with long nylon studs, Bournemouth did not have the footwear to cope with the frozen pitch that greeted their arrival at Sincil Bank. They could barely stand up, let alone play. Even so, this was beyond the pale – and now Allen had only one thought on his mind. 'Right,' he bellowed at his punch-drunk defence, 'they are not getting ten!'

'It really was tin hats,' says Allen. 'But nobody was to

blame. We left Bournemouth in lovely, glorious sunshine but by the time we got up to Lincoln it was frozen solid. We hadn't packed the footwear that you normally would for a pitch like that. We only had studs and our lads couldn't stand up. We held them for a while, but it just got worse as the afternoon progressed. The pitch got harder and harder, and they were wearing pimpled shoes. In the second half I just threw my boots off and donned two pairs of socks, because it was pointless trying to stand up. I think even their players must have got a little bit embarrassed about it – or I would like to think so – because it was just too easy for them. How we kept them down to nine was a minor miracle. It was good to get off the pitch. You could see Harry thinking "What have I done?"'

It was December 1982 and what Redknapp had done was to accept the caretaker-manager role offered to him by Harold Walker, the Bournemouth chairman, twenty-four hours earlier. The vacancy came about after a verbal dust-up between Walker and the club's erstwhile manager, Dave Webb, who walked out and was sacked a day later. As Webb's number two, Redknapp seemed the natural choice to replace him. 'Webby left and there was talk that they were going to advertise for a new manager,' recalls Allen. 'Harry was very popular with all the players, he made us laugh and he was brilliant with the coaching. So we said to him: "Hang on, why don't you apply for the job?" And he said: "Nah, I don't want to be a manager, it's not for me. I'm happy coaching." I said: "Yeah, but if a new manager comes in he might blow you out and bring his own man in." Anyway, Harry wasn't going to bother. So myself and John Impey, the club captain, went to see the chairman and we were instrumental in telling him that there was no need to look for another manager, because we had one. I don't know if Harry ever knew that. The chairman said: "Oh well, yes, if you're sure".'

Walker's offer left Redknapp in an awkward position, for the relief he felt at avoiding the axe was mitigated by a sense of regret about the departure of a good friend. 'I didn't want to be manager, I was very happy with Webbie,' recalls Redknapp. No wonder, for it was Webb – a fellow East Ender who made his name with Chelsea after failing to make the grade at West Ham – who had invited him back to Bournemouth in the first place. The offer to understudy Webb, which had come the previous season, was perfectly timed for Redknapp, who thus found himself swiftly re-employed after a miserable year spent treading the non-league backwaters as assistant manager to Bobby Moore at Oxford City.

It seems strange now, in an era when Redknapp is Britain's most expensive manager and England's World Cup winners are more venerated than ever, to imagine two of English football's most recognisable figures barking orders from the touchline of the now-defunct White House ground. At the time, though, neither could afford to turn down the opportunity. Infamously, Moore found employment hard to come by after hanging up his boots. When Tony Rosser, Oxford's affluent new chairman, offered to make Moore the figurehead of his new regime in the summer of 1980, he knew that the former England captain was unlikely to decline. Moore's new role in turn enabled him to fulfil a long-standing promise to Redknapp. 'He always said to me that if ever he got a job he'd like me to be his assistant,' says Redknapp, who at the time had just arrived back in England after the Phoenix Fire fiasco and was pondering his next move. 'He'd worked with me [in America] and I think he thought I knew what I was talking about, and we'd played together for years at West Ham and were great mates. I said "Great, I'd love that Bob". I enjoyed being with him, I loved him as a person, and so when he got the Oxford City job I went there with him.'

Neither man was cut out for life in the Isthmian Premier Division, and it wasn't long before things turned sour. 'We had been famous players, but we didn't know any players in the non-league system and we couldn't handle it,' recalls Redknapp. As City slid steadily down the league table and crashed out of the Cup to Bridgend Town in first-round qualifying, a horrified Redknapp could only look on as Moore, the man he revered above all others, was baited by non-entities not fit to lace his boots. 'Opposing teams would score a goal and make sure they ran from the other end of the pitch right to our dug-out to jump up and down in Bobby's face,' Redknapp wrote in his 1998 autobiography. Under the circumstances, relegation – and the perfect excuse to walk – came almost as a relief.

At the same time, Redknapp, who had subsisted on a weekly income of £120 while making a daily round trip of over one hundred and fifty miles from Bournemouth to Oxford, could ill afford to be without work. In the circumstances, Webb's offer of a return to the Football League with Bournemouth was like manna from heaven. When an injury crisis struck ahead of a League Cup tie against Manchester United, Redknapp even donned his boots again. 'I was in goal,' recalls Allen, 'and it was Harry's last professional appearance. He scored a goal at Old Trafford, but unfortunately it was at the wrong end! Harry tracked back Ashley Grimes, the United left-back – the only time he'd ever tracked anyone back in his life, he said – and he did a great job. But as Grimes crossed it from the by-line and I dived out to clear, Harry came sliding in and put it in the net. He just said: "Well, I won't do that again." And he didn't, because it was shortly after that that he was offered the job.'

It was touch-and-go whether Redknapp would take up that offer. 'Harry was reluctant to take the job, because he was loyal to Webby,' says Allen. 'But we all knew he would do a good job. And of course he did accept it, with a bit of persuasion, and everybody was delighted.'

Well, almost everybody. The nine-goal hiding at Lincoln was followed by another crushing defeat, 5-0 at Leyton Orient. Redknapp had put his stamp on the team, but hardly in the manner that Walker and his boardroom colleagues had anticipated. Publicly, Redknapp lost none of his natural bonhomie – 'there was a touch of offside about the sixth,' he quipped in a local radio interview after the Lincoln defeat – but inside the demons were gnawing away. 'I thought about jacking it in after the Lincoln match,' says Redknapp. 'On the way home it was like my world had come to an end.' Even his first win, 4-3 at home against Brentford on New Year's Day, was a showcase for Bournemouth's defensive frailties.

If anyone was more subject to introspection than Redknapp in the first few weeks after Webb's departure, it was Allen. In seven games under Redknapp's tutelage, the affable Teesside stopper was beaten twenty-four times. 'We must've had a defensive blip,' he ventures by way of explanation before muttering darkly of injury problems. Pressed, Allen concedes that Redknapp's appetite for adventure may also have contributed to Bournemouth's defensive travails. 'Well, you know what Harry's like,' says Allen, 'he always wanted to play football. Possibly – and this is only a guess – he was trying to coach the lads at the back to play it about. We had two big centre-halves who were used to just thumping it out, and they might have got caught out a few times trying to play it to each other. It was a time of adjustment: Harry was in charge, and he was putting his plans into action.'

If the early stages of Redknapp's tenure were a trial by fire, twelve weeks into his reign he was beginning to hit his managerial stride. As the Bournemouth team coach drew away from the Priestfield Stadium after a thumping 5-2 victory over Gillingham, he was taken aside by Alec Stock, the former Tottenham and QPR man who had preceded Webb as Cherries manager and was now a club director. Stock said he would use the following week's board meeting to press the case for Redknapp's permanent appointment as manager. A new career was beckoning.

Two days later, however, Bournemouth's ownership changed hands. Anton Johnson, a butcher-turned-businessman from Essex, bought out Walker and installed Don Megson, the former Bristol Rovers boss, as manager. Redknapp, who had been offered a role as Jimmy Melia's number two at Brighton, was ready to quit. He was prevented from doing so only by the intervention of Brian Tiler, the club's newly-appointed managing director. In Tiler Redknapp found the perfect boardroom foil, a man whose career mirrored his own and whom he could relate to both personally and professionally. Tiler had made his name as a defender with Rotherham and Aston Villa in the late sixties and early seventies. He later entered management with Wigan Athletic, spending two seasons at Springfield Park before moving to the NASL, where he was the head coach at Portland Timbers when the Seattle Sounders reached Soccer Bowl '77. Tiler's innate geniality struck a natural chord with Redknapp, and there was never any shortage of conversation when Harry passed his office of a morning. 'Brian was fantastic for me,' says Redknapp, 'he knew me inside out. He knew my moods, he knew when I had the hump. He never interfered in football, but he was always there if I needed advice. He was a good player, he captained Rotherham and Aston Villa and he knew the game.'

Under Megson's stewardship, Bournemouth finished the season in mid-table. Signings were thin on the ground that summer, but one new arrival was Ian Thompson, a £16,000 acquisition from non-league Salisbury City. The striker recalls walking into a side which already bore the stamp of Redknapp's coaching philosophy. 'Harry did most of the tactical stuff,' says Thompson. 'He was the brains behind the way that we played, and pre-season went really well. We beat Stoke and Southampton, we drew with Tottenham, and I think that series of games convinced Don that he had a pretty decent side, so he didn't really look to strengthen. But we then had a dreadful run. We lost to Preston 1-0 at home and then we went up to Burnley in midweek and lost 5-1. It escalated and we ended up bottom of the league with two wins out of eleven games. Obviously, it's the manager that takes the flak and something had to give.'

For Megson, that something came in the form of a P45 from Bournemouth's new owner, Peter McDonagh, a local builder who acquired the club when it emerged that Johnson had conflicting interests. Tiler's vocal boardroom support for Redknapp meant the identity of Megson's successor was not in doubt. 'There was never any real money at the club,' says Thompson, 'so they weren't going to look for a high-profile replacement – and Harry wasn't particularly high-profile at that stage. But he's always been a larger-than-life character, a real football guy, and he had the dressing room behind him. He had a few spats with people, but he matured into the role very quickly. He won't have a tactics board, but he will teach you how to be a professional footballer. His best quality was that he seemed to be able to coach people in every position. He would spend time on the training ground looking at each individual position and he would give you guidance on how to improve, which was fantastic.'

Redknapp's attentive support insured against a repeat of the teething problems that had blighted his first spell in charge. As then, Bournemouth's first game under Redknapp was against the league leaders – this time, Oxford United. Unlike then, Bournemouth's focus in the closing stages of the match was not whether they could avoid the embarrassment of a double-figure defeat, but whether they could stretch a 2-1 lead. 'In the last minute, they had a corner,' recalls Thompson. 'I picked the ball up on the edge of our box and started a counter-attack. I ran the length of the pitch, went round the keeper and scored. The crowd went wild. We'd won 3-1! But we got in after the game and it turned out the referee had blown [before I scored] and it was only 2-1. Harry was laughing, but he was happy because we'd won against the best team in the league and we'd played very well.'

Victory at the Manor Ground set the tone for an encouraging start to Redknapp's second period in charge, with losses few and far between in the early weeks. But when the new year began with a 2-1 reversal at relegation-haunted Port Vale, not even the most die-hard Dean Court disciple was contemplating anything other than two successive defeats. The FA Cup draw had thrown up a third-round clash against Ron Atkinson's Manchester United, a team packed with household names such as Bryan Robson, Ray Wilkins, Norman Whiteside, Arnold Muhren and Frank Stapleton. It was a daunting assignment. United were the holders. They had lost just once away from Old Trafford all season. And to compound Bournemouth's predicament John Beck, the captain, had gone down with the flu. Nobody gave Bournemouth a chance; nobody, that is, apart from Redknapp.

'We were together the Friday night before the game and he really had us believing that we could win,' recalls Thompson. Redknapp's message to his band of Third Division journeymen was simple. 'I'm going to ask you to do two things,' he told them. 'First, you're going to have to match them for work-rate. You can all do that. Second, just do the things you're good at. Go out there and believe you can win.' Within minutes of kick-off, it was clear that Bournemouth hearts were made of penetrable stuff. Superbly marshalled by their stand-in skipper, Roger Brown – who, like defensive partner

Everald La Ronde, defied an ankle injury to play – the Cherries made the most of a cautious start by United to reach the interval unscathed. When they entered the dressing room, the players found their manager in effervescent mood. 'Guys, you're going to win this game,' enthused Redknapp, 'I'm so confident.'

Fortified by Redknapp's enthusiasm, the players returned to the field brimming with belief. No one epitomised Bournemouth's defiance more than Ian Leigh, the callow but impressive goalkeeper to whom Redknapp had entrusted the number one shirt three months earlier. With the hour mark approaching, Leigh thwarted the visitors' first meaningful attempt on goal, a stinging effort from the Scotland international Arthur Graham. It proved a key moment. Three minutes later, Milton Graham capitalised on a mistake by Gary Bailey, the United goalkeeper, to bundle home a corner at the far post. The home fans' delirium had barely subsided when Thompson rattled home a rapid-fire second. Bournemouth were heading for a famous Cup upset, the reigning champions were on their way out, and – after just three months – Redknapp's management career was on a firmly upward trajectory.

'Once we were 2-0 up nobody ever thought we were going to lose it,' says Thompson. 'So credit to Harry for making a bunch of Third Division journeymen totally believe in themselves for ninety minutes. Man United didn't pay very well on the day, but we played out of our skins and that was down to Harry.' No one was more delighted with the win than Leigh. A local restaurant had promised him pizzas on the house for life if he kept a clean sheet, an offer that Bournemouth's gleeful goalie

Above: Harry Redknapp playing for his boyhood club West Ham, where he made 149 league appearances, scoring seven goals.

© *Cleva*

Below: At £31,000, Harry became Bournemouth's record signing when he arrived at Dean Court in 1972.

Above: Harry (*centre row, second from left*) and his West Ham team-mates ahead of the 1970/71 campaign.

Below: Tormenting a defender during West Ham's 3-3 draw against Derby County in January 1972.

Above: Having missed out on Ian Wright while in charge at Bournemouth, Harry finally got his man four years after his 1994 appointment as West Ham manager.

Below: Welcoming Florin Raducioiu (*left*) and former Tottenham apprentice Mark Bowen (*right*) to Upton Park in 1996.

Above: Harry makes a point in typically forthright fashion as West Ham struggle to secure Premier League survival during the 1996/97 campaign.

Below: Demonstrating that the old magic is still there on the West Ham training ground.

Above: Leaving the field alongside Sir Alex Ferguson after West Ham's 1-0 league victory at Old Trafford in December 2001.

Below: Harry issues some training-ground instructions as a young Joe Cole dreams of his first-team debut.

© *Action Images*

Above: A new chapter began for Harry when he joined Portsmouth as Director of Football in 2001.

Below left: Back in the thick of the action after taking over as Portsmouth manager in March 2002.

Below right: Applauding the Pompey fans after a victory – a routine that became ever more familiar as the promotion-winning season of 2002/03 unfolded.   *© Action Images*

Above left: The champagne-soaked celebrations begin as Harry is presented with the Division One Trophy after a 3-2 victory against Rotherham in April 2003.

Above right: After a flying start to the 2002/03 campaign, Harry receives the manager of the month award for August.

Below: A beaming Redknapp is mobbed by fans following Pompey's promotion to the Premier League.

A jubilant Redknapp celebrates as the final whistle confirms Portsmouth's 1-0 FA Cup win against Liverpool in February 2004.

was not about to pass up. 'Sure enough, he kept a clean sheet and for a little while he was getting free pizzas,' recalls Redknapp. 'The only problem was I bought that restaurant and that's when it stopped. I said: "Sorry, Ian, under new management. The old agreement doesn't stand." And boy, he could eat a pizza. He was a bit lumpy. He did like his pizza.'

Victory over Manchester United in only his thirteenth game in charge at a Third Division club put Redknapp firmly on the managerial map. On the Monday after 'the greatest day of my football life,' as Redknapp dubbed it, a wide-eyed Jamie, just ten at the time, watched in awe as the breakfast television cameras arrived on the family doorstep to interview his dad. But for all the media hoo-ha surrounding the win, Thompson has little truck with the suggestion that it was a watershed moment for his former boss. 'I think he was astute enough to realise that it was a one-off performance, just one rung on the ladder he was climbing,' says Thompson. 'He probably had more belief in his ability to motivate players for a one-off occasion, but I think he also accepted that it was just one game.'

Thompson's verdict is confirmed by Redknapp's own portrayal of the game as a footballing miracle. 'To this day, I still don't know how it happened,' says Redknapp. 'They were going well in the league, we were twenty-first in the Third Division and we won 2-0. Beat them easily. Our team that day was as bad a side as I've ever put out. Hopeless, they were – and they beat Manchester United. That shows you what can happen in the Cup.'

If a 2-0 defeat against Middlesbrough in the next round brought Bournemouth's players back down to earth with a resounding thud, Redknapp's feet had never left the ground in the first place. His long-term target was promotion. Yet Redknapp was a fledgling manager whose schooling under Ron Greenwood had been in the finer principles of the elite game. How would he fare in the earthier environs of the third tier? 'Harry was a realist,' reflects Thompson. 'He understood that you couldn't always play your way out of trouble in Division Three. He believed in getting the ball down and playing football and he also believed that the final ball into the box was the crucial thing, and he worked a lot on that in training. With us strikers, he worked on awareness in the box and finding that extra half a yard of space. So he believed in playing the game as the beautiful game should be played. But he also understood that we would be playing against teams like Wimbledon and Millwall, who would kick lumps out of you, and that trying to play around teams like that just wouldn't work. So he got a team together that could play both styles.'

It was a rocky road at times. As anyone who has crossed swords with Redknapp will attest, his temper can be explosive. 'When it goes,' says Jamie, 'it goes.' Thompson can vouch for that. He still recalls a trip to York's Bootham Crescent ground in March 1985. Five months earlier, Thompson had produced an outstanding home performance against the North Yorkshire club, scoring twice and creating another two. Redknapp's pre-match advice was unequivocal. 'Look Thommo,' he said, 'they're going to be scared to death of you, so you make sure that you're on your game.' Unfortunately, he wasn't. 'I had an absolute stinker,' recalls Thompson, who scored 'a really soft goal' in the final minute of a 4-1 defeat. As his dejected players tramped into the dressing room, a glowering Redknapp, cup of tea in hand, eyed them disapprovingly. 'As for you,' he loured, turning to face Thompson, 'I've never been so disappointed in one of my own players scoring a goal.' With that, the cup and its contents came flying towards Thompson, who ducked just in time.

Thompson believes that Redknapp's gradual recognition of how best to channel his emotions played a major role in his progress up the management ladder. 'He often used to lose his temper when he first took over,' says Thompson. 'As a coach he's a great communicator, but at first he dealt with things in a very up-front way and sometimes the shouting and the screaming and the tea-throwing went over our heads. But once he'd got to grips with that, he became an even better communicator, somebody who could understand players and how they would react in different circumstances. I think he learnt that at half-time he could have a real impact on you. And before a game he was always very calm and very clear about how he wanted us to play. He's very lucid and eloquent when he speaks on the football field. He might not consider himself a particularly educated man academically, but for football knowledge – football-speak and understanding of the game – he's head and shoulders above anyone I've ever come across. He would put a point over to you in a way that would make you understand, but he'd also do it in a way that would make you feel "Well, if I can't do it, there's something wrong with me, not you." In terms of his knowledge of the game and his ability to pick out things that don't look right tactically, he was tremendously astute. He would change little things in the middle of a game. So he was not just a great motivator and a good pick of players, he was also a really good tactical and technical coach.'

For all Redknapp's managerial gifts, Bournemouth's progress was solid rather than spectacular. The United victory merely papered over the cracks of another frustrating league campaign, although the disappointment of a seventeenth-place finish was partly assuaged by the club's first silverware since 1946. Having guided Bournemouth through the southern section of the inaugural Associate Members Cup (later known as the Football League Trophy), Redknapp was looking forward to crowning his first season as a manager with a trip to Wembley. But damage to the hallowed turf necessitated a switch of venue to Boothferry Park, the home of rival finalists Hull. 'We spun for venue and Hull won the toss,' recalls Redknapp. 'We travelled all the way up there and won [2-1]. On the way home, we stopped in a motorway service station for egg and chips and got back to Bournemouth at about five o'clock in the morning.'

Perhaps that indulgence blunted the side's appetite for Redknapp's first full season in charge. Either way, it was late October before Bournemouth shook off their early-season torpor to embark on a ten-game unbeaten run that carried them from third-bottom to ninth. It was as good as things got. Christmas defeats against Cambridge and Millwall arrested what little momentum had been established, Manchester United avenged the previous year's Cup defeat with a 3-0 victory at Old Trafford and, after failing to win any of their final four games, the Cherries were lucky to finish tenth.

Inconsistency likewise blighted the 1985/86 campaign.

The highlight of a season in which Bournemouth limped home fifteenth was Redknapp's £20,000 acquisition of Colin Clarke from Tranmere Rovers. Clarke first caught Redknapp's eye on a Division Four scouting mission. 'I remember the chairman telling me we couldn't afford him,' Redknapp explained to the *Daily Mail*, 'so I got three mates to put up five grand each and I then put up five grand and we were going to buy him between us. I told the chairman, Rodney Barton, but said: "If we sell him, we want a percentage." He then thought about it and came up with the money himself. I don't know if we would have been allowed to do it, but it seemed like a good idea.'

It was a good idea. Having ignored an eleventh-hour attempt by Chelsea to gazump the deal, Clarke banged in thirty-five goals, nailed down a place in Northern Ireland's World Cup squad and moved to Southampton the following summer for a club-record £400,000. Just as importantly, Clarke was instrumental in the recruitment of John Williams, the imposing Liverpudlian centre-half whom Redknapp regards as one of his best-ever signings. ('I think Paulo Di Canio might have one or two things to say about that,' says Williams of that accolade from his former manager, 'but it's a lovely thing and I understand the way Harry means it.') In the summer of 1985, after a season as team-mates at Tranmere, Clarke and Williams decided to leave Prenton Park. At a transfer tribunal in Birmingham, the Bournemouth-bound Clarke introduced Redknapp to Williams, who was on his way to Port Vale. Clarke left Redknapp in no doubt of his admiration for Williams, although the defender himself thought little more of the meeting until he was called into the office of

John Rudge, the Port Vale manager, one morning in December 1986. 'Harry Redknapp's made an offer for you, and we've accepted,' Rudge informed him breezily. 'So go to Bournemouth and have a chat with him.'

The Cherries were riding high in fourth place at the time, eight points adrift of Bruce Rioch's table-topping Middlesbrough side and harbouring genuine promotion prospects. The idea of stepping up a division appealed to Williams, as did the manifold charms of Bournemouth, a town that made the born-and-bred Scouser feel like he was 'on Broadway'. 'I had lunch with Harry and I don't think we even spoke about money,' he recalls. 'I knew I was going very quickly. Harry talked football constantly and explained what his plans were. He's very inspirational. I don't know if it comes across on television, but he's one of these people who makes you want to run through walls for him. He just has a quiet word, gives you a "Well done" here and there, and you feel like you're the only player at the club. That's what Harry does to you. He gives you an awful lot of confidence. He makes you feel that you're a better player than you are. He certainly did with me.'

Williams' impact on a side that had started to lose a little of its early-season momentum was remarkable. He scored on his Boxing Day debut at Bristol Rovers, and repeated the trick at home the following day against Fulham. It marked the beginning of a ten-game unbeaten run that hauled Bournemouth – who had lost four of their last six games before Williams' arrival – to the top of the table. A mid-February defeat to fellow promotion pushers Bristol City saw Redknapp's side temporarily deposed by Middlesbrough, but the response was emphatic: five successive victories, including a crucial home win over Boro, and only one more loss all season. It was enough to make Bournemouth champions; for the first time in history, Dean Court would stage Division Two football. Redknapp's reward was the third-tier Manager of the Year award and the cherished memory of an achievement that he still ranks among the proudest of his career.

'I managed to score in my first two games, which always helps,' recalls Williams. 'I don't think I played too well in those games, but people tend to remember the stats, not always what actually went on. But I remember I was very impressed with Harry. The thing about Harry is that he chooses the right players for the team he has at any given time. Although we won the league with a record number of points, there were no really outstanding players in our side. We were very much a team, and I think that's what Harry instilled in us. There were only thirteen or fourteen of us, so it was all about the [tactical] choices Harry made – and he got every one right.' None more so than those he made during the 3-1 win against Boro which, at the culmination of a season in which Rioch's side finished only three points adrift of Bournemouth with a superior goal difference, effectively proved the difference between finishing as runners-up and winning the title. 'That game was a sell-out,' says Williams. 'I was living down on the beach at Boscombe and there were Boro supporters everywhere. They said they let three thousand in, but I think it was an awful lot more than that. But Harry kept our feet on the ground, and it was a vital win. I think it really put one over on them.'

Another key figure in the thwarting of Boro's title aspirations was Jim Gabriel, who had come close to joining Rioch's Ayresome Park revolution on his return from America in December 1986. 'I was living in Bournemouth, I'd rented a place and my wife came over, but I needed a job,' recalls Gabriel. He was on the verge of accepting an offer from Rioch to become Boro's youth team coach when Redknapp, who had been lobbying hard for Gabriel's appointment as Bournemouth's assistant manager, informed him that he had been cleared to return to Dean Court. 'I knew Bruce well, because I'd worked with him in Seattle, so I phoned him to square things and he was fine with it,' says Gabriel. 'I went to work with Harry and it was great. We still had some laughs, but it was a lot more serious. Bournemouth were doing really well in the Third Division, but they had just lost a couple of games and been knocked out of the Cup [by Leyton Orient], so it wasn't a bad time for somebody new to come into the club. I'd like to think I helped. We went on a big run and ended up winning the division, which was fantastic.'

Years later, Rioch would confide to Williams: 'The one thing that Harry instilled in that team that was special was that they weren't only the best team when they had the ball, they were also the best team when they didn't have the ball.' Gabriel is in no doubt about the driving force behind that harmonious fusion of talent and industry. 'It all goes back to Harry's eye for a player. Harry's got a great understanding of what he needs in order to do well, and he put together a really strong team for that league. Harry has a bit of magic, and he can put that into a team. Players just shine under him. Like Sir

Matt Busby and Sir Alex Ferguson, he's got something that's a bit different. Managers like them can spot players and develop them, or they can buy players and make them play better. That's why they're top-class managers. And Harry's in that line; he can do all that stuff.'

Redknapp had started assembling Bournemouth's promotion-winning side the previous summer. A clutch of new players arrived including Tony Pulis, then a versatile midfielder for Division Three side Newport County, and Carl Richards, a £10,000 recruit from non-league Enfield. Richards' strike partnership with Trevor Aylott, who arrived from Chelsea, was a major factor in the club's ascent to the second tier, yielding a combined total of twenty-two league goals. At first, however, Richards' technical limitations left Redknapp aghast. Hardly the moment, then, for the burly striker to ask a favour. 'Boss, a mate of mine fancies a trial.' 'Is he as good as you?' asked Redknapp. 'No boss.' 'In that case, let's not bother.'

On August 9, with the start of the league season just a fortnight away, Bournemouth travelled to Crystal Palace for a friendly. Richards informed Redknapp that his pal would be playing up front for Palace. 'That's good news,' said Redknapp, 'he won't be a threat.' Come kick-off, however, Redknapp realised that Ian Wright was a little better than Richards had suggested.

Wright may have slipped through his fingers, but – as the Colin Clarke deal demonstrated – Redknapp was already beginning to forge a reputation as a shrewd operator in the transfer market. In January 1987, shortly after the recruitment of John Williams, he made another useful signing in the shape of Tottenham's Richard

Cooke. Cooke was an England under-21 winger plying his trade at a leading club, but Redknapp's powers of persuasion were such that he readily dropped down a couple of divisions to play for Bournemouth. 'David Pleat was the Tottenham manager, and he sent me on loan to Groningen in Holland,' recalls Cooke, who faced stiff competition for a place in the Spurs midfield. 'I was only twenty-one at the time, and I felt I was being pressurised into going over there. But I went over, had a week's trial and did really well. They wanted to sign me, but in the meantime Harry had got in touch with Tottenham. Bournemouth were on a good run at the time. The next thing I knew, I was in a meeting with Harry and after listening to him I signed straight away. He sold the club very well and told me he was looking for promotion, and he also sold me on Bournemouth as a place.'

After training alongside players of the calibre of Glenn Hoddle and Osvaldo Ardiles, Cooke could have been forgiven for thinking that life was about to become a little less challenging. Nothing could have been further from the truth. 'If training was ever lackadaisical, then you knew you were in trouble,' says Cooke, 'because Harry really is a perfectionist. I remember doing a crossing session with him one day. We were just inside the halfway line, and Harry said to me "Richard, I want you to pop this ball right on the penalty spot and then I want the centre-forwards to come in and score". I tried it the first time and I couldn't get anywhere near it. I tried it a second time and I could see he was getting outraged. By the third time I was starting to get more and more nervous. Then, when I missed it for about the fifth time he said: "For fuck's sake, this is how you do it" – and he just walked straight up and put it bang on the spot he wanted. I was gutted when he did that!'

As Williams' arrival strengthened Bournemouth's spine, so the presence of Cooke injected vital attacking impetus. The midfielder scored on his debut against Notts County and had stretched his tally to seven by the season's end. Redknapp could not have wielded the chairman's chequebook to better advantage. Yet there was nothing fortuitous about his successful transfer dealings. Those who witnessed Redknapp's managerial evolution at first hand will tell you that his status as the game's premier snapper-up of unconsidered trifles was hard won.

'People don't realise how many miles he covered,' says Williams. 'If he got a hint about a player, he'd be off and running. He was up and down the motorway constantly. Tony Pulis and I were in his office with him once. We tested Harry by going through names in the Rothmans Yearbook. He knew every player in that book from top to bottom, even if they'd only played two games for Scunthorpe two years before. His memory for players was absolutely incredible. If he hadn't seen them, he knew someone who had.'

Redknapp prepared for life in the Second Division by acquiring Shaun Brooks, an elegant playmaker whom he brought in from Leyton Orient, and the former England midfielder David Armstrong, a free recruit from Southampton. Such cultured additions ensured Bournemouth's fidelity to Redknapp's purist principles. But while his charges were easy on the eye, they found the transition to a higher level difficult. In a relegation dogfight by Christmas, Bournemouth were still mired in the drop zone a fortnight from the season's end. An immediate return to the Third Division looked likely until a run of four consecutive victories belatedly secured safety.

'Bournemouth had been down in the lower divisions for quite some time,' explains Cooke, 'so to suddenly be playing the likes of Leeds and Sheffield United was a struggle at times. Thankfully, though, we came through and a lot of that was down to the experienced players brought in by Harry. He knows the right time to play kids and when to play experienced players, and I think he's relied on that combination all through his career.'

Another constant has been the intensity with which Redknapp experiences each twist and turn in his teams' fortunes. Football means everything to him; he cares, and he expects his players to care too. 'When you hear that Harry's wife goes through it of a weekend, I can understand that,' says Cooke. 'If we ever got beaten in an away game, the coach home was a bad place to be. You just tried to keep away from Harry. You didn't even want to make eye contact. He really does take it personally. As a player playing for him, you definitely don't want to lose because you know that it's going to be a better weekend, and a better week training, when you come back in having won.'

With Bournemouth's Second Division status secure, Redknapp turned his attention to the necessary question of reinforcements. The signing of Ian Bishop, the former Everton midfielder for whom Redknapp paid Carlisle just £35,000, offered further evidence of his shrewdness in the transfer market. After smuggling Bishop into a Bournemouth hotel the night before a scheduled transfer tribunal, Redknapp received a call from Cliff Middlemass, the Carlisle manager. 'Harry,' said Middlemass, 'I need to get in touch with Bish because another club have come in with a hundred grand for him.' Reasoning that Middlemass could not sell a player he could not find, Redknapp replied that he had forgotten which of Bournemouth's eight hundred hotels Bishop was staying at. He then wished his Carlisle counterpart the best of luck and replaced the receiver. Redknapp signed Bishop the following day and sold him to Manchester City a year later at a profit of £465,000.

Redknapp's ability to generate such sums was needful. Boardroom turbulence and the introduction of an unpopular membership scheme, which caused attendance figures to dwindle, had left Bournemouth struggling financially. Consequently, Redknapp lacked leverage to secure the additional firepower that he craved and Bournemouth's limited attacking options demanded. Undermined by a pelvic injury, Thompson had returned to non-league football after just three seasons. Edwards, who had struggled to adapt to life in the second tier, had likewise departed, while Trevor Aylott was, by Redknapp's own admission, no more than 'an eight to ten goals a season man.' That left Brent Goulet, a United States international who had arrived on the south coast the previous November. Goulet was the first American player to receive a UK work permit, and Redknapp had high hopes of him. So too did Brian Tiler.

'The door was opened for us in the 1970s, and now maybe Brent will open the doors for Americans to come play in England,' said Tiler, once a player and coach at the Portland Timbers. 'We went after him because he has a real talent, with an eye for the goal. Harry comes back from training and will say: "He scored a couple more today," or "He had a fantastic goal today, you should have seen it." It's something you just haven't seen in an American up to now.' Nor was it something that was seen much subsequently. Goulet did not live up to his reputation, failing to score in six appearances before he was dispatched on loan to Crewe. Redknapp had nonetheless set a significant precedent, his willingness to delve into the American market clearing a path since trodden by more successful US imports such as Kasey Keller, Brad Friedel and Brian McBride.

Bournemouth's midfield creativity earned them plenty of plaudits for artistic merit, but in the absence of a proven goal-scorer the more tangible currency of league points proved elusive. When the club's second tilt at Division Two began badly, Redknapp responded by splashing £60,000 on Luther Blissett. The former England striker's November arrival raised more than a few eyebrows. At thirty, Blissett's best days were surely behind him. Six years had elapsed since he marked his international debut with a hat-trick midway through a season in which his twenty-seven goals for Watford made him the First Division's leading marksman. In the interim, Blissett had never come close to recapturing that form, a barren run for England earning him the moniker 'Luther Missit' while a miserable year at AC Milan culminated with a tail-between-the-legs return to Vicarage Road. His stock had since fallen so low that he found himself in Watford's reserves. With money tight at Dean Court, the received wisdom was that Redknapp had made a calamitous mistake.

CHAPTER FOUR

Even a debut goal did little to allay the doubters' concerns, particularly since it was scored during a 5-2 defeat at Barnsley which left Bournemouth dangerously close to the drop zone. Four days later, however, Redknapp's decision to purchase Blissett was vindicated in spectacular fashion, the striker rattling home four goals in a 5-1 demolition of Hull. By February, when Bournemouth renewed hostilities with Manchester United in a fifth-round FA Cup tie – Brian McClair's lone strike won an Old Trafford replay after a 1-1 draw at Dean Court – Blissett had scored eleven goals in fifteen appearances.

'Everyone thought he had gone,' recalls Redknapp. 'Dave Bassett is a mate of mine. He had him for a spell at Watford and he advised me not to sign him, but I was looking for a striker and people were asking £250,000 for ordinary players, so I thought I'd take a chance on Luther.' With two months of the season remaining, Blissett's remarkable run of form had hauled Bournemouth to the vertiginous heights of fifth, just two points off the third automatic promotion spot with a game in hand. 'It was a great achievement by Harry to get us into a position where we were looking at the First Division,' says Williams. 'I remember Leeds coming down and Billy Bremner said: "There's a miracle going on at Bournemouth." He was right, when you look at what Harry had done. He'd taken us from nowhere.'

A late loss of impetus saw the Cherries' promotion hopes fade, but Blissett's twenty-one goal haul proved the difference between a relegation battle and a respectable twelfth-place finish. 'It was an inspired signing,' says Williams. 'Luther was seemingly on his last legs at

Watford. Harry went and picked him out, and I think he's some sort of record goalscorer for Bournemouth with the amount of goals he got in such a short space of time. He was a great lad to have around the place, both on and off the pitch. Harry picks players who fit into teams that he has in his head, and I think that's his biggest thing: he chooses the right people for the team that he has at any given time.'

The following year, a spate of late-season injuries sent Bournemouth into a fatal tailspin. With six games left Redknapp was even forced to hand his sixteen-year-old son Jamie his professional debut – ironically, against West Ham. Redknapp Junior acquitted himself well, but a 4-1 defeat did nothing to ease Bournemouth's problems. On the final day of the campaign, Leeds United travelled to Dean Court for a May bank-holiday match that would either seal the Yorkshire club's promotion or consign Redknapp's men to relegation. The scene was set for an unforgettable afternoon, but the showdown was to be remembered for all the wrong reasons. In the hours before the game the visiting Leeds fans ran riot, shattering the south coast town's customary tranquillity as surely as Lee Chapman's winner broke Bournemouth hearts.

'They took the town over and smashed the place to pieces,' recalls Redknapp. 'It was a horrendous day. There weren't any Bournemouth supporters in the ground, because people were coming in and they just took the tickets off them. Every car in the car-park got smashed to pieces. They charged the police – the police took a bit of a beating that day, I think. It was a mad day, it was a bank holiday, the sun was out and they got on the beach and got on the booze. They were horrific that day, Leeds; it was a sad day for football.'

'It went right down to the last day and obviously everybody was devastated,' recalls Williams. 'But we had an awful lot of injuries and even Harry couldn't do anything about that. I dislocated my shoulder and the captain, Mark Newson, got an injury, as did Shaun Teale and Paul Morrell. It really decimated the team and the season just fell away. In his heart of hearts, Harry will know that if we'd had four or five of the injured players fit, there's no way in the world we would have gone down.'

Jimmy Gabriel likewise acknowledges the adverse effects of a lengthy injury list, but also believes that Bournemouth's parlous financial state was a major factor in the club's demise. 'The only thing that stopped Bournemouth staying in Division Two was money,' says the Scot. 'It was tough for us because we weren't getting huge crowds, so Harry couldn't go out and sign big players. He had to go and scrap it out and get players for virtually nothing. He was trying to turn Bournemouth into a team that could get into the First Division. It was a really tough task, but I think he would eventually have done it if it hadn't been for that one year where we got unbelievable injuries. When you're a club like Bournemouth, you've got maybe fourteen players who you can count on to be up to the standard to get you where you want to go. If six of them get injured for most of the year, the likelihood is that you're going to go down – and we did.'

Relegation was an unwelcome addition to Redknapp's CV, but it paled into insignificance beside the tragic events that unfolded fifty-one days later. Accompanied by a small group of friends, Redknapp travelled to Italy for a busman's holiday at the World Cup finals. Among the party were Brian Tiler – who, having decided to tread an alternative career path within football, had recently stepped down as Bournemouth's managing director – and Michael Sinclair, the York City chairman. It should have been a dream break. The group booked into an idyllic coastal retreat, were ferried to the tournament stadia in a hotel minibus, and had tickets for every round of the event. But in the early hours of Sunday July 1, after a trip to the Stadio Olimpico to see the quarter-final between Italy and Ireland, the group's bus was passing through the province of Latina, fifty miles south of Rome, when a car containing three young Italian soldiers ploughed headlong into them at 70mph. The three youths were killed instantly, as was Brian Tiler.

Redknapp, who had drifted into a deep sleep before the collision and was subsequently knocked unconscious, recalls nothing of the moment of impact. But Sinclair later described how the vehicle was flipped into the air, landing on its roof before sliding some fifty yards along the road. Although doused in petrol, Sinclair bravely pulled Redknapp clear of the wreckage. He also rescued the Aston Villa chairman Fred Whitehouse and his son. Redknapp suffered a hairline fracture of the skull, a broken nose, cracked ribs and a severe gash to his left leg. He lost his sense of smell permanently and temporarily lost the ability to taste. Like the emergency services, who pulled a blanket over his head, the doctors who treated him on his arrival at hospital initially believed him to be dead. Redknapp recovered consciousness two days later, but was at first told nothing of Tiler's death.

CHAPTER FOUR

'I had just dozed off when the accident happened and I woke up two days later in hospital,' Redknapp told the *Bournemouth Echo* after regaining consciousness. 'The people who pulled me out thought I was dead. Everyone has been magnificent – very, very kind. I have a top doctor looking after me. My main worry is my leg, which has a terrible gash in it. But basically I'm just very glad to be alive. Doctors have told me I will have to rest up for quite a while, so that is what I will do. But after that I will be back to work. I don't expect I'll be putting a track suit on for quite a while though.'

Redknapp's skull injuries meant he was unable to return home on an ordinary flight. But a fortnight after the accident, Bournemouth paid £10,000 to have him flown into nearby Hurn Airport on a special low-altitude aircraft. He was finally released from hospital ten days later, although specialists advised that he would be unable to return to work until October. 'Maybe now you're going to take it easy,' implored Sandra, whom Redknapp had prevented from accompanying Jamie and Mark when they flew to Italy in the immediate aftermath of the accident. Some hope.

'We played a pre-season game at Aldershot,' recalls Williams. 'They put half the reserve team out and half the first team. I was sitting in the stands with some of the lads, and with twenty minutes of the game gone, who should pop his head around the corner but Harry. He wasn't supposed to be there, but he came and sat at the back of the stand with us. He looked an awful lot better, although there was still a lot of recuperation to come over the next few weeks. It didn't take him too long to get back to his old self football-wise, but I think the loss of Brian was devastating for him. His strength of character shone through – he came back to football as quickly as he could and just got on with it.'

Seven years later, Alan Hudson suffered horrific injuries after being hit by a car while crossing the Mile End Road in London. He narrowly avoided having both legs amputated and did not fully regain consciousness for almost three months. When he finally came round, Redknapp was soon at his bedside; he knew, better than most, what Hudson had been through. 'One of Harry's strong points is that he really couldn't have a bigger heart,' says Hudson. 'When I'd got through the coma, he came to the hospital to see me. He brought champagne and couldn't do enough for me. He said to me: "All the wife's done is give me a bollocking that I don't come and see you enough." Later, when I was going back into hospital to have operations, I was going to West Ham every home game and Harry really looked after me. He was brilliant. Even if I had an operation on the Thursday, I'd be at West Ham on the Saturday. After the game I'd be in the office with him and [Sir Alex] Ferguson or whichever manager was in town, and it was really good therapy for me. It got me away from the hospital and everything else, and it brought a lot of things back to me on the football side.'

Hudson believes that the accident totally redrew Redknapp's world picture. 'It shook Harry up big time,' he says. 'He was close to death's door and I think he appreciates life a lot more now. Not that he didn't before, but he really took it to heart. He warned players about the dangers of drinking and driving, that they shouldn't do this, shouldn't do that. I think it really changed him.'

Others are not so sure. Richard Cooke, who moved to Luton the season before Redknapp's accident but returned two years later, found no discernible difference. 'When I came back, he was the same old Harry,' says Cooke. John Williams agrees, adding that if the tragedy changed Redknapp it did so positively, igniting the embers of a previously latent ambition. 'People have said that he's changed since the crash but I can't honestly say I've found that,' says John Williams. 'He's as passionate now about the game and about training players as he was when I first met him in 1986. At times, when he's on his own, I'm sure he has thoughts of what happened and reflects on it. But I don't think he's changed. He's just as passionate now, if not more so; passionate to strive and to be manager of England. Perhaps if that crash hadn't happened he'd have been happy with whatever cards life dealt him, but I think he's a bit more ambitious now because of what happened.'

Chapter Five

'If you don't do it,' urged the voice on the other end of the line, 'someone else will. And you're the man for the job.' It was a strangely resonant choice of words, one which cast Harry Redknapp's mind back to a similar moment five summers earlier. John Lyall had just parted company with West Ham after failing to avert relegation to the Second Division. A radio interviewer asked Bobby Moore who should replace him. 'There's only man for the job,' replied Moore, 'and that's Harry Redknapp.' On that occasion, with the Upton Park throne vacant and his managerial star on the rise, Redknapp felt humbled to have an ally of such stature. This time round, the support of a close friend weighed upon him like a millstone. To Redknapp's mind, West Ham had a manager. His name was Billy Bonds, and he was not only a long-standing pal – Redknapp had been best man at his wedding over two decades earlier – but also an Upton Park legend. Bonds had been at the Boleyn Ground, man and boy, almost three decades, setting a club record for appearances, captaining the side to two FA Cup victories and, as manager, twice leading the Hammers out of the Second Division. And now here he was on the phone, just hours after leaving the club, trying to convince Redknapp to take over as manager.

Bonds had talked about packing it in before, but Redknapp hadn't expected this. Only three months earlier they had watched together from the sidelines as the Hammers ended the 1993/94 campaign with a 3-3 draw against Southampton. They were united by a sense of nostalgia that day, as Upton Park – soon to be redeveloped in compliance with the terms of the Taylor Report – bade farewell to the Chicken Run, the notoriously feisty lower-east-tier area they had once patrolled with distinction. A game of high drama provided a fitting swansong, with a premature pitch invasion temporarily halting the goal glut before Southampton scored a late own goal that might have sealed their relegation had results elsewhere gone differently. 'Fortunes tend to come and go for you so dramatically in this game there is no telling what might happen next,' Bonds mused afterwards. How prophetic those words seemed now. 'Look Bill,' said Redknapp, 'if I take this job it's going to look like I've stitched you up.' Bonds told him not to worry. 'Take it,' he implored, adding that they knew the truth and that was all that mattered. Redknapp was not convinced.

A few days earlier, Redknapp had been contacted by Geoffrey Hayward, the former Bournemouth chairman. Hayward was part of a three-man consortium attempting to persuade Norman Hayward, his most recent successor at the head of the boardroom table, to sell his majority stake in the club. A £100,000 deal had been agreed, and Hayward wanted Redknapp, who was on West Ham's pre-season tour of Scotland at the time, to return to Dean Court as manager-director. It was a tempting offer. Redknapp had recently signed a new three-year contract as Bonds' number two, but his home was on the south coast and his old club was offering similar money. In the two years since his July 1992 return to West Ham, the club had won promotion from the Second Division and then finished a respectable thirteenth in the Premier League. Redknapp's contribution to that success, both on the training pitch and through his canny manoeuvrings in the transfer market, had burnished his standing as one of the country's brightest young managers.

As Redknapp weighed up the competing claims of the two clubs that had defined his career – and, by extension, his life – he would hardly have been human had the whirligig of conflicting emotions he experienced not included a latent sense of achievement. At forty-seven, the man once sacked by Seattle Sounders of the North American Soccer League was suddenly in demand. It was the deserved outcome of a lifelong adherence to the work ethic exemplified and instilled by his parents. Modern management may be increasingly the preserve of retired stars high on profile and low on experience, but Redknapp had won his spurs the old-fashioned way, through accumulated knowledge and long-term endeavour. In the process he had earned the respect not only of Bonds but also of Alvin Martin, the former England centre-half who enjoyed a nineteen-year career at Upton Park and shares with Bonds the distinction of having been awarded two West Ham testimonials.

'Harry did it the hard way,' says Martin. 'He is now incredibly successful, but he's getting the rewards of his experience. He didn't get a job in the Premier League to start off, he earned his stripes in the lower divisions. That's the most difficult way of doing it. Any job in football is difficult, whether it's in League One or League Two. But the higher up the leagues you go, the more support you get – even though there's the same pressure and the same difficulties managing lower down. At that level, it's nearly impossible to stay successful over a period of ten years. You might have a run where you manage to get some talented players together who are better than the rest have got, and that might keep you going for two or three years. But to do it over the amount of time that Harry did it, you've got to have real talent. One thing he's done really well is kept his persona the same. He's still approachable. If you took a poll of the managers that the press most want to deal with, Harry would be at the top of that. He's kept his accessibility and kept his feet on the floor. But he's also got a hard side – people don't recognise that, but he's certainly got that because you don't survive in his line of work without it.'

Torn between the opposite poles of a natural loyalty to West Ham and the tantalising prospect of a return to his beloved Bournemouth, Redknapp was soon forced to draw on that natural resilience. Bonds' reaction to the prospect of losing his trusted lieutenant was mixed. He understood Redknapp's desire to return to the south coast, but stressed that their fortunes were inextricably entwined: if Redknapp left Upton Park, so would he.

Redknapp was still wrestling with that dilemma when it became clear that news of Bournemouth's approach was about to be made public. He was ushered into a hastily-convened meeting with the West Ham chairman Terence Brown at which Bonds and Peter Storrie, the club's managing director, were also present. The situation as Brown saw it was simple: Redknapp's desire to move on was motivated by a desire to become manager. Brown's remedy was equally straightforward. Bonds would make the proverbial move upstairs, taking a paid directorship, and Redknapp would step into his shoes. The problem for Brown was that neither man cared for the proposed reshuffle. While Redknapp was mortified at being offered his friend's job, Bonds was affronted by the implied suggestion that he was a lesser manager than his number two. With nothing resolved, the party returned home from Scotland to mounting newspaper speculation about Redknapp's future.

That Saturday, with Bonds growing increasingly disenchanted, West Ham continued their pre-season preparations with a visit to Portsmouth. The manager's mood was not improved by a lacklustre display from Joey Beauchamp, a left-sided winger signed from Oxford United for £1m earlier that summer. Beauchamp had done little to endear himself to the Hammers hierarchy. He complained after his first training session that he was feeling homesick and should have signed for Swindon instead. He was given permission to commute in from Oxfordshire, but then blamed the stresses of negotiating the M40 for his failure to make training one morning. When Redknapp later suggested that Bonds became 'fed up with people who didn't show the same standards as he did,' it didn't require much imagination to guess who he had in mind. Was it the Beauchamp affair that finally tipped Bonds over the edge? Whatever the truth, three days later – and despite a last-ditch effort by Redknapp to dissuade him – Bonds left the club. 'Billy Bonds has decided to call it a day after twenty-seven years' service as player, youth coach and then manager,' West Ham announced in a statement. 'He fully supports the appointment of Harry Redknapp and wishes him every success for the future.'

Redknapp was immediately installed as Bonds' successor, but his misgivings were plain. He sympathised with the subsequent groundswell of support for Bonds, who responded to the official version of events by emphasising that 'the board wanted to reshuffle the pack' and stressing that he had declined the proffered directorship 'because I still feel that I have something to offer as a manager.' The ink had barely dried on Redknapp's five-year contract before he was threatening to resign. 'I have never felt so bad about anything in my life,' he said. 'The way I feel at the moment I am going to pack it in. The truth is I pleaded with Bill to stay. I wanted things to continue as they were. But Bill had had enough. He would not be budged. I can't go on in this job knowing people might think I stitched Billy up. How am I going to take training? How can I look the players in the eye? It was suggested, nothing more than that, that there might be a change with me as team manager and Bill as a paid director. Nothing was set in concrete but Bill said he was going to step down. He'd had enough. I tried to talk him out of it. I want the truth to be told because if people think I've stabbed my best friend in the back then I can't stay at the club. My friendship with Bill is worth more than anything to me.'

Redknapp's loyalty to Bonds was reflected in the dressing room. 'I think we were all placed in a similar position,' recalls Martin. 'It was a difficult time for Harry and for everybody. Personally, I had a tremendous amount of respect for Bill. He wasn't just a manager, he was a friend. Bill did a great job, and I think he's still admired and fondly remembered at West Ham, both as a player and as a manager. So it was a situation that none of us wanted – me especially, being the oldest pro at the club. But my take on it was that we all knew the industry, we knew what could happen. Departures, sackings and comings and goings happened all the time. My stance was "I'm on a contract and I'm being paid to give one hundred and ten per cent for the club. That one hundred and ten per cent doesn't rely on who is manager, it relies on me pulling a shirt on and doing everything I can to help us win football matches." You focus on what you need to do for the club.'

With the season looming, what West Ham needed above all was a clear sense of leadership. Redknapp's recruitment two summers earlier had been well received, with Martin not alone in welcoming the arrival of a 'bubbly, chirpy character' who became 'the life and soul' of the dressing room and offered a wealth of experience. 'Harry was a good person to have around the place, but I think what he also brought in from West Ham's point of view was a knowledge of the lower leagues,' says Martin. 'He recommended several players – Peter Butler [a combative midfielder from Southend United], [Bournemouth midfielder] Matty Holmes, Mark Robson [a lively winger rescued from Spurs' reserve team] – and they all did well.'

The unlikeliest of Redknapp's recruits was Steve Davies, a West Ham fan who spent the opening half of a pre-season friendly against Oxford United chastising Lee Chapman. At the interval, Redknapp turned to the heckler. 'Can you play as good as you talk?' Davies, a former parks player, replied that he could. So Redknapp handed him a strip, and a quarter of an hour later Davies was making his West Ham debut. 'We didn't know what was going on,' recalls Martin. 'I was playing in the game and I remember thinking when the lad came on: "Who's that?" I just assumed that he was a trialist who I hadn't seen before. It soon became apparent that he wasn't very good. There was a bit of banter flying around the ground, and then we realised what had happened. But it was typical Harry. There's a lighter side to him that's quite unpredictable; he sees the funny side of the game.'

While the manner of Bonds' departure allowed little scope for levity, such antics ensured that the players were more than averagely acquainted with the new gaffer by the time all concerned gathered to discuss the crisis. 'We had a meeting in the dressing room, a private discussion about what had gone on,' recounts Martin. 'We were all very much in the dark about the circumstances but, in situations like that, everyone needs to know who's going to be taking over. Harry was the man who the club had approached. He'd been offered the job, but he felt unsure about whether he was going to take it. The feedback in the meeting was that whoever took the job would get backed one hundred per cent by the players.'

As the players threw their weight behind the new man,

so too did Bonds. 'There is absolutely no animosity between Harry and me,' he insisted. 'We are the greatest friends and always will be. Nobody wants him to succeed more than I. He is the best man for the job.' There could be no denying that Redknapp and West Ham were indeed a perfect fit. As Bournemouth manager, Redknapp had forged a reputation for entertaining, attack-minded football. A Redknapp team did not just hoof the ball forward or defend in numbers and play on the counter. Raised on traditional Upton Park virtues, his sides consisted of technically-gifted players who made creative, intelligent use of possession and placed a premium on delivering the final ball with accuracy and intent. Inevitably, this aesthetically-pleasing brand of football was achieved at a price: capable of beating the best, Redknapp's sides were equally prone to the odd shocker. But a belief that losing beautifully was preferable to winning ugly had been a central dictate of the West Ham manifesto since the days of Ron Greenwood. Redknapp, an ex-Hammer whose veins coursed with claret-and-blue blood, understood that creed as well as anyone.

The opportunity to manage his boyhood club came at an auspicious time for Redknapp. Two years earlier, just weeks before Bonds invited him back to Upton Park as his number two, the newly-formed Premier League had agreed what was then the most lucrative broadcasting deal in the history of British sport. BSkyB, together with the BBC, paid £305m for the rights to exclusive match coverage over a five-year period. Suddenly, the game was awash with money as never before; those who prospered in this brave new world would reap untold wealth. Had it not been for a terminal falling-out with Ken Gardiner, a Bournemouth director whom he grabbed by the throat after taking exception to a remark about Brian Tiler, Redknapp might have missed the gravy train. Instead, his acceptance of Bonds' offer of a return to East London signalled the beginning of a long and lucrative career in the top flight.

On a personal level, however, Redknapp's ascent to the Upton Park throne had less palatable consequences. Beneath the public show of amity that accompanied his exit, Bonds was far from happy about the alleged doctoring of the original statement announcing his departure. He also took exception when Redknapp later asked him to appear in a photograph alongside him, branding the request 'selfish' in an interview with the *Sunday Mirror*. Six years later, Redknapp's well-meaning offer of a return to West Ham, made publicly in his autobiography, also caused offence, as did the book's portrayal of a drinking culture at Upton Park during Bonds' tenure. The net result was the fracturing of a friendship of three decades' standing.

The soul-searching that preceded Redknapp's eventual decision to take the West Ham job was plain. 'Nobody has suffered more than I have in the last two weeks,' he confided on the eve of the new season. 'No one wanted Bill to leave this club, no one wanted him to stay here more than I did. But Bill's not here. I'm very positive about the job and I have no doubts I will make a big success of it. Last season we were favourites for relegation and this time it is even more the case. We've had a nightmare pre-season and haven't won a single game, even against non-league opposition. But we've got to pick ourselves up and get on with it.'

Martin believes that Redknapp was ideally equipped for the challenge. 'What I personally liked about Harry is that he's a very good motivator,' he says. 'He makes it easy for you to enjoy your football, and I think players respond to that. We all come into the game to enjoy it. The pressures that surround it, the ups and downs, are not like they might be with an athlete, where you have five or six months to train for an event which then goes by and you get over, football is constantly picking yourself up off the ground. Unless you're lucky enough to play for one of the top four and you win the majority of your games, you're continually having to pick yourself up after being beaten and make sure you're up for the next game. I think that's something that Harry was really good at – he got the balance right between working the players and lifting them.'

Redknapp's first major decision was to install Frank Lampard Snr as his number two. The defensive expertise of the former Hammers right-back provided the ideal counterpoint to Redknapp's natural attacking instincts. Lampard's presence also deepened the sense of continuity between the club's past and present. 'There was a genuine trust between Harry and Frank,' says Martin. 'Frank's reputation and his experience as a defensive player certainly helped, and Harry was good at taking on board advice. He wasn't a dictator, he would always listen to what people had to say. That's part and parcel of being a manager. Harry didn't want people around who were never going to disagree with him. He didn't mind people piping up and saying something, he would encourage that. Frank offered a new dimension when he was looking at games because of his defensive attributes, and with the connection between Frank and the crowd as well, it was a nice balance.'

The campaign got underway with little sign of the close season turbulence abating. Redknapp's first match in charge, a goal-less home draw against Leeds, was a far cry from the nine-goal mauling with which his Bournemouth stewardship commenced. But the Hammers, bullied by Howard Wilkinson's side throughout, were fortunate to escape with a point. Redknapp's post-match assessment was typically candid. 'I need a striker,' he concluded after a laboured performance by the front pairing of Trevor Morley and Lee Chapman, 'someone who can score goals and make things happen around the box.' Results over the next three weeks confirmed that analysis. A run of three successive defeats was punctuated by just one entry in the goals-for column; even that was a penalty. 'The players asked me to stay on after Billy left but they have a funny way of showing they want me,' mused Redknapp.

With five games gone and only two points to show for their efforts, the closest West Ham had come to scoring in open play was when Morley hit a post at Maine Road. When the burly forward subsequently suffered a knee injury, Don Hutchison, the attacking midfielder acquired from Liverpool for a club-record fee of £1.5m, was pressed into service as an ersatz striker. Clearly, the need to replenish West Ham's ailing attack had gone up a notch in urgency. 'We need a couple of front men and fast,' Redknapp re-iterated. 'I need to do some wheeling and dealing in the transfer market. I've been trying to shuffle the pack but there's not much more shuffling I can do.' As it turned out, there was: full-back David

Burrows was shuffled off to Everton, with Upton Park alumnus Tony Cottee and £500,000 coming in the opposite direction.

Cottee's readmission to the West Ham fold, although it began in unpromising fashion with a red card at Anfield, proved an inspired move on Redknapp's part. A week later, the prodigal son – for so the match-day programme labelled him – marked his return by swivelling to drive home a close-range winner against Aston Villa. The goal, the first of thirteen in the league for Cottee, lifted Redknapp's side out of the relegation zone for the first time in almost a month. Without Cottee's marksmanship, the Hammers would almost certainly have been facing a return to the second tier. 'Harry saw where there was a weakness in our team and found a solution to it,' says Martin. 'These days, there are many times when supporters look at players who are brought in and think "We don't really need him, do we?" But with Harry there was always an obvious reason why a player was in our dressing room.'

Despite Cottee's contribution – and a six-game unbeaten streak – only goal difference separated West Ham from the drop zone by the time Blackburn Rovers, the league leaders, arrived at the Boleyn Ground in late April. With four games remaining after that match – and Liverpool, Manchester United and fellow relegation strugglers Crystal Palace still to face – victory was crucial. Yet Kenny Dalglish's side had lost only three times all season away from Ewood Park, and for all Redknapp's bullishness – "We are unbeaten in six and we have every chance of survival," he declared on the eve of the game – it was difficult to see where the eight points he deemed necessary to reach safety would come from. The initial outlines of an answer were sketched by Marc Rieper, the Denmark international defender signed on loan from Brondby the previous December, who headed the Hammers in front. The picture was subsequently completed by Don Hutchison, who applied the *coup de grâce* seven minutes from time. 'Why are people surprised?' enquired Redknapp afterwards. 'To come to Upton Park with a full house behind the Hammers is a very difficult place to win. Having said that, we'll probably get relegated.'

The gallows humour proved unwarranted. Despite a defeat at Crystal Palace that ended West Ham's unbeaten streak at eight games, victory over the title favourites gave Redknapp's side the belief to reach the finish line. A 3-0 win over Liverpool four days later preserved West Ham's top-flight status, and if victory tasted sweet to Hutchison, who scored a brace against his former club, for Redknapp it came as a mighty relief. 'I can now get some sleep,' he said. 'It's been a great performance by the lads because ten games ago we looked dead and buried. I think we were four-to-one on to go down – in fact I know we were, because I had a tenner on myself.' Redknapp celebrated survival by masterminding a 1-1 draw with Manchester United on the final day of the season that denied Sir Alex Ferguson's side the title. By then he had also persuaded Rieper, whose outstanding form at the heart of the Hammers defence had attracted covetous glances from various Premier League rivals, to sign a permanent deal. In every respect, the old gambler had once again defied the odds.

As Upton Park aficionados will attest, not all

Redknapp's foreign signings took to the English game with the alacrity of Rieper. Still smarting from the previous season's goal-scoring travails, Redknapp prioritised the summer acquisition of a new striker. His natural inclination was to buy British, but a lack of funds thwarted a bid to sign Bristol Rovers' Marcus Stewart. Instead, Redknapp decided to hazard £800,000 on Sparta Rotterdam front man Marco Boogers, a player he had seen only on video. It was another roll of the dice. 'Only time will tell how well Marco does,' said Redknapp. 'But I think it's good value compared to what players in Britain are going for. You're being asked to pay £1.5m for strikers who haven't even had Premier League experience.' Time did indeed tell, and quickly too. Sixteen minutes after coming on as a late substitute at Old Trafford in the second game of the season, Boogers scythed down Gary Neville to earn a red card. Fined a fortnight's wages, he subsequently declared himself mentally unfit to play before fleeing to Holland. 'I made a mistake in the transfer market,' Redknapp later conceded.

Other foreign signings left Redknapp similarly exasperated. One was Florin Raducioiu, the Romania forward. Raducioiu arrived from Espanyol in the summer of 1996, but returned to Spain six months later after missing a League Cup tie at Stockport in favour of a Harvey Nichols shopping trip with his wife. Equally eccentric was Paolo Futre, the Portugal attacker who stormed out on learning that he did not have the number ten shirt. 'Eusebio number ten, Futre number ten,' explained the former AC Milan man in his halting English. The bizarre spat was later resolved in an appropriately novel manner when John Moncur agreed to relinquish the shirt in exchange for a free holiday at Futre's luxury villa on the Algarve.

Such signings were largely the result of financial constraints, although Martin insists that Redknapp's purchases were rarely without merit. 'There were very few players that Harry brought in who didn't have something,' says Martin. 'He'd bring them in and you'd train with them for a week, and you'd think "Yeah, they're decent players." There was the odd one who couldn't apply his ability to the English game, but you could always see why they were there. Marco Boogers, for instance, was big and strong and he'd done well in Holland, so you could see why Harry brought him in. And let's not forget that Harry also made some inspirational signings like Paolo Di Canio and Stuart Pearce. The more chances you take [with signings], the more chance there is of you getting some wrong. Nobody ever gets them all right, but I would have thought that Harry's percentage in terms of risky transfers is better than anyone in the business.'

Redknapp's youth-development record merits similarly favourable comparison with most of his peers. A couple of months before Raducioiu's arrival, West Ham's youth team, already winners of the South East Counties League, reached the final of the 1996 FA Youth Cup. Their success was the first evidence that a renewed emphasis on the cultivation of home-grown talent was having the desired effect. According to Tony Carr, the club's Director of Youth Development, the rekindling of West Ham's once celebrated youth policy was strongly influenced by Redknapp's return. 'Because Harry was an ex-West Ham youth product himself, he took an active interest in what we were doing,' says Carr. 'He liked to have input into how the system was running, and it was his impetus and enthusiasm – and, it would be fair to say, disappointment, because at the time our youth production line had slowed to a crawl – that made us reassess how our system worked. Harry is passionate about the game, he loves to see good players. He used to come and watch the coaching, and maybe he was a little bit disturbed with the quality that he saw when he first arrived. He was a senior member of staff and he wasn't afraid to tell people what he thought wasn't right or what needed to be improved. It's fair to say that the whole system got a bit of a shake-up when Harry arrived. We invested a bit more and re-structured the recruitment and development side of things. It was the kick up the backside that the club needed.'

Among the early products of West Ham's revitalised approach was Rio Ferdinand, who first impacted on Redknapp's consciousness as a fifteen-year-old. Ferdinand lined up in midfield for West Ham's youth side when they travelled to Chelsea for the second leg of the 1994 Southern Junior Floodlit Cup final. First-team commitments prevented Redknapp from attending the game but, after a heavy first-leg defeat for West Ham, he was expecting the worst when his father called with an update later that night. 'I've just seen the best player I've seen in years,' enthused Harry Snr, almost neglecting to mention that the Hammers had staged a dramatic turnaround to win on penalties. A bemused Redknapp began wracking his brains. None of the suggested contenders rang a bell with his father. Finally, Harry Snr unearthed the match programme. 'He's called

Ferdinand,' he said. 'Ferdinand? He's a schoolboy,' replied Redknapp, 'he won't have played.'

As Redknapp subsequently discovered, however, Ferdinand had played, bestriding midfield with a poise and elegance that won rave reviews from Carr. 'Rio was a schoolboy at the time and had been a substitute in the first leg, where we'd been beaten quite heavily,' recalls Carr. 'I decided to give the young players a chance, so I played Rio in midfield and he was outstanding. We'd been playing him as a defender but on the night he played fantastically well in midfield. Harry knew who Rio was, but he wasn't aware of how good he was. He couldn't see the boys play because we played on Saturdays, which was when the first team were playing. But Harry's father watched the game that night and he said to him: "I tell you what, Harry, there's a bloody good player playing for your youth team".'

Alongside Ferdinand that night was Frank Lampard Jnr, who converted the cup-winning penalty. Unsurprisingly, Lampard's talents had long since registered on his uncle's radar. 'I never had any doubt that Frank would make it,' said Redknapp when Lampard later underlined his burgeoning potential with a League Cup hat-trick against Walsall. 'Frank has always had the ability to run all day but now he's got stronger and bigger. I always knew he was going to be a player.' Redknapp also took the opportunity to cock a snook at those sections of the West Ham crowd who attributed Lampard's presence in the team to nepotism. 'I am especially pleased for Frank because, let's be honest, when he first got in the side he did not get a very good reception, which we were all disappointed about. People maybe thought something stupid like he was getting his chance because his old man is the assistant manager here, but that's rubbish.'

'There was some ill feeling with young Frank, which I could never understand,' says Martin. 'West Ham had a player who scored a lot of goals for them from midfield and brought a lot of money in. If they could do that with another twenty players, it wouldn't be a bad thing. So it's a shame that young Frank isn't really held in the esteem he deserves.' Lampard made his first-team debut as a substitute against Coventry City in January 1996, while Ferdinand took his bow late on against Sheffield Wednesday on the final day of the same campaign. Their blooding served notice to the outside world that the Academy of Football was once again up and running. Inside three years, seven of the young hopefuls who appeared in the 1996 Youth Cup final had played in the Premier League.

'We could attract the best youngsters because Harry has a reputation for putting them in the first team,' says Carr. 'There's no one better than Harry [at handling that transition], because if he believes in a youngster then he'll push him and give him every opportunity. When Harry became manager, there were a lot of players that made their debuts at a very young age, and that's because Harry believed in them. He's always done that; he did it with his own son, Jamie, down at Bournemouth. Harry wants to see homegrown kids do well. It takes courage, because they're not going to go in there and immediately make a massive impact. You have to nurture them, they take time – you have to dip them in and dip them out. There's an art to knowing when the time is right, because if young players aren't given the chance at the right time, then sometimes it can bypass them – and it might take years, or a switch to another club, before they get the opportunity again.'

Carr's views are echoed by Alvin Martin. 'A lot of credit has got to go to Tony Carr and his team, but I think what Harry recognised is that the players were ready to play,' says Martin. 'Harry is one of the great managers who will play young players even though his job is on the line. It takes courage to play youngsters because they make mistakes. Harry had the courage to [alternate between] playing them and resting them, and that's where his management skills came in. There was a balance there. It's easy for managers to want experienced players, because they know what they're going to get. They also know that these players are making decisions on the pitch that are born of experience. But what Harry did was to take some young players, who he knew were going to make mistakes, and still play them. I had a lot of respect for that.'

Redknapp's willingness to give youth its head regardless of consequence was emphasised when he sent on Lampard and Ferdinand for the final twenty minutes of the 1995/96 campaign. At stake was the possibility of clinching West Ham's highest league finish for a decade. That milestone was reached, but even tenth place was not enough to insulate Redknapp from the criticism that greeted his foreign signings the following season. Lofty expectations had been raised around Upton Park, and Redknapp's hastily-assembled band of hired mercenaries were unable to meet them. A knee injury forced Futre to hang up his boots. Raducioiu went shopping. Illie

Dumitrescu, another misfiring Romanian forward, was shipped off to Mexican side Club America. 'I've been very disappointed with some of the players I've brought to the club, players who have failed to live up to their reputations,' said Redknapp. 'It has all gone wrong.'

The scale of the problem was underlined by a wretched run over the festive season that brought a humbling League Cup exit against lowly Stockport County, defeat at the Boleyn Ground to relegation-threatened Nottingham Forest and a devastating FA Cup loss against Wrexham. By now the fans were baying for the dismissal of Redknapp, who candidly described the Wrexham result as the worst of his career. 'I can understand their frustration,' he said. 'We finished tenth last season, spent £4m during the summer and I suppose the fans thought we were getting somewhere. I just feel I've let them down and I like the people here too much to have them think ill of me. I don't want to stick around if I'm not wanted, but I can't see where I'm going to get a goal right now and it's an impossible situation. This time last year we were on the way to finishing tenth in the Premier League and our kids reached the FA Youth Cup final – and then, bosh, it all goes boss-eyed. Most people wake up in the morning wondering whether to have cornflakes or toast for breakfast, but I woke up this morning and wondered where our next goal was coming from. I'm not a quitter by nature, but sometimes you have to accept what's going on. If the chairman decides I have to go, then I'll accept it.'

Under the circumstances, agreeing a deal with Everton for the sale of Slaven Bilic, the centre-half whose outstanding form for the Hammers had earned him a place in the Croatia side, was not good news. Joe Royle, the Everton manager, had got wind of a clause in Bilic's contract stating that any offer over £4.5m would trigger the defender's release. For Redknapp, the only up side was the big Croatian's decision to remain at Upton Park until the end of the season. Losing a key player in such a manner could be regarded as a misfortune; using the money from the sale to buy two players struggling to hold down a regular first-team place at their respective clubs looked like rank carelessness. That, though, is precisely what Redknapp did, splashing £2.3m on the Newcastle front man Paul Kitson and a further £5m on Arsenal's John Hartson.

While Redknapp hailed the arrival of 'two young strikers [who] can benefit West Ham not only this season but also in the long term', others weren't so sure. The Celtic manager Tommy Burns, who had also contemplated a move for Hartson, described Redknapp's investment in the Welshman as 'a huge gamble'. When Hartson received a debut booking at Derby, bringing his total for the season to eleven and so triggering an automatic two-game suspension, it looked like Burns could be right. Then, one wet Monday night in late February, with West Ham mired in the bottom three, Tottenham came calling at Upton Park. In one of the season's most memorable games, home debutants Hartson and Kitson both made the score-sheet as Redknapp's side ran out 4-3 winners. 'John's not just a big lump,' Redknapp enthused after an eye-catching performance from Hartson, who also won the decisive penalty. 'He can move, has pace, and is a real handful for defenders.' It proved an accurate appraisal. By the season's end, Hartson had scored five goals in eleven games. He was outshone only by Kitson, who netted eight times in fourteen games as West Ham reached safety with a game to go.

'I said when we signed Hartson that we had got a bargain but I think a few people thought I was barmy,' said Redknapp, who was further vindicated when Hartson bagged a twenty-four goal haul the following season. 'But I could see what he could do for us alongside Kitson. I knew I had to do something. The chairman backed me and for the first time since I've been at the club I was given decent money. It would have been tempting to have just rushed in and bought the first available players, but I managed to keep my nerve and got Hartson and Kitson. Even though their fees weren't big compared to what some clubs can pay, it was a huge amount for us and if it hadn't come off I would have been out of the door.'

Interestingly, West Ham's 1996/97 campaign is remembered not for the fact that Redknapp preserved the club's top-flight status – under the circumstances, finishing fourteenth was not an achievement to be sniffed at – but as the era of Upton Park's foreign flops. History has afforded primacy to the problem (Boogers and co), not the solution (Hartson and Kitson). But the best in the business make mistakes. Sir Alex Ferguson once made the error-prone Massimo Taibi Britain's most expensive goalkeeper, and yet Manchester United's 1999/2000 campaign is rightly recalled not for that rare lapse of judgement but for the club's sixth Premier League title under the Scot. Ferguson escaped censure because Ferguson did what Ferguson does: he won the title. Yet in 1996/97, when Redknapp performed his own party piece by defying the odds to keep West Ham in the top flight for the fourth successive season, the talk was all of dodgy foreign signings. Clearly, different standards of evaluation are at work.

'Outside the game, Harry really hasn't got the credit he deserves,' says Shaka Hislop, the goalkeeper whose summer 1998 arrival at Upton Park coincided with the dawn of West Ham's brightest season for a dozen years. 'I think people within the game appreciate Harry more than people looking in from the outside. He makes a team better than the sum of its parts. A lot of managers try to buy big-name players and spend a lot of money, whereas Harry does the exact opposite: he gets the best out of a number of less expensive players. He built a team at West Ham that was a whole lot better than it should have been when you looked at it on paper.'

The construction process that would culminate in the club's return to European competition after an eighteen-year hiatus had begun in earnest the season before Hislop's arrival. Eyal Berkovic, the Israeli playmaker who cut his Premier League teeth while on loan to Southampton from Maccabi Haifa, brought verve and creativity to midfield. David Unsworth, who arrived from Everton along with a cheque for £1m in exchange for the midfielder Danny Williamson, added steel and experience to the Hammers' defence. Trevor Sinclair expanded Redknapp's midfield options, weighing in with an impressive return of seven goals from fourteen games, while the Hammers' cutting edge was further sharpened by the arrival of French forward Samassi Abou. The payoff was a quarter-final berth in both domestic cups and an eighth-place league finish.

CHAPTER FIVE

'I'm disappointed that we didn't get into Europe but if you'd said at the start of the season we would finish eighth, not many people would have believed it,' said Redknapp, who compensated for the subsequent loss of the homesick Unsworth by signing Javier Margas and Neil Ruddock in a summer sales spree that also included Ian Wright, the Arsenal striker. 'We've taken a massive step forward this year as a football club. We have a couple of kids who are going to be big players and all our signings have been successes. Our form at the end of last season was excellent and we just carried on in the same way this season. We've been beaten at home in the league only twice, and the fans have seen some great football.'

Shaka Hislop thus joined a team brimming with potential, a point underlined at the outset of the 1998/99 campaign when the Hammers, not normally a byword for obduracy, kept three successive clean sheets from an early run of fixtures that included two away games and a visit from Manchester United. Any notion that defensive solidity would be the keynote to life under Redknapp was quickly dispelled, however. 'We hadn't conceded a goal in the first three games of the season,' recalls Hislop, 'but then we were 3-0 up against Wimbledon, conceded one just before half-time and lost 4-3. But I don't think that game was a fair reflection of Harry or West Ham at the time. It was just that Harry believed in the attacking traditions of West Ham. Sometimes we'd get tanked, but more often than not it worked well and we were a better team for it. The players prefer it that way and, although as a goalkeeper it's never nice to concede, when you play for Harry sometimes you just have to accept it when things go against you. We managed to keep something like seventeen clean sheets that season, but at the same time we conceded four or more goals eight times. They say that to win championships you need to build from the back, but that is not Harry's style and it is not West Ham's style. West Ham would never be happy with a Bolton style of football, even if it brought trophies. It's just not how West Ham play and it's not what the fans expect. They want to come to Upton Park every other Saturday and see attacking football. On the other side of the coin, I remember we went to Liverpool and were 2-0 down at Anfield and came back to draw 2-2. We did the same to Newcastle when they were flying. That's just part and parcel of Harry Redknapp football.'

West Ham swiftly returned to winning ways following the Wimbledon setback, Hartson and Berkovic putting the league leaders Liverpool to the sword in an impressive 2-1 victory at Upton Park. 'The key was the players' attitude,' Redknapp reflected. 'I didn't give them a rucking after Wimbledon because I probably wouldn't have got the right response. We've got a great dressing room full of bubbly, positive people.' This considered approach to handling adversity is a quality that Alvin Martin remembers with particular fondness. 'I look back and think about the times when Harry rollicked us after a game, but in a positive way,' Martin recalls of Redknapp's first season in charge at Upton Park. 'We were in a relegation battle and he didn't have any room to manoeuvre. He couldn't go out and spend £10m, so he was stuck with this group of players that had just lost a game. What he did was to keep the morale up after a game and get us to look forward to the next game. He didn't panic, he didn't take the easy route, which was to lambast his players. In an indirect way he would be rollicking you, but he'd also be saying "We're better than that, I expect more from you." You'd go out with your self-esteem still intact, ready for the next game.'

The methods that led to survival on that occasion served Redknapp equally well as he set his sights on European qualification. So effectively did he shepherd his players through heavy, potentially confidence-sapping defeats against Blackburn, Charlton and Leeds that West Ham entered the new year in sixth spot. The achievement was all the more notable for Redknapp's largely successful negotiation of the potentially damaging off-field episodes that blighted the early months of the campaign. The season was little more than a month old when Hartson went in hard on Berkovic during a training session at Chadwell Heath. Berkovic, who stayed down, reacted angrily, swearing and swatting his team-mate's thigh. In response, Hartson aimed a brutal kick at the Israeli's head, catching him flush on the jaw. 'If my head was a ball,' said Berkovic, 'it would have been in the top corner of the net.'

The unsavoury incident left Berkovic streaming with blood and Redknapp facing a dilemma. The episode had occurred on the training ground, away from the public eye; open condemnation would only highlight it. But while instinct told Redknapp to keep things in-house, the presence of Sky TV cameras meant it was only a matter of time before the truth came to light. In the end he steered a middle course, attempting to play the episode down – a decision that Hislop believes was a mistake. 'John Hartson was very much in the wrong,' he says. 'Eyal Berkovic is a very slight man at best and John is a big strapping man. Eyal was on the floor. I have to say it's the one real complaint about my time at West Ham – I don't think that, initially, it was handled correctly. There were some personality conflicts, particularly between John Hartson and Eyal Berkovic, and it came to a boil. I don't think anyone could have anticipated it happening the way it did, but I think Harry could have handled the situation differently. The initial response, not only by Harry but by the whole coaching staff, could have been a little bit stronger in terms of their approach to John Hartson.'

Redknapp eventually fined the Welshman £10,000, the maximum penalty allowed under the rules of the Professional Footballers' Association. But his difficulties with the player did not stop there. Having lost fitness over the summer, Hartson made a subdued start to the following campaign. His form and confidence on the wane, he looked a shadow of the free-scoring player of the previous season. So when Wimbledon came in with a January offer of £7.5m, Redknapp was not about to decline. 'Every player has his price,' he reflected, denying that Hartson's departure was connected with the Berkovic incident. 'It was a good offer and I just felt I want to strengthen my team in two or three positions. I'm sorry to see John go. We have done well out of him. We bought him from Arsenal and we have doubled our money and he kept us up a couple of years ago with his goals.'

Two months after the Berkovic affair there was further controversy when, despite Redknapp's protestations, Andy Impey, the winger signed from QPR fourteen months earlier, was sold to Leicester City in order to balance the books. Informed by the club hierarchy that Impey would be unavailable for an away trip to Derby, Redknapp reacted with fury, sparking a war of words with Peter Storrie, the West Ham chief executive. 'If he doesn't like it, he'll have to lump it,' observed Storrie, explaining that Redknapp's summer transfer activity had been conditional on a player being sold by the end of November. 'I'm not a mug and I don't need a job that badly that I'll let people walk all over me,' Redknapp countered. 'If someone walks in and says they are selling Rio Ferdinand without telling me, then I'll resign. They probably thought it was alright to sell Andy because the fans don't like him too much and no one will really care, but I feel I have been undermined in front of my players and everyone else. The day I stop choosing who I buy and who I sell is the day I am not managing a football club anymore.'

Redknapp, who was promptly linked with a move to Blackburn, subsequently apologised for his outburst. Yet, with a stellar generation of youngsters emerging from the club's academy, it was a bad time for West Ham to be perceived as a selling club. Within days of the Impey uproar, Storrie was forced to rebuff a bid from Tottenham for Frank Lampard – as clear a sign as could be of the dangers of going over the manager's head.

The need to protect the club's crown jewels was all the more pronounced for the emergence of a third budding talent, a youngster expected to outshine even Lampard and Ferdinand. 'I remember the very first time Harry set eyes on Joe Cole as an eleven-year-old,' says Tony Carr. 'We said to him: "Harry, you've got to come and have a look at this trial game, we've got a kid on here who we think is a very good player." He stood on the sidelines and watched Joe do this run and dummy that you wouldn't expect a kid of his age to do. Harry said: "Get a copper, lock them gates. No one leaves this training ground. Don't let that kid out." That was Harry – he could spot talent a mile off, and he wasn't far off when he saw Joe.'

Six years later, Cole was introduced to the first team in circumstances that once again emphasised Redknapp's faith in Carr's colts. With West Ham trailing Swansea by a goal to nil in a third-round Cup tie at Upton Park, Redknapp handed Cole a twenty-five minute cameo. That the youngster comfortably held his own came as no surprise to his team-mates, who had been spellbound by his precocious talent from the moment Redknapp invited him to train with them two months earlier. Ferdinand drew comparisons between Cole and the England playmaker Paul Gascoigne, while Steve Lomas, the Hammers' captain, spoke of the seventeen-year-old's ability to do things with the ball which 'leave you gasping.' Redknapp, meanwhile, did what he could to alleviate the burden of expectation. 'Joe was in the squad on merit,' he said. 'He's got a good attitude and good talent and he didn't look out of place.' Four months on, he didn't look too bad in the FA Youth Cup final, either. Pulling the midfield strings in tandem with Michael Carrick, another future England international, Cole produced a mesmerising second-leg display as West Ham obliterated Coventry 6-0 to complete a 9-0 whitewash over the two legs.

Cole made a further eight first-team appearances that season, but was spared the full glare of the media spotlight by Redknapp's late-January recruitment of Paolo Di Canio. The controversial Italian had not been spotted in the Premier League since his infamous shove on referee Paul Alcock at Hillsborough the previous September. That incident – which increased Di Canio's notoriety exponentially – earned the maverick Sheffield Wednesday front man an eleven-match suspension. Di Canio then took it upon himself to prolong his absence, citing stress and depression as he refused to return from Italy. Many felt Redknapp was playing with fire. 'Everyone has got opinions,' he said at Di Canio's unveiling. 'I expect that but I'm not afraid to take the chance. That's how I am. I spoke to Tommy Burns who was his manager at Celtic and he told me he was the best player he ever worked with. When I told my players he was coming they were absolutely delighted. People like Ian Wright and Rio Ferdinand just can't wait to play with him. He can play like you can't believe and do things most people only dream of doing. His skills are frightening. It will be great to have someone in the side who can produce a flash of genius and turn the game upside down for you. You will all have your opinions, but in the end I'll be right.'

He was. Despite a four-month layoff, Di Canio scored four times in twelve starts as West Ham ended the season fifth, the second-highest finish in the club's history. 'People are now saying my gamble in buying him has worked but, as far as I'm concerned, it never was a gamble,' said Redknapp, who subsequently guided his side safely through the InterToto minefield and into the Uefa Cup, ending the club's eighteen-year European interregnum. 'Defences better watch out when he's back to one hundred per cent, because there's even better to come. I like good players, ones who get you off your seat, ones who can do what you could never do, and Paolo's different class. There are players who have cost three times [as much] who couldn't lace his boots.' Redknapp's feelings were mirrored by the Upton Park crowd, who readily identified with the aberrant Italian entertainer. Extravagantly gifted, exhilarating to watch, Di Canio was a player cast in the West Ham mould, a free-spirited attacker who played the game as it ought to be played. Redknapp, the arch-custodian of football exotica, had found the perfect centrepiece for his E13 exhibition hall.

Redknapp had also hit upon a player whose intense emotions – passionate but temperamental, vivacious but volatile – rivalled his own. 'Like Harry, Paolo wore his heart on his sleeve,' says Hislop. 'You never knew what you were going to get out of him.' At his best, Di Canio was irresistible. The following season he scored sixteen league goals in twenty-nine starts, including two in a mesmerising performance against Arsenal that gave West Ham their first home win against the Gunners for twelve years. 'Di Canio is a genius,' purred Redknapp. And he was – but of the flawed variety. In Di Canio's first full season at Upton Park, his travel itinerary failed to take in Anfield, Old Trafford, Stamford Bridge and four other away grounds. In those seven games West Ham registered just one victory. That disappointing return proved costly when the Hammers finished ninth, missing out on an InterToto Cup place by three points.

Nor were Di Canio's absences limited to crucial away games. When Bradford City visited the Boleyn Ground in February 2000, he briefly went missing before a crowd of twenty-five thousand. Denied a penalty for the third time by the referee Neale Barry, the disconsolate front man sank to his knees before signalling to Redknapp that he wanted to be taken off. 'He wanted to be substituted but Harry refused to substitute him,' recalls Hislop who, having broken his leg in the second minute, was as bemused a spectator as any. 'Paolo just sat on the pitch for five minutes, quite literally, while the game went on around him. It was the most surreal thing I've ever seen in the professional game at the top level. But that was Paolo. He was passionate, sometimes to a fault, but equally talented.'

Both aspects of the Italian's persona were on show that afternoon. On finally hauling himself to his feet, Di Canio showcased his genius by orchestrating a thrilling comeback from 4-2 down. He converted a penalty after wrestling the ball from the grasp of Frank Lampard, then centred for the England midfielder to slam home the winner in a 5-4 victory. In his autobiography, Di Canio attributes his belated show of spirit to Redknapp's refusal to substitute him: 'Seeing that this man, this middle-aged figure who had faith in me thirteen months earlier when to most Britons I was either a madman or a disease blighting the national sport, still believed in me was the adrenalin injection I craved.'

Redknapp's ability to get the best from Di Canio was highlighted again the following month when the Italian cracked home a breathtaking scissors-kick volley against Wimbledon. 'It was a fantastic goal,' enthused Redknapp of a strike that was later voted the season's best. 'They come here to see special things and moments of magic and he hardly ever lets them down.' More special things followed. Redknapp thought it was pretty special when, the following December, Di Canio elected to catch the ball rather than bundle it past Paul Gerrard, the injured Everton keeper. Victory would have lifted the Hammers into a European place but, with Gerrard lying prone, Di Canio deemed it unsporting to capitalise and the game ended 1-1. 'I'd be lying if I said I was cheering what Paolo did at the time,' sighed Redknapp. 'It was sportsmanship of the highest merit and it's nice to know that kind of thing exists in the modern game. We would have had three points in the bag, but I am not going to throttle him for it. Still, I have never seen anything like it on a football pitch before. I think my players are still kicking him.'

'Everybody understood Paolo's gesture, how sporting it was, but at the same time, in terms of survival we were more concerned with our own plight,' recalls Hislop. 'It was met the same way by both the players and Harry. You couldn't really lose it with Paolo, because you understood the gesture, but at the same time we knew exactly how much two points meant. Nobody knew what to say, so we just accepted it, but we were all left scratching our heads. Harry's a good judge of those situations, though. At times he took Paolo aside quietly and had a word with him, at times he'd let his feelings be known because he had to show that he was still the boss. So it was well played by Harry.'

Alvin Martin likewise admires Redknapp's dextrous approach to dealing with the game's more colourful characters. 'Harry handles players like Di Canio really well,' he says. 'He gets players in with great talent, but usually there's baggage to go with them. What he's very good at is being able to handle people in terms of their character and personality, but still being able to manage the dressing room. Sometimes you make special dispensations for people like Di Canio and that can upset the rest of the dressing room. But Harry's good at getting that balance right.'

Whatever demands Di Canio made on Redknapp's man-management skills, the means almost invariably justified the ends. 'Di Canio is an absolute screwball,' Redknapp told the audience at an awards ceremony shortly before the Everton episode. 'This morning he was all happy – tomorrow morning, who knows? But he is a great player.' Events at Old Trafford in late January doubtless reinforced Redknapp's admiration. Ignoring an audacious offside bluff by Fabien Barthez, the Manchester United goalkeeper, Di Canio scored the only goal of the game to fire West Ham into the fifth round of the FA Cup. It was the second time in his career that Redknapp had put paid to United's hopes in the competition, with victory all the sweeter this time round for coming just ten months after a 7-1 league spanking at the same venue. 'I would say this is my best win,' said Redknapp. 'We've had a couple of beltings here, we had an awful lot of injuries, and it was a makeshift team. So it's a great result. I was manager at Bournemouth when we beat Man United 2-0 in the Cup when they were holders and we were a very poor Third Division team. That was a great day for us but, given United's status now, this is my greatest win as a manager.'

The result reflected the full gamut of Redknapp's managerial traits. Most strikingly apparent was the familiar blend of experience and youth. At the back was the hoary defiance of Stuart Pearce and Nigel

Winterburn, the veteran defensive duo Redknapp had snapped up for nothing. At the other end of the age spectrum was the youthful midfield trident of Lampard, Cole and Carrick, a potent mixture of relentless industry, audacious skill and precocious tactical maturity. Galvanising the whole was the same infectious belief that had underpinned Bournemouth's famous victory against United. Young and old alike responded to Redknapp's pre-match clarion call, buoyed by a confidence that remained unshaken even in the face of an injury crisis which ruled out a glut of key players, necessitating an impromptu switch to a three-man central defence. 'We worked at things during the week,' said Redknapp. 'I told them I didn't want them to lie down.' He need not have worried on that front. True to Redknapp's own natural exuberance, West Ham carried the fight to United from the first whistle; they had come to play, not cower. 'Winning at Old Trafford is a fantastic achievement, a once-in-a-career happening,' says Hislop. 'You have to survive an almighty onslaught whenever you're at Manchester United. We managed to do that, and then Paolo grabbed that goal where Barthez tried to freak him out. We were ecstatic. It really meant a lot and we started to believe that, if we could beat United, we could go on and win the Cup. But it just didn't work out that way.'

Not much was to work out in the months ahead. Having entered the new year in eighth place after a 5-0 Boxing Day thumping of Charlton, it was late February before West Ham next registered a Premier League win. By then, they had slipped to thirteenth, effectively putting paid to hopes of a fourth consecutive top-half finish. 'We won't win championships but we do give our fans plenty of entertainment and I couldn't send out a team to play boring football,' said Redknapp. 'Unfortunately, some people have a false idea of where this club should be. Even when Bobby Moore, Martin Peters and Geoff Hurst were playing, our average league position was seventeenth, which shows how useless the other eight of us were.'

As the malaise continued, even the art of losing beautifully eluded West Ham. The show went on, but Redknapp's motley troupe of entertainers were fluffing their lines. Di Canio, his licence to improvise now shared with Cole and Frederic Kanoute, looked a shadow of his normal self. Cole, despite being called into Sven Göran Eriksson's first England squad along with Lampard and Carrick, struggled to impose his impish talents. Above all, a defence shorn of Rio Ferdinand mustered only one clean sheet in a dismal run of eighteen league games which brought just three wins. Ferdinand's move to Elland Road the previous November, in an £18m deal which broke the British transfer record, was beginning to look more costly for West Ham than Leeds.

'It is very hard to see someone like Rio go,' Redknapp said at the time of Ferdinand's departure. 'We've known him since he was thirteen and he's a lovely lad, but it was a crazy offer by Leeds. I have a feeling of satisfaction that he made it. I have rucked him up hill and down dale in an effort to make him the player he is, and he has never once answered me back. And let's face it – how could we turn down £18m? We just had to make one of the kids we have brought through pay. I'll just have to wait and see how much of it I get to spend on new players. That's what the fans will want to see.' Yet the players who came in subsequently – Rigobert Song, Titi Camara, Svetoslav Todorov and Christian Dailly – struggled to make an impression. Already low on confidence, West Ham suffered a further loss of impetus when Spurs ended their Cup odyssey at the quarter-final stage. 'The lads are very low,' said Redknapp after a defeat that effectively signalled the season's conclusion, 'I'm very low.'

Two months later, he was even more dispirited. When safety was belatedly secured with a 3-0 win over Southampton on the penultimate weekend of the 2000/01 season, Redknapp's thoughts turned immediately to the future. 'There's talent in the squad but the keeper's a free transfer, Pearce is thirty-nine, Winterburn's thirty-eight. I haven't gone out and bought superstars. It's about being a team. We've got a lot of free spirits and when you don't keep the ball you get punished. It's not an ideal balance. I don't want to sell the Coles, the Lampards, the Carricks or the Sinclairs. But if I can get one or two in and find the right shape for the team, it will make a big difference. If I don't do that, we are in for another tough season.'

It was with the need for reinforcements in mind – not to mention a proposed extension to his contract – that Redknapp entered a seemingly routine meeting with Hammers chairman Terence Brown five days later. He left the rendezvous minus his job. The soundtrack to the exchange was provided by the same rumblings of financial discontent that had been echoing around Upton Park for several months. Money was tight. Building work on the Boleyn Ground's west stand was already underway as the club pressed forward with plans to expand the stadium's capacity from twenty-six thousand to thirty-five thousand. That project, combined with the modernisation of the youth academy, would cost around £27m. The previous day, after Redknapp had released a tranche of players including Davor Suker and Sebastien Schemmel, the club's managing director, Paul Aldridge, had remarked: 'Our wage bill is the seventh highest and you obviously look for your league position to mirror that.' The implied suggestion that Redknapp had underachieved struck a jarring note. Of West Ham's seven previous managers, only John Lyall had emulated Redknapp's feat of finishing in the top half of the table for three successive seasons. Did Aldridge seriously imagine that one bad campaign was the measure of the manager?

Even Brown saw beyond such simplistic logic. 'The last three seasons' final league positions of eighth, fifth and ninth represent the club's best league performances since its formation in 1895,' he told the club's annual general meeting the previous December. 'In total we have spent forty-five seasons in either the old First Division or the Premier League, nine between 1895 and 1958 and thirty-six since. During those forty-five seasons we have finished in the top half of the table on no more than fourteen occasions. Four of those occasions have occurred during the last five seasons. Such statistics put into perspective all the club has achieved under the management of Harry Redknapp at a time when funds have had to be carefully apportioned between the team, the stadium and revamping our famous academy.'

Brown might equally have adduced another statistic in support of his portrayal of the Redknapp era as a resounding success. Despite the popular perception that the manager's transfer activity had left the club out of pocket, Redknapp's frenetic wheeler-dealing – sixty players in and sixty out during his seven years in charge – had delivered an £11m profit. Small wonder, then, that Redknapp felt confident enough to request the £12-14m summer transfer kitty he deemed necessary to take West Ham forward. There was scope for manoeuvre, he felt, since he had spent little over a third of the money brought in from the Ferdinand sale. The club, however, saw things differently, suggesting that his expenditure was closer to £15m.

'Nonsense,' Redknapp told *Over Land and Sea*, a club fanzine, in an interview that he has since identified as a contributory factor in his departure. 'I don't want to argue with the chairman or anybody else. I think they are genuine people who support the club as well, but I certainly haven't spent £15m of the Rio money.' Redknapp was equally forthright when asked about an undercurrent of discontent within the Hammers' support. 'It just shows how fickle people are,' he said. 'I have a bad month and suddenly I have got to go. Let them do what they want to do. Redknapp out, get someone else in. See how well they do. See where you are in four years' time, but I doubt that I will still be the manager. I'll probably be booted out before then.' Like Bonds before him, Redknapp's musings proved prophetic. 'I've had a chat with the chairman and just feel it's been a tough season,' he said in a statement shortly after meeting Brown. 'The last eight weeks or so of the season haven't been particularly enjoyable and I feel that, maybe, it's time for a change.'

The repercussions of Redknapp's departure were keenly

felt in the dressing room. 'I owe my whole career to Harry, so I could never imagine going back to the club if he is not there,' lamented Di Canio. 'I love him now as if he was my own father. He was my saviour in football and I'll be forever in his debt. I would do anything for him.'

Di Canio's dismay was shared by Hislop. 'It was a shock,' he recalls. 'It was a big, big blow and I don't think anybody saw it coming. We didn't have a great season, there's no doubt about it. We narrowly avoided relegation. But still, you just felt that given Harry's history with the club, given how well we'd been playing a couple of seasons before, we could have taken it in our stride and done better the following season. Afterwards, Harry spoke to all the players privately at a function in London where we had a long talk about everything. I'm absolutely certain that Harry was devastated. It was a big shock and the club struggled to cope with it for a long time.'

That summer, Frank Lampard Jnr, whose father had left the club along with Redknapp, joined Chelsea for £11m. Two seasons later, West Ham were relegated to the Championship, where they remained for two years. When they returned to the Premier League in 2005, Redknapp was among the first to offer his congratulations. 'I was very down when I left,' he has since admitted. 'It was difficult, because I loved it there and was just about to sign a new four-year contract. They had been asking me to sign it for six months, but I said some things I shouldn't have and made a mistake. But that's life. I don't look back and regret anything. You get on with your life.' None more so than Harry Redknapp.

Chapter Six

They say a week is a long time in football; to Harry Redknapp, it must seem like an eternity. His wife, Sandra, once suggested his life story should be entitled *Never A Dull Moment*. It is easy to see why. In the forty-three days that elapsed between Redknapp's departure from West Ham and his re-emergence as Portsmouth's director of football, he maintained a frenetic level of activity. He 'sat down, had a glass of wine and talked football' with the Southampton chairman, Rupert Lowe, who was looking for a new manager after Glenn Hoddle's defection to Spurs. He joined his son, Jamie, in supporting a campaign to raise awareness of testicular cancer. He enjoyed a day out at the races in Salisbury with Alan Hudson. He reportedly became a target for non-league Yeovil. He took up an informal scouting role with Notts County, where his old West Ham pal Peter Storrie, the executive deputy chairman, enthused about his 'knowledge of the game' and ability to 'throw a few names to us'. He maintained a high media profile, continuing to write his regular *Racing Post* columns while pontificating on a bewildering array of subjects elsewhere in the national press. Frank Lampard's switch to Chelsea? 'It's a smashing move, he will be perfect for them.' West Ham's struggle to find a new manager? 'I would have thought that people would be falling over backwards to take the job.' Glenn Roeder, his eventual Upton Park successor? 'You couldn't meet a nicer fellow.' Like a beaten prize fighter refusing to look back, Redknapp, so recently laid out on the Upton Park canvas, was keeping busy.

Nor did he eschew the bright lights of the television studio. In a Channel Four documentary, Redknapp described the corrosive effect of foreign players on traditional team spirit. 'In the old days you'd have a golf day, or a day at the races, and we'd all go out and have a crack,' he said. 'Then maybe on the way home you'd stop at a pub somewhere and have a drink. But with the foreign players it's more and more difficult. Most of them don't even bother with the golf, and they don't want to go racing. They don't even drink, most of them. So the sort of team spirit you could get a few years ago has disappeared.'

Redknapp was harking back to an era when drinking was so commonplace among players that, from a manager's perspective, it was more easily harnessed as a mechanism of team bonding than contained. Ron Atkinson, for instance, routinely turned a blind eye to the institutionalised drink culture at Manchester United, allowing his players to enjoy benders of epic intensity so long as their bar-room bonhomie was indulged at a safe distance from match days. Memorably, Brian Clough even instigated the drinking on occasion, most famously when he plied his Nottingham Forest players with champagne the night before the 1979 League Cup final in a bid to ease pre-match tension. Thirty years on from Forest's nerveless if bleary-eyed victory over Southampton, a similar scenario is unimaginable. The continental influence on English dressing rooms and the need for the modern player to be as much athlete as footballer have irrevocably altered the game's relationship with alcohol. Every British manager from Sir Alex Ferguson down has welcomed that change, and Redknapp is no exception. He may once have been open to the potential benefits of a little boozy camaraderie, but Redknapp has long viewed out-and-out alcohol abuse as the antithesis of professionalism.

Towards the end of the 2008/09 campaign, the Tottenham captain Ledley King was pictured dishevelled and partially un-trousered outside a London nightspot, where he was arrested in connection with an alleged assault. Redknapp afterwards pledged to impose an alcohol and nightclub ban on his players. 'Footballers should not drink,' he said. 'You shouldn't put diesel in a Ferrari. I know it's hard but they are earning big money, they are role models to kids. I don't want what happened to Ledley to happen again.' As some in Fleet Street cried foul, the Channel Four interview was dredged up as 'evidence' that Redknapp's attitude had undergone a sea change. Not so. Even in his Bournemouth days, Redknapp had no time for drunken inanity.

'He was always strict about drinking,' says John Williams. 'In our championship season we'd played Port Vale on the Tuesday night and we were playing Carlisle on the Saturday, so we stayed in Blackpool to cut the journey up. We relaxed on Wednesday and trained on Thursday, when everybody was meant to be indoors by nine o'clock. Three or four of us were a wee bit late getting back and we'd decided we might have another drink downstairs at the bar. I'd gone back to my room and Richard Cooke, my team-mate, was in bed. He said that Harry had been on the phone asking where I was. I thought "Uh-oh, there's trouble." So I said to Richard: "I'm just going downstairs to tell the others to get to bed because Harry's looking for us." I jumped in the lift, which went downstairs to the bar area. The doors opened and Harry was standing there with Jim Gabriel. He got stuck into me, he gave me abuse like you wouldn't believe and I just had to stand there and take it. He frightened the living daylights out of me that day. Harry's got a venomous tongue when he wants to.'

As he demonstrated on exchanging tracksuit for lounge suit, Redknapp can be equally silver-tongued. 'It is not easy for Graham, and I understand his situation,' he said in June 2001, reflecting on his appointment as boardroom foil to the Portsmouth manager Graham Rix. 'When someone tells you there will be a director of football coming in, who will be responsible for buying and selling players, you suddenly think: "Hang on, what's going on?" But I had a meeting with Graham the other night and the one thing he does know is that I don't want his job. I don't want to be the manager. When I left West Ham I wasn't sure if I wanted to get back into football. I'd had enough of the aggro, sitting in the dug-out shouting and screaming. Sometimes it felt like there'd been a death in the family when we got beaten on a Saturday. So I know what Graham will be going through and I'll be with him all the way.'

In retrospect, Redknapp was showing a natural awareness of pitfalls that he would later face himself. Yet Rix had always known that Milan Mandaric, the Serbian-American computer entrepreneur who rescued Pompey from bankruptcy two summers previously, intended to appoint a director of football. The former Arsenal and England midfielder asked only that the new man be someone he could work alongside and respect. Redknapp, whom Rix hailed for his wealth of 'experience and expertise', seemed to qualify on both counts. If Rix harboured private misgivings about working alongside someone more accustomed to front-line management, or Redknapp wondered how effectively he would cope with the transition from boot room to boardroom, neither man was saying so. Time would tell whether two strong characters could dovetail effectively.

Mandaric had no doubts about the viability of the new set-up, even cancelling a family holiday to ensure that he got his man. 'Harry is someone who has been there and done it and has an understanding of football,' says Mandaric. 'He's somebody who knows a lot of players and has a lot of character. I needed that at Portsmouth, because nothing was moving in the right direction. That's what prompted me to go with him. I first met Harry in America, when I owned a club in the North American Soccer League [San Jose Earthquakes]. We didn't really know each other that much in America, but of course I knew Harry for what he'd done in football and I'd followed his career. I was making some decisions with

Portsmouth – do I make commitments, make some major changes and bring in some capable people, or do I leave England? That particular year was a breaking point for me. I didn't have room for a manager at that time [but] when I found Harry was available, I called him immediately. I didn't really know what he was going to do, I just yanked him in to be somebody that I could lean on, if nothing more. "Look," I told him, "I want to get together with you." So we met down south in a really prestigious hotel – you know Harry, he doesn't just want to meet in an ordinary pub – and talked.'

The pair got on like a house on fire. Two hours passed. Finally, it was time to go.

'Harry,' said Mandaric as they prepared to leave, 'I'd like you to come and help me.'

'I'd like to come and work with you,' replied Redknapp.

'Would you come as a director of football, just for a while?'

'Yeah, why not?'

At fifty-four, Redknapp had hit upon a new vocation. Or so it seemed. One late November afternoon five months after he had signed on at Fratton Park, Redknapp was chatting with Mandaric in his office. 'By the way,' he enquired with an air of insouciance, 'can you tell me what the director of football job is?'

A smile plays across the features of Mandaric as he recalls the exchange. Yet before Redknapp's arrival, he had found little enough cause for mirth at Fratton Park. His reward for ploughing over £20m into the club had been unmitigated mediocrity. In the first year of his ownership, Pompey finished eighteenth in the First Division. In the second, Rix averted relegation only on the final day of the season. It was the third time in six years that Portsmouth had escaped at the death, a clear sign that – for all the owner's investment – the club was standing still. Mandaric was crying out for someone who could stop Pompey haemorrhaging soft points and hard cash. Redknapp, he felt, with his astute transfer dealings and proven ability to bring through youngsters, was the man for the job. 'Those things – together with his record with West Ham and his knowledge of the game and the players – made me want to bring Harry into the organisation at that time,' says Mandaric. The new man wasn't complaining. Though buffeted by the slings and arrows of managerial misfortune – and for all his insistence on wanting to take a back seat – Redknapp wasn't about to turn his back on the game he loved. Nor had adversity drained him of ambition. 'It's about time Milan and the supporters had some success and I want to help them achieve that,' said Redknapp. 'I've not come here to be part of a failure.'

That much quickly became clear. Fans accustomed to welcoming more workaday talents suddenly found themselves contemplating the possible arrival of David Ginola. The idea of signing the mercurial French playmaker – past his best, but still of quality enough to inflict damage at First Division level – had Redknapp written all over it. 'I'm not here to mark time,' Redknapp reiterated. 'It would give everyone a boost if we could get the lad.' It wasn't to be, the need to match Ginola's hefty Aston Villa salary proving an insurmountable obstacle. Portsmouth did, however, succeed in capturing Peter Crouch, the former Tottenham reserve and future England international, in a club record £1.25m deal with

Queens Park Rangers. 'With his height he ought to win most things in the air, but he has a good touch as well,' said Redknapp, establishing a refrain that others would later echo with increasingly dreary monotony.

Further evidence that Mandaric had found himself a smooth transfer-market operator arrived in the form of Alessandro Zamperini, a promising young defender signed from Roma. Though only eighteen, the ambitious Zamperini had already sought advancement by defecting from Lazio to the Stadio Olimpico, where he impressed Fabio Capello enough to make the bench several times during Roma's scudetto-winning 2000/01 season. Zamperini's stay on the south coast lasted only a season, but the limited nature of his contribution was less significant than the newfound willingness of Pompey, a club accustomed to foraging at the lower end of the football food chain, to do business with Europe's elite.

Nonetheless, the signing of Zamperini paled into insignificance beside that of Robert Prosinecki. At thirty-two, the chain-smoking Croatia playmaker's best years were behind him, yet he remained a monster of a player. A decade earlier Prosinecki had captained Red Star Belgrade to European Cup victory, showcasing an intelligence and midfield craftsmanship that would subsequently earn moves to Real Madrid and Barcelona. During his time in Spain, he had supplied the ammunition for Pichichi winners like Emilio Butragueno, Ronaldo and Ivan Zamorano. When Redknapp told Mandaric, whose Balkan connections were the pivot upon which the deal turned, that it would be 'a miracle' if Pompey were to lure the player from Standard Liege, he merely stated what most were already thinking. Yet the miracle became manifest.

Prosinecki was not much to look at. With his spiky, unkempt blonde hair, unshaved jowls and lived-in features, he appeared more like a libertine freshly returned from a night on the tiles than a modern-day magician. He would not have set any records for distance run or tackles made, and his penchant for Marlboro Reds was matched only by his thirst for espresso, which he drank by the bucket-load. But Prosinecki had a deftness of touch that could make the ball talk. His lavish technical gifts drew comparisons with Eric Cantona that Redknapp felt were not unwarranted. Certainly few First Division players had faced such a talent. On one occasion against Rotherham, Prosinecki turned the increasingly disoriented Alan Lee four times in quick succession, his touch so adhesive that the ball seemed glued to his boot. On the fourth occasion, the Croatian's hapless victim landed on the seat of his pants. Redknapp's verdict? 'He's one of the best players I've ever seen.'

Like Zamperini, Prosinecki would spend only a season in Hampshire. Yet his signing marked a key moment in Portsmouth's evolution. It gave weight to Mandaric's suggestion that Pompey were once again becoming a serious club. Redknapp – who hailed the midfielder as 'a massive signing, a world-class player' capable of having 'the same impact Di Canio did when I was at West Ham' – had 'a major influence' on the successful completion of the deal according to Peter Jeffs, the club's communication manager. 'Graham Rix had very little to do with transfers,' says Jeffs, 'so as director of football it was down to Harry to see it through. Harry was thrilled to have Prosinecki at the club and was well aware of the sort of quality we were getting.'

If Mandaric received a swift return on his investment in Redknapp, it was not all plain sailing. As the transfer whirlwind subsided and a season brimming with eastern European promise loomed, rumours surfaced of internal discord. One newspaper reported that Redknapp's wheeling and dealing had put Rix's nose out of joint, sparking a quarrel that culminated with Redknapp suggesting a play-off between the manager's signings and his. True or false? Certainly Redknapp was unimpressed when Pompey were beaten by Yeovil in a pre-season friendly. 'It was inept,' he snapped. 'It doesn't matter if it is a friendly or not, we should always try and win. If you ask me, Yeovil looked the better side.' The speculation intensified when Redknapp publicly questioned how long he would remain at the club. 'I still have to discover what it means to be director of football,' he said. 'Being the buffer between the manager and the chairman is new to me. I could be here seven years or six weeks. I don't need the money. It's all about satisfaction and I will see how it goes over the next two months.'

He would soon discover that old addictions die hard. Pompey started the league season solidly, but as late autumn faded into early winter, Redknapp became uncharacteristically restive. A makeshift office had been set up for him at the Pompey training ground, but Redknapp was reluctant to give the impression that he was looking over Rix's shoulder. His appearances became so rare that staff grew perplexed about the nature of his role. Redknapp shared their bemusement. For almost four decades, first as a player and then as a manager, football had dictated the rhythm and tempo of his life, the similarity-in-difference of each campaign creating structure, routine, purpose. The passing years had been a relentless treadmill of challenges to be met, of battles to be won, lost or drawn. As a dressing-room insider looking out, Redknapp had occasionally wondered what life might be like upstairs, sipping a glass of Amarone and making post-match chit-chat in the directors' lounge before returning home to a stress-free life. Now he knew. The cushioned fall of leather on deep-pile was no substitute for the clack of match-day studs. 'I'm used to being on the training ground and I admit I miss it,' said Redknapp. 'I miss picking the team and all the aggro that goes with it. The life I've got now is much easier with no aggro or pressure, but perhaps I thrive on them. Portsmouth are a terrific club with great support but it's not easy when you're used to being manager. It can get boring. If something comes along, then who knows?'

With Peter Taylor under increasing pressure at Leicester, that was a question most sports editors were only too happy to answer. It is a truth universally acknowledged within the Fourth Estate that when one manager is struggling and another is unhappy with his lot, change is in the offing. An impressive cameo as caretaker manager of the England team had earned Taylor the Leicester job, but poor purchases and worse results meant City were facing a relegation fight. Redknapp's disquiet tipped the rumour mill into overdrive. He had an escape clause in his three-year Pompey contract and had already held clandestine preliminary talks with Leicester, claimed reports; only rival candidate George Graham could pip him to the post. Not so, countered the man at the eye of the storm. 'There have certainly been no hush-hush talks,' said Redknapp. 'I've been too busy with Portsmouth. Leicester have a manager. Peter Taylor needs a result right now and let's hope he can get one.' He couldn't. Days later, Taylor was sacked. 'If they want to speak to me, I'll see,' said Redknapp.

Leicester's offer – a short-term contract, a transfer kitty of no more than £2m and a bonus dependent on avoiding relegation – left Redknapp cold. So too did the thought of letting down Mandaric, for the duo had established a genuine rapport. At first glance, the Serb from Novi Sad and the East End lad were unlikely bedfellows. Yet both had forged a path to success from humble beginnings. Redknapp rose from the Burdett Estate to become the five-million-pound man, while Mandaric transformed his father's machine shop into Serbia's most prosperous business before striking gold in Silicon Valley. They shared personal characteristics, too, each sporting heart prominently on hand-tailored sleeve. Passionate and unpredictable, theirs would be a love-hate relationship. For the moment, however, goodwill was in the ascendant. Within days of meeting Leicester, Redknapp withdrew from the race to succeed Taylor. 'I feel I owe some loyalty to Portsmouth and to Milan Mandaric,' explained Redknapp, who had also been linked with Coventry in the wake of Gordon Strachan's departure. 'I have had only two clubs in twenty years and I preach loyalty to players. Milan has become a close friend of mine and he brought me to Portsmouth to do a job and help them achieve a goal.'

Had Mandaric fretted that the Redknapp era might be

over before it had truly got underway? 'Yes, that was definitely the case,' he recalls. 'I didn't realise at the time, but Harry had a job more or less nailed down with Leicester. He changed his mind at the last minute after he met me. I heard the rumours at that time, and I was worried. But I knew what I wanted to do at Portsmouth and I explained to Harry the help I needed. I thought I had a good chance to get him to [stay and] work with us, because Harry's a people person. He needs to be loved, he needs to be understood, and then he can respond and be successful.' Among Redknapp's early successes was persuading his chairman of the pleasures of the turf. 'Harry likes a bit of betting, so he took me to the races,' recounts Mandaric, who arrived at Doncaster to find that an aptly-named colt was the favourite in the St Leger. 'There was a horse called Milan. We put money on it, and the horse won the race. That Saturday, we played a game and the supporters were singing "Milan, there's only one Milan." I said "Harry, don't be jealous – these guys love me and one day they'll sing about you." He said, "Don't be silly Milan, they all put twenty quid on that horse last weekend".'

The banter at Redknapp's new club was in pointed contrast to the sombre mood at his former stamping ground. West Ham had made a faltering start under Glenn Roeder, with the season six games old before he achieved his first win with a 3-0 success against Newcastle. Victory failed to turn the tide, however: two crushing away defeats followed, 5-0 at Everton and 7-1 at Blackburn. Throughout, a verbal feud had been simmering between Redknapp and Roeder; when Roeder insinuated that the Hammers' slump was due to his

predecessor's poor signings and the sale of Rio
Ferdinand, it finally boiled over. Having brought Roeder
to Upton Park in the first place, Redknapp was not about
to see his reputation besmirched. 'It's absolute rubbish to
suggest the rot set in when I was there,' Redknapp
retorted. 'He [Roeder] has got Joe Cole, Michael Carrick,
Trevor Sinclair and Freddie Kanoute – all absolutely top-
class players. But he's blaming everyone but himself. The
fact is, there's no excuse for getting beaten 7-1 at
Blackburn. Accept it. He's saying he wants more money
for players, but the board have backed him. He has spent
£14m on players already this season. How many
managers can spend £14m these days?'

Redknapp also had to contend with sniping from other
claret quarters. The former West Ham defender Tony
Gale weighed in with criticism of Redknapp's legacy, as
did assistant manager Paul Goddard. Both were put
firmly in their place. 'Paul Goddard has never signed a
player and maybe Tony Gale should have a crack at
management if he thinks he's so smart. There seems to be
some sort of vendetta going on.' That impression was
underlined when the West Ham chairman Terence Brown
complained in his annual statement to the club's
shareholders that Redknapp had 'bought and sold
virtually a team every season' at a 'net deficit' of £16m.
'Such expenditure cannot be justified,' wrote Brown.

As Redknapp pointed out, Brown's views had
undergone a dramatic transformation. 'In his statement
last year, Terry Brown said I was the most successful
manager in the club's history, so I don't know why he has
changed his attitude. I think it is him trying to justify
getting rid of me. But it's sad. West Ham have always

been my club, but I must admit I am a bit disillusioned. They say I cost us £16m, but they sold Frank Lampard almost straight away and that got them £11m. If they now sell Sinclair – who I bought – they will have a profit. Show me another manager who has achieved what I did in the Premiership with those kind of figures.' Time bore out his reasoning. Within three years Joe Cole, Glen Johnson and Jermain Defoe had followed Lampard through the Boleyn Ground exit. The combined total received in transfer fees for the quartet – each of whom made his Premier League debut under Redknapp – was £30m. By then, the club was playing First Division football, a reality that put the relative merits of West Ham managers past and present firmly in context.

In the meantime, Portsmouth had their own problems. As form became indifferent and results variable, the club slid out of the promotion picture. Speculation was rife that Rix, the fifth manager of the Mandaric era, would make way for Redknapp. 'We are not giving our supporters what they deserve, especially at our home games,' complained Mandaric. 'We should be participating in a higher position in the First Division, and I am not a happy man right now.' He had further cause for despondency when a festive run of five defeats in six games was followed by a 4-1 Cup humbling against Leyton Orient. Surely now Redknapp was a shoo-in for the manager's job? Had Mandaric had his way, it would have been a foregone conclusion, but his entreaties fell on deaf ears. 'If Graham left and Milan asked me to be manager then I would take it,' said Redknapp. 'I would be the obvious choice. But I want Graham to stay and keep his job and be a success at this club.' Privately, it is understood, Redknapp was dismayed by Rix's failure to adopt a more hands-on approach in training, but his public show of solidarity earned Rix a stay of execution. 'Graham stays on the advice of Harry,' said Mandaric. 'It would have been the easiest thing in the world to pull the trigger.'

Instead, when February brought another dismal run, Mandaric pulled the plug – on the players' wages. Neither Rix nor his squad would be paid for the preceding month, announced Portsmouth's disenchanted owner. Only Redknapp – who had been linked with yet another managerial vacancy, this time at Aston Villa – avoided the impromptu introduction of performance-related pay. 'We won only one match in February and that shows the players have not been trying in the other four we played,' said Mandaric, who was particularly incensed by a 5-0 hammering at the Hawthorns. 'I regard it as extortion. These players expect to go through the motions and not give anything like one hundred per cent and then expect a huge wage packet. This will make them think, I hope. Why should I just keep on bankrolling non-triers?' It proved the proverbial storm in a teacup. 'The players got their cheques after a meeting and, to be honest, there was never any doubt that they would,' wrote Redknapp in his *Racing Post* column a couple of days later. 'It was a heat of the moment thing, an idle threat.' Maybe so, but it was also an indication that Mandaric was not prepared to tolerate poor results indefinitely.

The end finally came for Rix in late March. This time, not even the last-minute intervention of a deputation of players led by Shaun Derry, the club captain, was enough to save him. With Pompey hovering nine points above the relegation zone, Mandaric axed the beleaguered Rix and then summoned Redknapp to his office. The moment had come to test his director of football's resolve anew. Would Redknapp now take the job he had turned down two months earlier? 'Harry was reluctant,' says Mandaric, 'because he didn't want to be a threat to somebody and take their job. I said no, Graham has gone, you're just going to help me and we're going to work for the future, bring in some players and try to get out of the division. We talked about lots of things – ideas, what was happening, what I wanted to do – and then we shook hands. We talked for two hours, but we made a deal in five minutes.'

While Redknapp's decision was motivated principally by a desire to return to management, he was also conscious that Pompey had been living on borrowed time. Mandaric had grown weary of the club's relentless drain on his resources, and Redknapp knew it. From Portsmouth's perspective, his appointment was a reprieve, a chance to put the listing ship back on an even keel. 'When the job is in your blood it stays there,' said Redknapp. 'When I first came here as director of football I had no intention of returning to management. But I don't know what a director of football is supposed to do. I'm looking forward to getting on the training ground again, but, to be honest, I don't need this job. The club can do without me, Graham or anyone else, but if Milan walked away that would be it. I could have taken over after we lost to Leyton Orient in the FA Cup, but I said no. When the job was offered I wasn't sure, but Milan said he would walk away if I didn't take it.'

The challenge differed from any Redknapp had faced previously. At Bournemouth, where overnight miracles were more a matter of hope than expectation, the relationship between club and manager had been largely symbiotic, the Cherries' fortunes ripening as Redknapp himself gained experience. At West Ham, where he inherited the makings of a good squad from Billy Bonds, Redknapp's frequent sorties into the transfer market were counterbalanced by a long-term emphasis on youth development. But at Portsmouth the demands of the here and now were paramount. Survival was the priority – and beyond that, promotion. It was a make-do-and-mend assignment; the bigger picture could wait.

Redknapp's first task was to prune a squad bloated by the largely ineffective transfer dealings of his predecessors. Peter Storrie, who renewed his working relationship with Redknapp following Mandaric's decision to recruit him as chief executive, had warned on his arrival of the need to 'drastically reduce the wage bill' before bringing in reinforcements. Redknapp took him at his word: Crouch, whose tally of nineteen goals in thirty-nine games made him Portsmouth's most valuable player, was sold to Aston Villa for £5m. 'Sometimes in football you have to make financial decisions,' said Redknapp, who can hardly have imagined that the arrangements surrounding the deal – his contract entitled him to a percentage of sell-on fees from outgoing transfers – would later attract the alleged scrutiny of Her Majesty's Revenue and Customs. What he did know – as many disgruntled Portsmouth apparently fans did not – was that the club already had a capable alternative in place. A week earlier Svetoslav Todorov, the Bulgaria international who first arrived in England towards the end of Redknapp's West Ham tenure, had been reunited with his former manager. Once billed as the new Hristo Stoichkov, Todorov looked anything but in the few pedestrian appearances he made for the Hammers. Yet he arrived at Fratton Park nursing a sense of grievance that West Ham had not kept him on, and would go on to make his point emphatically, scoring twenty-six times to finish the 2002/03 campaign as the First Division's leading marksman.

Portsmouth's real problems lay at the back. Defensive frailties had been a key factor in the club's season-long inconsistency, and Redknapp sought swift redress. In the seventy-two hours between his appointment as manager and the closure of the transfer window, Eddie Howe was recruited from Bournemouth. So too was Scott Wilson, a loan signing from Rangers. Both were central defenders. They were joined by Mark Summerbell, a defensive midfielder borrowed from Middlesbrough. With four games of the season remaining, the anxiety to consign five-nil capitulations to the past was palpable.

For a manager typecast as a firefighter, Redknapp traditionally makes a lousy job of beginnings. The opening weeks of his Tottenham reign were the exception that proved a rule established by Bournemouth's nine-goal battering at Lincoln and reinforced by the five-game winless streak with which his West Ham stewardship began. Portsmouth were not exempt. But if a 2-0 debut defeat at Preston was predictable, the long-term injury sustained by Howe and the dismissal of Todorov were less so. Did Redknapp have second thoughts? Did he hell. 'Instead of standing in the boardroom sipping a glass of wine, I've just had half a heart attack,' he enthused. 'If I was ever going to forget what it is like standing on the touch-line, I have been reminded. You miss the action when you're away. I've had twenty years of it and I love it. It becomes your life. I'm not saying I will take us to the Premier League, but I will build a good team. I am now in the mood to give it a right good go. All we need is a new stadium, a new training ground and half a new team. Apart from that, we're not in bad shape.'

Todorov ensured that Redknapp's Fratton Park debut went more smoothly by scoring the equaliser in a 1-1 draw with promotion-chasing Burnley. 'I don't think Burnley were any better than us and they are fourth in the table,' said Redknapp. His upbeat verdict gained credence when Pompey likewise finished all square against Birmingham, the eventual play-off champions. But if Redknapp's confidence encouraged Portsmouth's band of serial underachievers to believe the new boss was a soft touch, they were disabused of the notion after losing 1-0 to Watford in the final home game of the campaign. 'We have been shocking all season,' Redknapp remarked acidly as he recalled humiliating defeats against Crewe, Leyton Orient and Colchester. 'How the players had the nerve to go on a lap of honour, I'll never know.'

By September, fifteen players had gone. Among them was Prosinecki. Redknapp had originally intended to refashion his team around the Croatian, who had become a cult figure among supporters, but a lucrative – and, ironically, abortive – offer from the Japanese side Nagoya Grampus Eight persuaded Prosinecki to weigh anchor. Without him, Redknapp faced an unenviable task. Portsmouth's seventeenth-place finish was their highest in five seasons. The club's last major piece of silverware, the old First Division championship, had been won over half a century earlier. Branded a sleeping giant, Pompey's narcolepsy was bordering on the terminal. Yet circumstances conspired in Redknapp's favour. Two days after his appointment, ITV Digital, the UK broadcaster that had signed a three-year deal worth £315m to show Football League games, went into administration. Clubs that had budgeted on the basis of television income were thrown into financial disarray, with many brought to their knees by the burden of huge wage bills. Redknapp, a team-builder *par excellence*, found himself backed by a multi-millionaire in a buyer's market devoid of buyers. It was a combination to rouse hope in even the most battle-weary Pompey heart.

From the mingled yarn of youth and experience, Redknapp wove a team that took the division by storm. It was metamorphosis on an Ovidian scale, a transformation so radical that only one player, Nigel Quashie, started both the last match of the old campaign and the first of the new. Redknapp's powers of persuasion were writ large in the relative quality of the newcomers. The Australia international Hayden Foxe, a West Ham alumnus who had previously plied his trade in Australia, Holland, Japan and Belgium, eagerly embraced the opportunity to be reunited with his former manager. Arjan De Zeeuw, a veteran of Barnsley's 1997/98 Premier League campaign and a consistently impressive performer for Wigan, brought steel and experience to the heart of defence. From Juventus came loan signing Vincent Pericard, a gifted young striker who had caught Redknapp's eye on Champions League duty against Arsenal. Lured from Bournemouth was Richard Hughes, a promising midfield anchorman and future Scotland international. From West Ham to Wigan, Turin to Dean Court, Redknapp left no stone unturned in the quest for talent.

Notably, however, for all Pompey's financial leverage, Redknapp made little recourse to the chairman's chequebook. For the most part, he opted instead to snap up free agents or to make loan signings which limited the club's financial obligation to around half of the borrowed player's salary. By late autumn – and after an equally wholesale exodus of unwanted players – Mandaric was noting with astonishment that Redknapp had spent less money than any of his predecessors. Most of what was invested went on Matthew Taylor, the out-of-contract Luton full-back. Taylor's formidable left foot and impressive turn of pace were coveted by several Premier League clubs, including Tottenham. The Luton manager Joe Kinnear prized Taylor accordingly, placing a £1.5m price tag on him. Unperturbed, Redknapp sparked a transfer tribunal with a substantially lower offer, eventually whittling the price down to £600,000 plus add-ons. It was daylight robbery. Literally, so far as Kinnear was concerned. 'At least Dick Turpin had the decency to wear a mask,' he muttered.

The nature of the Taylor transfer drew a wry smile from Wilf McGuinness, Redknapp's erstwhile England youth manager. 'Harry was a wily bird in his early days at Portsmouth,' says McGuinness, who was surprised to bump into Redknapp when paying a social visit to Kenilworth Road one afternoon. 'I saw him outside the ground and we were chatting. I said to him, "What are you doing here?" and he said, "Well, I shouldn't be here really. But the chairman wanted me to come down because he didn't want to come on his own, so I've ended up here". I thought "Well, that's a funny story." A day later, they signed Taylor. Harry knew I was connected to Manchester United still, and he'd sold me a red herring! He wasn't going to let it out of the bag that he'd come to watch Taylor.'

The subsequent recruitment of Shaka Hislop offered further evidence of the seriousness of Redknapp's intentions. Hislop, a goalkeeper of proven calibre, had been edged out of the first-team picture at West Ham by David James, just as he had once been supplanted at Newcastle by Shay Given. Like Todorov, he had a point to prove – and with Redknapp confident that he could turn Portsmouth into promotion contenders, the big Trinidadian had no qualms about dropping down a division to do so. 'I wanted a fresh challenge and Harry offered that to me,' says Hislop, who played behind a three-man defence that included Linvoy Primus – another of the few Pompey veterans to survive Redknapp's summer cull – and Gianluca Festa, the veteran Middlesbrough defender once of Internazionale and Roma, who later arrived on a free. 'The time I'd had with him at West Ham was a big contributory factor. There's no gimmicks to Harry, he's very straight. He wanted me to join the club, he showed faith in me. Harry assured me that he was going to turn things around at Portsmouth, although to be honest I'm not sure that he thought we'd have as great a season as we did.'

Redknapp's ability to spot the right players and lure them to Portsmouth at minimal expense was impressive, but the more telling achievement was in forging a team of substance from his disparate band of new recruits. The frenzied summer of trading had seen Redknapp cast as a glorified commodity broker, yet he revealed himself to be as much team-builder as team-buyer. Hislop believes that the key to Redknapp's success in infusing a group of strangers with shared purpose and belief lay in his instinctive grasp of character and psychology. 'Harry's strength is that he understands people and knows how to get the best out of them,' says Hislop. 'He understands English football and he's good tactically, too, but above all he's a people person. That factor was a big part of our success.'

So too was Paul Merson. With Pompey's curtain-raiser against Nottingham Forest only days away, Redknapp lacked a regime-defining player, a headline act to fill the void left by Prosinecki. Various luminaries had been linked with the role. There was talk of Romario, the legendary Brazil forward, trading the Copacabana for the Solent. The Ginola link resurfaced only to be scuppered once again by the Frenchman's wage demands. Money likewise ruled out a move for Fabrizio Ravanelli, the gifted but outspoken Middlesbrough marksman. The thirty-four-year-old Merson, though, was a viable target. Under John Gregory, he had been Aston Villa's creative heartbeat. But when Gregory was replaced by Graham Taylor, who was intent on constructing a younger side, Merson became *persona non grata*. Taylor stripped him of the captaincy and made it clear that first-team opportunities would be limited. Unimpressed and available on a free transfer, Merson had no hesitation in signing for Redknapp. 'Harry Redknapp is one of the best managers around and I have total respect for him,' said the former Arsenal and England midfielder. The feeling was mutual. Redknapp hailed Merson as 'a fantastic signing' who would 'give [Pompey] Premiership quality and do the job that Robert Prosinecki did last season.' In truth, Merson's lineage went back considerably further. John Williams at eighties Bournemouth, Paolo Di Canio at nineties West Ham, Merson at noughties Pompey: Redknapp had found his talisman.

'You have to say that Paul Merson was an absolute gem of a signing for Harry,' says Hislop. 'He convinced Paul to come to Portsmouth and I think that transformed the way the team played. We weren't overly direct. We had a team that could play the route-one football needed to get out of the First Division, but we also had players who understood the game as it should be played: with the ball on the ground, played quickly, attacking. We didn't lump it, we played; we overran teams. We had a good defensive understanding, too. We had two centre halves in Arjan De Zeeuw and Linvoy Primus who liked to stay at home while the others attacked. So we were a Premier League club in all but name.'

It showed. By the end of August, Redknapp's hastily-assembled side were unbeaten and top of the table with five wins from their first six games. It was Portsmouth's best start since the championship-winning season of 1948/49. With Christmas looming and his team still setting the First Division pace, Redknapp had his sights trained firmly on the Premier League. 'At the start I thought we could push for a play-off spot,' he said, 'but these players just keep getting better. We will never have a better chance of going up.'

Redknapp's bullish appraisal was all the more credible for the presence alongside him of Jim Smith. The recruitment of Smith, for whom the invitation to work as Redknapp's number two proved more alluring than semi-retirement on a Spanish beach, was typically sharp-witted. Smith was one of English management's elder statesmen, a former Portsmouth manager who knew both the club and the division. A decade earlier, with an FA Cup semi-final already on his Pompey CV, he had led the club to the brink of automatic promotion, losing out on goal difference to West Ham, where Redknapp was in his first year as assistant manager. At Derby, where he subsequently enhanced his reputation by winning promotion to the Premier League, a status the club retained for five successive seasons, Smith had been a worthy adversary. Now he would prove an equally formidable ally. Together, Redknapp and Smith brought over half a century of football knowledge to the blue corner; if Pompey fell short, it would not be for want of experience.

Among the most impressive aspects of the partnership was the ability of two accomplished football men to work fruitfully in tandem. The infamous deterioration of Joe Mercer's working relationship with Malcolm Allison at Manchester City is merely the most vivid example of the basic footballing truth that two into one won't go. Redknapp and Smith were never destined to go the same route. Their friendship dated back almost three decades, to Smith's stint as Colchester manager in the early seventies. Redknapp would joke that he had intended to recruit somebody funny and knowledgeable, but settled for Smith instead. In reality, they were united by the shared experience of careers played out in parallel and by a mutual commitment to attacking football. Smith was a confidante, a sounding board, someone Redknapp could trust and rely upon. Hislop detected in time present more than a hint of time past. 'Jim Smith played a role similar to Frank Lampard Snr in our time at West Ham,' says Hislop. 'He would be a go-between, a second set of eyes, someone Harry could speak to and who could advise him. And Jim was absolutely fantastic. His reputation in the game is well deserved. He had a big part to play.'

When Pompey were drawn away to Manchester United in the FA Cup, Sir Alex Ferguson paid warm tribute to the Redknapp-Smith axis. 'The odd couple have done a fantastic job and I suppose you have to say it's amazing what experience can do,' said Ferguson. 'Portsmouth have tried a variety of managers over the years and now they have got Harry in and Jim at his right hand and it's that experience that has helped them. They also know the market and where they can get value and you can see the results.'

In the event, Old Trafford proved a barren hunting ground. Yet the 4-1 score-line failed to reflect Pompey's spirited response to an early phase in which they were overwhelmed by United's superior passing and movement. Had Nigel Quashie converted a glorious opportunity to pull Pompey level at 2-2 midway through the second-half, you would not have ruled out another famous Cup upset. 'If we had equalised, who knows?' mused Redknapp.

Success against United with a third different team could wait, however. After five draws in six games, Portsmouth's seven-point lead at the First Division summit had been cut to four. The United game was followed by a home defeat against promotion rivals Sheffield United, the only time Redknapp had presided over successive losses all season. When Pompey then drew against bottom-placed Brighton, the received wisdom was that Redknapp's side had hit a wall. Merson, for whose influence opposing managers had begun to make tactical provision, was struggling to sustain his early-season form; as he became the butt of fans' distemper, he briefly contemplated quitting. At the same time, Todorov experienced a five-game goal drought, the longest he would go all season without scoring. It was hardly a crisis, given the speed with which Redknapp had transformed Pompey from First Division stragglers to title favourites. But if Premiership dreams were to become a reality, fresh impetus was required.

It arrived in the imposing form of Yakubu Ayegbeni. The powerful Nigeria international had first come to Redknapp's attention the previous October, when he scored a Champions League goal for Maccabi Haifa against Manchester United. When Redknapp called Ferguson to get a second opinion on the twenty-year-old, the response was unequivocal: 'Harry, get in your car and get him now.' No further endorsement was required. Having signed on loan from Maccabi, Yakubu marked his first start, against Grimsby in early February, with a fourth-minute goal. It was the prelude to an electrifying display. 'I thought it was Thierry Henry out there for a moment,' said Redknapp. 'He was so quick and he had a real va-va-voom about him. If he was a racehorse, I would say he will come on for the run.' He did. The following week, Yakubu scored two and made three in a

6-2 romp against Derby. By the season's end, he had netted seven times in fourteen appearances.

If Yakubu eased the burden on Todorov up front, Tim Sherwood performed a similar service for Merson in midfield. Sherwood, at whom Redknapp had been casting covetous glances for six months, brought experience and composure to the Pompey engine room. His signing from Spurs meant that stopping Portsmouth no longer hinged on stopping Merson. 'Harry has done it again,' said Merson, who revelled in the greater space and freedom created by Sherwood's presence. 'Tim is just the sort of player we needed at this stage of the season and has been brought in at just the right time.'

Yakubu's pace and Sherwood's experience put the pomp back in Pompey. While the first two months of the year had produced just one win, March brought fifteen goals in six games. By mid-April, Portsmouth were on the threshold of the Premier League. The malignant fate that had long shaped the club's destiny briefly intervened again when relegation-threatened Sheffield Wednesday snatched an improbable late victory to deny Redknapp's men promotion. But this time fortune could only delay the inevitable. Three days later, Todorov's twentieth goal of the season saw off Burnley; for the first time in sixteen years, Pompey were back in the top flight.

'I didn't expect it,' says Mandaric, recollecting the emotion of a jubilant night under the Fratton Park floodlights from the relative tranquility of his office at Leicester's Walkers Stadium, where he is now chairman. 'I knew that Harry could budget and put players together and play good football, and I knew that playing good football would get us out of that league. But I did not realise that he was going to be able to do it at the first attempt.' Nor, it seemed, did Redknapp. 'I went to the playoff final between Birmingham and Norwich last season,' he reminisced on the eve of promotion. 'My chief scout, Stuart Morgan, turned to me and said: "You'll be here with Portsmouth next year." I told him: "You must be joking." When I took over we were struggling at the bottom of the division. I'd have been happy with mid-table mediocrity, but we've had a fantastic run and I can't believe how well things have gone.'

Attention turned almost immediately to Redknapp's plans for the following season. With West Ham facing relegation, Paolo Di Canio and Joe Cole were added to a list of rumoured targets that included Kevin Phillips, Martin Keown and Jermaine Pennant. But before Redknapp could fortify his side to withstand the rigours of Premier League combat, there was the necessary question of the First Division title to be considered. A post-promotion letdown at Ipswich on Good Friday briefly handed Leicester the initiative in the championship race, but Portsmouth regained the lead on Easter Monday and clinched the title with a 3-2 home win against Rotherham. With a game to go, Redknapp had delivered the club's first silverware in two decades. Todorov, who scored twice against Rotherham after winning an early penalty, had no doubts about where the credit was due for 'a great achievement.' 'Harry brought in a lot of good players and made the difference,' said the Bulgarian, who would sign off with a hat-trick in a 5-0 win against Bradford the following week. 'He's the man.' That verdict is endorsed by Mandaric. 'Harry's number one strength is man management, really getting the best out of people,' says Mandaric. 'A lot of people would have written off some of those players, they wouldn't have given them the time of day. But Harry saw a lot more in people like Paul Merson, Steve Stone and Tim Sherwood, all players who had a tremendous amount of quality and experience.'

The city celebrated extravagantly. Overjoyed fans snapped up tickets for a medal-presentation ceremony at the local town hall. They were out again in force for the club's victory procession, forty thousand lining the streets as Redknapp and his players paraded the First Division trophy from an open-top bus. As Redknapp stood flanked by Jim Smith and Milan Mandaric, the feeling that he had written an indelible chapter in the club's history was inescapable. Along with guiding Bournemouth to promotion and leading West Ham into Europe, he ranked the achievement among his top three. Yet in a wider sense, it was an ephemeral triumph. Football clubs, by their very nature, exist in a perpetual state of flux. As Redknapp appreciated, he had done no more than meet the demands of the moment. He had built a team to escape the First Division, but another cycle of regeneration and renewal lay ahead; revolution complete, evolution beckoned.

The need to rebuild was underlined by the departure of Merson. The midfielder had a year remaining on his contract, but the die was effectively cast on his future when he skipped the promotion party to watch his son play rugby. A fortnight earlier, he had bared his soul to a Sunday newspaper, revealing that Redknapp had released him from training for a week to undergo treatment for a gambling addiction. Under the circumstances, Merson's desire to work closer to his family home in the Midlands was understandable. In July, he left the south coast for Walsall. Portsmouth would be 'forever indebted' to him, said Redknapp.

The breach was filled by another celebrated thirtysomething. When Glenn Hoddle decided not to renew Teddy Sheringham's White Hart Lane contract, Tottenham's loss became Portsmouth's gain. A prominent contributor to Manchester United's treble-winning 1998/99 season and former footballer of the year, Sheringham was, as Redknapp put it, a player who had 'been there and done it all.' Like Merson before him, the former England international would make a mockery of the theory that he was past his sell-by-date, his leadership, predatory instincts and cerebral orchestration in the final third richly rewarding Redknapp's faith that, at thirty-seven, he could still cut it at the highest level.

Even with Redknapp's ability to patch up the deficiencies in his squad, Portsmouth had the air of gatecrashers at the Premiership party. In a summer when the arrival of the Russian billionaire Roman Abramovich at Chelsea reconfigured the financial landscape of English football, Fratton Park seemed an incongruous addition to the roster of top-flight grounds. With nary a prawn sandwich or an executive box in sight, Pompey's ramshackle old home – all peeling paint, chafed carpets and primitive dressing rooms – was an anachronism, a throwback to the days before football was ruled by the money men. Yet if some regarded Portsmouth as artisans among aristocrats, no one could deny that a club with more league championships than Chelsea was rich in tradition. Redknapp and his men

Above: Harry's appointment at Southampton in December 2004, just a fortnight after leaving local rivals Portsmouth, marked another dramatic twist in his career.

Below left: Like father, like son: reunited at St Mary's, Harry and Jamie celebrate a rare moment of joy during the 2004/05 campaign.

Below right: Enraged Portsmouth fans were not slow to display their anger and sense of betrayal over Harry's switch.

Above: Southampton fans were dismayed when Harry returned to Portsmouth after less than a year at St Mary's.

Below left: Harry Houdini talks to the media after returning to Portsmouth to mastermind the great escape.

Below right: The signing of Sol Campbell in summer 2006 marked a turning point in Pompey's fortunes.

Above: After more than a quarter of a century in management, Harry finally lands his first major trophy as Portsmouth beat Cardiff 1-0 to win the 2008 FA Cup.

Below: Painting the town blue: fans line the streets as Redknapp and his players celebrate aboard Portsmouth's Cup winners' bus.

Above: Harry and Portsmouth chairman Alexandre Gaydamak pose with the FA Cup against the background of a jubilant dressing room.

Below left: Child's play: Harry shares a playful pitch-side moment with his grandson, Charley, who was named after Louise Redknapp's late grandfather.

Below right: Harry Redknapp made the best start to a managerial reign in 110 years after taking over at Tottenham.

Above: Harry keeps a watchful eye on proceedings as he presides over a training session at Spurs Lodge.

Below: Ten months after leading Portsmouth to glory at Wembley, Harry returns with Tottenham for the 2009 League Cup final against Manchester United. © *Action Images*

Above left: Redknapp made old ally Kevin Bond his first coaching appointment at Tottenham.

Above right: Harry's animated presence on the sidelines wrought a rapid upturn in Spurs' fortunes.

Below left: Posing with the Football Writers' Association Tribute Award in January 2009.

Below right: Redknapp moved swiftly to re-sign Robbie Keane from Liverpool.

Harry's experience and old-school management style have reinvigorated Spurs, who finally look set to mount a genuine challenge to the top four.

© *Action Images*

With the larger-than-life figure of Harry Redknapp at the helm, Tottenham's future is in good hands.

quickly emerged as worthy custodians of that history. Supported by another crop of seasoned performers that included Patrik Berger, Sebastien Schemmel and Dejan Stefanovic – respectively lured from Liverpool, West Ham and Vitesse Arnhem – Sheringham began the season in imperious style. His forward partnership with Yakubu, who together with Vincent Pericard had been signed on a permanent basis over the summer, gave Portsmouth a winning blend of guile and pace. 'Teddy is going to make sure we compete with anybody in the Premiership,' declared Redknapp after the striker had opened Pompey's Premier League account in a 2-1 win against Aston Villa. 'Nobody thought we would do much at the beginning of last season, but we brought in a few players, including Merson, and his ability and experience inspired us to win the First Division title. Now I think Teddy is capable of something similar in the Premiership. The other players look up to him like they did with Merse and now we've also got Berger in there. You can't beat that sort of experience.'

For a month, you literally couldn't. As Sheringham scored five goals in five games, winning the August player of the month award in the process, Portsmouth briefly topped the Premier League table. For euphoric fans, it was an unexpected chance to dust off the previous season's signature tune, 'Top of the league, with Harry and Jim'. For Redknapp, who had never before occupied such a lofty position, it was a freeze-frame moment – although he was hardly getting carried away. 'It's a fantastic feeling being top,' he said, 'but we know it's an awfully long season.'

A subsequent haul of two points from a possible

fifteen emphasised the need for caution. Even so, Portsmouth were still in the top half of the table with ten days of October remaining. By then, Redknapp had pulled off another remarkable transfer coup by securing Alexei Smertin, the Russia captain, on a season-long loan from Chelsea. Smertin, who was acquired by Chelsea from Bordeaux as a £3.5m 'investment for the future,' slotted into midfield alongside Amdy Faye, the Senegal international whose tenacious performances had earned him glowing reviews following his summer arrival from Auxerre. Both signings stretched credulity. While Smertin would have walked into most Premier League teams, Faye's move was sealed only after late interest from Middlesbrough prompted Redknapp to place the midfielder under the guard of his pet bulldogs. As Redknapp explained to *Mirror* journalist Oliver Holt: 'I'm going round to Jamie's house for a barbecue and get a call saying Amdy's done a runner out of the hotel in Portsmouth and is on his way to Heathrow in a taxi. I said to my wife, Sandra, "Forget the barbecue, quick, we're going to Heathrow". We get there, looking for Amdy. I ring his phone number. He answers and says he's on his way to Paris. I find him, capture him and say, "Amdy, you've got to come with me". I bundle him into the car and take him to my home. We've got two bulldogs and I say, "Amdy if you escape, one of these dogs will bite your legs, the other will bite your bollocks".' Unsurprisingly, Faye signed the next day. As Steve Stone put it: 'Nobody else had heard of people like Amdy Faye and Alexei Smertin. Harry nicked Smertin off Chelsea for nothing when they'd just paid three and a half million for him. How does that happen? He can do that and nobody else can. He obviously has an eye for a player to do a job for a certain amount of time and I think he thrives on it, although it probably gives him a few sleepless nights.'

With Portsmouth in danger of a nosebleed, a likelier cause of early-season insomnia was the television pundit Andy Townsend, who suggested that Portsmouth would adopt a rudimentary approach to securing survival. Having won promotion by playing attacking rather than attritional football, Redknapp's verdict was withering. 'He's on the box talking about kick and rush,' he said. 'I've never had a team like that in my life. Kick and rush? He must be thinking it's Harry Bassett of Wimbledon rather than Harry Redknapp.' Yet while the ball remained on the Fratton Park turf, a team assembled for little more than £3m could not defy gravity indefinitely. Portsmouth's first victory against Liverpool for forty-three years, a resilient performance capped by a Patrik Berger goal, was followed by a barren run that brought only two more league wins all year. Predictably, Redknapp did not let the opening of the January transfer window pass unmarked. Seven new players arrived on the south coast, including Eyal Berkovic, the midfield schemer who had served Redknapp so successfully at West Ham, and the Newcastle striker Lomana LuaLua, who was brought in on loan. Nor was Redknapp slow to recognise where he had recruited badly. The most notable departure was that of Boris Zivkovic, the Croatia international signed on a free six months earlier. Shipped back to the Bundesliga after eighteen underwhelming performances, Zivkovic took a parting swipe at Redknapp, complaining that the manager spent more time on his mobile than coaching. 'I was on the phone trying to find someone to replace him,' Redknapp retorted.

For once, though, Redknapp's managerial alchemy failed to yield instant gold. Another victory over Liverpool took Portsmouth into the FA Cup quarter-finals, where Fratton Park's raucous refusal to be bowed in the face of a 5-1 drubbing by Arsenal drew unstinting praise from Thierry Henry, but league form remained indifferent. By mid-March, with ten games remaining and a south-coast derby against Southampton in the offing – not to mention visits from Manchester United and Arsenal – Redknapp's men were in the relegation zone, two points adrift from safety. 'It was a difficult feeling, a difficult situation,' recalls Mandaric. 'Portsmouth's supporters are among the best, if not the best, in the country. But it was an experience and we did go through difficult times. It's one thing to be successful and to get to the Premier League, and another situation to stay up there. Many times people told me, "You will stay up, because your manager is a lucky manager". I said: "What do you mean, lucky manager?" It was the first time I'd heard that. They said: "Harry's got that thing, he's a lucky man – luck goes on his side when it's needed." There's something in that, to be honest.'

A lengthy casualty list suggested otherwise. Injuries had interrupted Hislop's season, prematurely curtailed the involvement of Sherwood and Berger and effectively ruled out Todorov and Pericard for the entire campaign. Yet it is not without reason that Jim Smith refers to Redknapp as 'golden bollocks.' With the home straight beckoning, Lady Luck obliged the prognosticators by making a belated arrival at Redknapp's side. Portsmouth had a late scare against Southampton when Kevin Phillips hit the woodwork in injury time, but held out to claim their first win against the Saints at Fratton Park since 1963. At Ewood Park, Andy Cole wasted a simple chance to pull Blackburn level in the dying moments as Portsmouth clinched their first away win of the season. The good fortune continued when a linesman's flag denied Paolo Di Canio a probable winner against his former manager at Charlton. By the time the Birmingham goalkeeper Maik Taylor had been controversially dismissed at Fratton Park, swinging a tightly-contested game in Pompey's favour, ten points had been garnered from a possible twelve.

Milan Mandaric was thus in good heart as he boarded a plane for Dubai shortly before Manchester United's visit to Portsmouth. Or he was, until a member of staff pointed out that Mandaric was not the only south-coast representative whose pleasure lay in the east.

'Mr Mandaric, one of your players is here.'

'Impossible. Which one?'

'Steve Stone, sir.'

'No, no, that's not possible. It's Wednesday. We have a game on Saturday against Manchester United, and Steve Stone is in the team.'

'No, he's there on the beach.'

Weaving his way through the sun loungers, Mandaric spotted a distinct bald dome. 'I went up behind him,' he recalls, 'but I thought maybe it was a mistake.' There was no mistake.

'Steve, hi.'

'Oh, hi Mr Chairman,' Stone replied breezily, 'how are you doing?'

'What are you doing here, Steve?'

'Well, the gaffer told me I can take a rest for two or three days this week and to be sure that I'm back on Friday.'

Mandaric retreated a safe distance before punching Redknapp's number into his phone.

'Harry? Steve Stone's in Dubai.'

'Oh yeah, yeah, I know,' said Redknapp. 'He's got tired legs. But he's going to come back and play, don't worry.' That Saturday, Stone scored the decisive goal in a one-nil win against Manchester United at Fratton Park. It was a landmark victory. While no stranger to bettering United in cup combat, it was Redknapp's first league success against them in sixteen attempts. Portsmouth were top of the form table and, more importantly, five points clear of the relegation zone. 'That's Harry for you,' says Mandaric.

'Teams who go up invariably come down,' reflected Redknapp in the aftermath of the United win. 'I know people call me "Harry Bare Bones", but I walked from the training ground every day midway through the season and saw eight or nine players having treatment. It was a problem. We've exceeded our expectations and to stay up will be a terrific achievement.' Victory at Leeds the following weekend followed by a point against Fulham – the seventeenth from a possible twenty-one – secured safety with three games to go. Portsmouth had confounded all predictions.

'It was a surprise to stay up,' concedes Hislop, who epitomised the team's spirit of defiance by playing through the pain of a broken finger for the final three months of the season. 'For a very long time, we were staring relegation in the face, and then we won six out of ten games. That's how we survived. We started well and we finished well, but we didn't have a good middle. But that's what you'd expect in your first season in the Premier League.'

What nobody could have expected was that seven months later Redknapp would be leading a team out at Fratton Park as Southampton manager.

Chapter Seven

As the penultimate game of the 2004/05 season dawned, Harry Redknapp's drawn countenance bore testimony to a season of turmoil. His wife, Sandra, knew the symptoms of old. She had seen the same hollow expression a decade earlier, when West Ham likewise faced relegation with two games to go, just as she had seen it before the defeat against Leeds that consigned Bournemouth to the drop in 1990. Somehow, though, this was worse; this time, the anxiety had roots deeper than football. Redknapp's defection from Portsmouth to Southampton the previous December had been at the upper end of the scale from impulsive to rash. Predictably, given the traditional hostility between the two clubs, he became an overnight pariah in the eyes of most Pompey followers. Dubbed a 'Judas' and forced to change his mobile number after its posting on a Portsmouth website resulted in a string of abusive phone calls, the man who introduced a 'u' to Poplar suddenly found himself on unfamiliar ground. Had he foreseen that he would be travelling to Crystal Palace for the penultimate game of the season with the Saints' twenty-seven year stay in the top flight at stake, perhaps even he would have thought twice about taking over at a club third from bottom of the Premier League. 'Harry,' said Sandra, 'this will help you.' Redknapp glanced down. His wife had handed him a white plastic angel.

Beyond Chez Redknapp, faith was in short supply. Southampton were clear of a tightly-bunched relegation zone by the slender margin of a one-point goal difference; on the final day of the campaign, they would host Manchester United. After a season of wretched performances and worse luck, it was not a scenario to encourage optimism. Yet only eighteen months earlier, Southampton had been fourth in the table and casting surreptitious glances at Champions League qualification. To understand what went wrong in the interim, it is necessary to go back to February 2004, when Gordon Strachan announced that he was standing down as manager for family reasons. Once synonymous with stability – only nine men had taken charge of the club in the post-war period to 1996 – Southampton had become noted for a high turnover of managers under the chairmanship of Rupert Lowe. For over two years, Strachan had bucked that trend. His shrewd stewardship brought renewed steadiness to the club, and with it came an upturn in fortune that included an eighth-place Premier League finish and a run to the 2003 FA Cup final. When Strachan left, form and confidence plummeted. Paul Sturrock and Steve Wigley came and went in quick succession and, by the time Redknapp became Lowe's eighth appointment in nine years a fortnight before Christmas, Southampton had won only seven times in the league all year.

Compounding the club's woes was a long-term knee injury to the tousled-haired Sweden international Michael Svensson. With Svensson in the team, Southampton had conceded under a goal a game; without him, a defence that Redknapp found far too quiet for his liking was breached seventy-two times in forty-four league matches. Attempts to sign a stop-gap were consistent with a wider tendency, epitomised by the signing of the thirty-four-year-old Graeme Le Saux as a replacement for Wayne Bridge, to bring in players of lesser influence than those who were sold. The conclusion was inescapable: rather than using the impressive progress made under Strachan as a springboard for further achievement, Southampton were content to tread water.

Even without this background, there is mileage in the argument that Redknapp was on a hiding to nothing from the day he stepped foot in St Mary's. His appointment was greeted with reluctance by Lowe, who had championed the return of former manager Glenn Hoddle only to be overruled by his board. It is doubtful that Lowe has Redknapp's mobile number on speed dial. 'He wasn't really my choice,' says Lowe, 'but the board wouldn't support my wish to reappoint Glenn Hoddle. I probably should have resigned when the board wouldn't do what I wanted to do with Hoddle, but being a team player I followed the board's wish and ended up working with Redknapp – much to my regret.'

The lazy view attributes the lack of chemistry between

Lowe and Redknapp to the chalk-and-cheese combination of former public schoolboy and archetypal East Ender. Yet Redknapp had overcome greater boardroom hurdles in his time. A more significant threat to smooth relations lay in Lowe's innate scepticism about Redknapp's managerial acumen. 'Journalists write very good things about him all the time because he spends his life giving them stories,' says Lowe. 'As I said to him on one occasion, if he spent five per cent as much time coaching the side as he did schmoozing the media, we might actually get somewhere. I think his public persona, as [the media] all show him, is very different to his private persona. I think he's a rather miserable chap, not remotely the happy-go-lucky cockney that you might think. He doesn't manage football clubs in the way that I think they should be managed. Ultimately, he has his favourites. He's not a great man-manager in my view, he's lazy.'

Given the trademark tendency of those within football to churn out platitudes like confetti, Lowe's candid critique deserves a fair hearing. The unflattering picture he paints is all the more compelling for the readily recognisable sketch that lies beneath its surface; it is the interpretation, rather than the delineation, that invites challenge. Take Lowe's appraisal of Redknapp's relationship with the media. Redknapp's ability to hold a room is not in question. Catch him in the right mood and the stories – of players past and present, signings made and missed, battles won and lost – flow freely. Catch him in the wrong mood and you're walking on eggshells, running the gauntlet of a famously fiery temper that makes a mockery of the notion that he is a serial schmoozer.

CHAPTER SEVEN

'He doesn't suffer fools gladly – he can be a moody guy, and he can take that out on the media,' says Peter Jeffs, who witnessed Redknapp's dealings with the press at close quarters during his spell as Portsmouth's communications manager. 'He will take a journalist to pieces if it suits him.' Jeffs vividly recalls one such occasion. 'He came into the press room and his face was a picture. You could tell that plenty had been said in the dressing room. This wasn't the time to put a foot wrong; you had to be careful what you asked. One radio journalist, who was a bit wet behind the ears, piped up and said: "It's one win in six now – are the wheels beginning to come off?" Harry went ballistic, he tore the bloke to pieces. He asked him if he'd ever played football before, if he'd managed before, and once he'd slaughtered him he marched off in an enormous fit of pique.'

With 'onest 'Arry, then, what you see is what you get. And during prolonged rocky periods, what you get from a man whose mood is invariably a barometer of his team's fortunes is football's answer to Victor Meldrew. 'I can't switch off,' admits Redknapp, whose ability to lift the mood on his arrival at a new club contrasts pointedly with the more strained figure he cuts when things go badly over the long haul. 'I take all the problems home with me and I suppose I must be awful to a lot of people.'

It requires no great leap of the imagination to believe that Redknapp was, as Lowe suggests, 'a rather miserable chap' during Southampton's scrap for Premier League survival. He has form for putting himself through the mill in similar circumstances. When West Ham made a faltering start to Redknapp's first season as assistant manager, Tony Gale branded him 'a miserable bastard'. Similarly, Sandra Redknapp remembers him being 'a miserable sod' at the height of Portsmouth's struggle to survive their first season in the Premier League. Yet these comments are in the public domain because Redknapp put them there – hardly the act of a media Jekyll determined to conceal his managerial Hyde.

'You get what you see with Harry,' says the former Bournemouth striker Ian Thompson. 'He'll say it as it is. I think he recognises always where he's come from. He's an East End boy and he had an upbringing that was quite tough, and I don't think he'll ever lose sight of those roots. Wherever he's gone, whenever he speaks, he speaks the truth. What you see when he comes out on TV is the real person. He's no different on camera than he is person to person. It's a genuineness of character that is embedded in his roots as an East End boy who's made good. I can't speak highly enough of him, I think he's a terrific guy.'

Thompson's insistence on his former mentor's warts-and-all sincerity, which echoes the testimony of most Redknapp alumni, flies in the face of Lowe's suggestion that Redknapp's geniality is a facade. It also goes a long way towards dispelling any doubt about his man-management skills: bad bosses, particularly those guilty of favouritism, are rarely described by their employees as terrific guys. Nor do they draw the kind of lavish praise with which the striker Kevin Phillips greeted Redknapp's arrival at Southampton. 'Harry has come to this club and given everyone a lift,' said Phillips. 'I must admit I am delighted about his appointment. We now know we have a manager. No disrespect to Steve Wigley, who was a fantastic coach, but he was always under this illusion of whether he was the manager or not.'

No such doubts surrounded Redknapp's appointment. But while his command of the dressing room was never in question, in a broader sense he too struggled to exert his influence fully. Whereas at Portsmouth his ebullient persona had become woven into the club's DNA, a reality that made his defection all the more unpalatable to the Fratton faithful, at Southampton it barely ran skin-deep. The Saints needed a manager who could dig them out of a hole and Redknapp, still smouldering after an acrimonious split from Portsmouth, fancied the challenge. The result was a marriage of convenience that never felt natural or even comfortable. In other circumstances, things might have gone differently. Southampton was ostensibly an ideal destination for Redknapp: a big club, right on his doorstep, with a solid infrastructure, a flourishing academy and an established top-flight tradition. But his Portsmouth links dictated the dynamics of the relationship from day one. While the emphasis at Redknapp's first press conference as Portsmouth manager had been firmly on the future, his Southampton unveiling was more about the past than the present, with the new man forced to mount a spirited defence of his Fratton Park legacy. 'I took that club from fourth bottom of the First Division to mid-table in the Premiership,' said Redknapp. 'If I had walked away leaving them in dire straits, it might have been different. But everyone knows the job I did. I have nothing to be ashamed of.' On his first day as Southampton manager, Redknapp was talking about Portsmouth: it was no way to open a supposedly new chapter. The animus emanating from along the M27, and the media hysteria it occasioned, only added to the obvious difficulty of coming in mid-campaign to fight a relegation battle with limited transfer funds. There would be no clean slate, no honeymoon period, none of the feel-good factors normally associated with the arrival of a new manager. Redknapp's tenure was effectively tainted before it had begun.

By the time Southampton arrived at Selhurst Park in early May, the signs of strain were visible. With eighteen minutes to go, Nicola Ventola waltzed almost unopposed through the Saints' defence to give Palace a 2-1 lead. As Redknapp's blood pressure rose off the scale, Sandra's angel, which he had superstitiously grasped throughout, was moments from meeting its end. Salvation was at hand, however, in the unlikely form of Danny Higginbotham. In Redknapp's first game in charge, against Middlesbrough, the former Manchester United defender's late own goal cost Southampton a victory that would have lifted them out of the bottom three. More recently, he had put through his own net against fellow relegation contenders Norwich. So when Higginbotham turned home a Kevin Phillips cross to equalise against Palace with only seconds remaining, it was a cathartic moment. Hapless blunderer turned improbable hero, he had thrown Southampton a lifeline, ensuring that the four-way relegation tussle with Palace, West Brom and Norwich would go down to the final day.

Afterwards, Harry's angel took centre stage. 'With a minute to go it was about to go flying on to the pitch,' said Redknapp. 'I was thinking "You can stick your fucking angel" but suddenly it was "Well done" and I put it back in my pocket. I believe in fate. That's how silly it is. It's crackers, really. If we win and stay up we can put that angel on display on the mantelpiece, maybe give it a name. But I never thought I'd end up holding a plastic angel in my hand all game.'

Until Milan Mandaric began mooting the appointment of the former Yugoslavia international Velimir Zajec as Portsmouth's director of football, Redknapp probably hadn't contemplated managing Southampton either. The first signs of tension between Mandaric's long-term thinking and Redknapp's more immediate and pragmatic focus on Premier League survival had come at the end of the 2003/04 campaign. Concerned about the scale of Portsmouth's transfer activity, Mandaric revealed plans to overhaul the club's coaching structure, with Jim Smith and Kevin Bond potential casualties. 'The way we have stayed up this season is by signing nineteen players,' said Mandaric. 'We cannot do that again next year. We need to reorganise and to bring in a top coach. We need more coaching and to build up our youth system, so I am looking at the whole coaching structure.'

In response, Redknapp mounted a typically robust defence of the existing set-up. 'The chairman wants to bring in a European super-coach,' he said. 'Me and Jim have been a team from day one and taken this club forward so far. But he's the chairman and he makes the big decisions. Me, Jim and Kevin have turned things around and I don't see any reason to change that. Jim Smith is my mate and I have told him what was happening. Jim has done nothing wrong. He's been terrific. I simply don't understand it. It's bemusing. No one could have done anything more.'

Smith and Bond remained, but by November rumours

about Zajec's impending arrival were beginning to test Redknapp's patience. His own unhappy spell as director of football had hardened a natural suspicion about the role into full-blown scepticism. 'You tell me one time in England when a manager and a director of football combination has worked,' said Redknapp. His doubts seemed well founded. Could Zajec, with no previous experience of English football, realistically be expected to prosper in a job that had strait-jacketed a seasoned domestic campaigner like Redknapp?

A fortnight later, when a Sky television reporter thrust a microphone in his face after a 2-1 defeat at Southampton, Redknapp could no longer contain his frustration. 'Well, I suppose we could do better,'" he replied with caustic irony on being asked if he was happy with his staff. 'We were fourth from bottom of the First Division when I took over, then we won the league, then we finished thirteenth in our first season in the Premiership and this morning we were tenth. So, yeah, there's room for improvement.'

Ask Mandaric today about the gradual souring of a richly successful relationship and his reply is tinged with palpable regret. 'I thought maybe I could help Harry by bringing in somebody to worry about things, mainly outside of the country and things like that,' he says. 'Harry and I got along well, but he didn't see it that way, so there was a little bit of a misunderstanding. We went our different ways and I felt bad about that, because I did like him personally, we'd become friends. The situation really didn't help me and it didn't help Harry either.'

Hindsight has evidently dulled the acute sense of grievance that, at the time, earned Redknapp a sharp rebuke from his employer. 'I really disapprove of Harry's angriness,' said Mandaric following Redknapp's television outburst. 'There is no room for that. We are enhancing the structure of the club and enhancing Harry's situation as well. I honestly don't think there is any threat to Harry's job. There is no way we will bring over some players and tell Harry: "These are your players." No, no, it doesn't work that way. They will work together and Harry will have the decision firmly.'

Redknapp called the shots in no uncertain fashion: on November 24, he quit. 'I won't tell lies,' he said. 'I was disappointed with the way [the Zajec affair] was handled. I picked up a newspaper on Thursday and I was manager of the month. We'd just beaten Manchester United. Suddenly, I'm down the pan. The other man coming in has made it a bit of a soap opera.'

'Harry left under a cloud,' recalls Shaka Hislop. 'They brought in a director of football, which he didn't agree with, and I'd have to say that I'd side with Harry on that one because he'd achieved so much success for the club in such a short time. I couldn't understand why somebody else should be needed, looking over Harry's shoulder. I don't think he deserved that and I don't think it was right. So there was a big cloud over his departure and it came as a shock. Having said that, I think you could see it coming once the director came on the scene. It changed the relationship between Harry and the chairman, and I think everyone knew it was going to be sooner rather than later that Harry would depart.'

Jim Smith, who along with Kevin Bond followed Redknapp through the Fratton Park exit, confirmed that the boardroom plotting centring on Zajec had played a key role in the souring of relations. 'That was a major effect,' said Smith. 'That decision was not the only effect, there were other undercurrents. But when he arrived we felt the writing was on the wall. What Harry achieved was a miracle. Four or five years ago it was just crap football and he took this club to another level. It's hard to believe there was anybody who failed to appreciate what he did for the club. But some who should have appreciated it didn't.'

For all his frustration over the Zajec affair, Redknapp struck a conciliatory note in his final media briefing as Portsmouth manager. 'I've had a fantastic two-and-a-half years and I'm not going to start slagging anyone off,' he said. 'It's nice to walk away from a club in great shape on the field. I've taken them from the bottom of the First Division to the Premiership playing fantastic football. We're on TV more than Coronation Street. No one pushed me out, I've been thinking about it for a while. I just thought I wanted a break.'

Sandra thought otherwise. 'You'll be bored within four weeks,' she warned her suddenly ubiquitous husband. As things turned out, she erred only on the side of caution.

Three months earlier, the curtain had fallen on Paul Sturrock's Southampton tenure after just thirteen games. Steve Wigley was promoted from assistant coach to the top job, but the former Nottingham Forest man embarked on a wretched fifteen-week run during which the only win came, ironically, against Redknapp's Portsmouth. Two candidates emerged as potential successors. Neither appealed to Southampton fans. On the one hand there was Glenn Hoddle, the former manager who had done little to endear himself to St

Mary's regulars by upping sticks for Tottenham four years earlier. On the other there was Redknapp, a figure synonymous with the club's bitterest rivals.

While the Saints marched inexorably towards the drop zone, the Redknapps left England for a sunshine break at their holiday home in Marbella. They touched down in Andalucia on Friday, two days after Redknapp's resignation. A little after seven the next morning, Sandra called her husband into the living room: 'Harry, you'd better come and see this.' Redknapp hauled himself out of bed. As he wiped the sleep from his eyes, he was surprised to be greeted by the news that his name had been dragged into a brewing controversy. 'We have spent £3m on agents' fees in the last couple of years,' a television report quoted Mandaric as saying. 'I know Manchester United are spending a lot more money on some heavy-duty players, but this is Portsmouth we are talking about.' The quotes came from a back-page article in the *Daily Mail* headlined: '£3m, that's what Harry's special agents have cost me over two years, says Mandaric'. Never mind that Mandaric himself, in tandem with Peter Storrie, the club's chief executive, had overseen the relevant transfers. Never mind that Redknapp had led Pompey from the foot of the Championship to a mid-table Premier League spot at minimal expense. Redknapp, who subsequently referred to the episode as 'my worst moment in football', was seething.

Within the hour, Mandaric was on the phone from Dubai. 'Harry, I never said any of this.' Redknapp was having none of it. He had never felt comfortable with the wheeler-dealer image cast upon him by the media; now he felt that his integrity had been impugned to boot. Three days later, at a hastily-convened Fratton Park press conference, Mandaric publically clarified his comments. 'Harry was never involved at any time on any transfer and contract negotiations throughout his period at the club,' he affirmed. 'At no time did I ever imply that there was any wrongdoing by Harry Redknapp in these transactions. I was simply saying that agents take so much out of the game. I want, along with all my fellow Premier League chairmen, to reduce their influence in all club finances.'

Redknapp, meanwhile, made his feelings clear. 'I'd never been so shocked and disgusted in my life,' he told the assembled media. 'Innuendos and all that are no good. I don't deserve that. I needed to clear the air. That's what Milan has done.'

That Saturday, Southampton travelled to Old Trafford, sliding to a 3-0 defeat as they failed to muster a single shot on target. 'I am at my lowest point,' admitted Wigley. Not quite. Four days later, he became the eighth managerial casualty of the Rupert Lowe era.

On Monday morning, Redknapp's telephone trilled. Surprisingly, it was Dennis Roach, the agent who normally acted on behalf of Glenn Hoddle. The previous day, Hoddle had completed a move to Wolves that was brokered by Roach; now, Roach wanted to know if Redknapp would be interested in having a chat with Rupert Lowe. That evening, Redknapp drove up to Lowe's house in the Cotswolds. 'Redknapp had fallen out with Mandaric and our board was attracted to him because [of what] was said [about] his man-management skills, that he knew football and all the rest of it,' says

Lowe. The question, then, was simple: would Harry be interested in taking over at St Mary's?

There were reasons enough for Redknapp to decline. There was no way of predicting how he would gel with Lowe. A twenty-game punditry deal had been agreed with Sky. That Wednesday, he and Sandra were due to board a plane to Dubai for a pre-Christmas trip with Jim Smith and his wife. Above all, Redknapp had pledged to the Pompey faithful that he would never 'go down the road.' Then, though, he had been contemplating leaving the game for good. Now he was angry. Angry at Mandaric's perceived ingratitude. Angry at the besmirching of his reputation. Two days later, Redknapp signed an eighteen-month contract with Southampton. A predictable wave of antipathy rolled in from Portsmouth, with Terry Brady, a club director, branding his switch 'the highest betrayal possible.'

'I don't see it as an act of betrayal,' countered Redknapp. 'I don't owe anybody anything. It's my life and this is a great opportunity for me. I left Pompey a couple of weeks back with them half way up the Premiership table. I had taken them from fourth from bottom of the First Division into a mid-table Premiership team two years running. Then circumstances at the club changed. A new chap was director of football, which wasn't a situation that suited me. I decided to move on and walked away without wanting to blame anybody or cause any aggravation. I left Portsmouth saying all the right things and a week later I got badly hurt by people, so I am angry.

'I've sat at home for the last two weeks watching football on TV and didn't enjoy it. I felt myself getting bitter and twisted, I got this offer and I jumped at it. There's nothing to be ashamed of. It was sad when it all ended, very sad. It was sad for me and I didn't deserve what happened to me at the end. If I had walked away from Portsmouth leaving them in dire straits it might be different. But I know the job I did there and so does everyone involved in that football club.'

Redknapp's defection caused few ripples in the Fratton Park dressing room. 'The fact that Harry joined Southampton was not a shock because he's always lived in Bournemouth, his house is still there, and I don't think that he ever wanted to leave the south coast,' says Shaka Hislop. 'But Harry was forced out of Portsmouth and Southampton was a viable option at the time.'

The early days of Redknapp's Southampton tenure were promising, notwithstanding the late collapse against Middlesbrough that denied him a winning start. His predecessors had been reluctant to deploy Peter Crouch in attack, but Redknapp immediately recognised the potential benefits of pairing the six-foot-seven forward with the nippier, more modestly proportioned Kevin Phillips. Crouch writes in his autobiography of how Redknapp took the duo aside during his first session at Southampton's Marchwood training ground. 'From now on, you are my two main men up front,' he told them. 'I know what you can do, you're both goal-scorers and you'll be the two who will get us out of this mess.'

The little-and-large partnership, redolent of the attacking alliance Phillips had forged to such profitable effect with Niall Quinn at Sunderland, reaped immediate dividends. Fed by long, diagonal balls from the flanks, Crouch and Phillips tormented the Boro defence in

Redknapp's debut game. The duo scored a goal apiece to ensure that the Saints, despite the absence of the injured James Beattie, did not lack a cutting edge. For Crouch it was the beginning of a journey that would bring fifteen goals in twenty-four games, culminating in his England debut the following summer.

For Beattie, a different journey lay ahead. Asked about rumours linking the striker with a January move to Everton, Redknapp said: 'We need him to stay here, to let him go in January would be a disaster. He can score goals and he is vital to us.' Within a month, however, Beattie was sacrificed on the altar of financial expediency as Redknapp – his hand forced by the need to raise funds – reluctantly accepted a £6m bid from Everton. With Liverpool, Arsenal, Manchester United and Chelsea still to visit St Mary's, he knew he was in a dogfight. 'Make no mistake, we are involved in a relegation battle,' said Redknapp. 'We have played most of the teams at the bottom here and we only have thirteen points.'

Less than half the money raised by Beattie's sale was rechanneled into transfer fees, and there is a school of thought that says underinvestment was a significant factor in Southampton's subsequent travails. Lowe bridles at the suggestion. 'We supported Harry absolutely to the hilt,' he says. 'We signed all the players that he wanted including Henri Camara [the Senegal international who was brought in on loan from Wolves] and Olivier Bernard.'

Yet Leon Crouch, the local businessman and Saints devotee who would later become club chairman, believes that if Redknapp had received greater backing in the transfer market, the relegation crisis that ensued might have been avoided. 'I think that Harry Redknapp has proven his ability to come into clubs when they're in a difficult position and rescue them,' says Crouch. 'He did it at Portsmouth, he's done it more recently at Tottenham, and I see no reason why he shouldn't have been able to do it with Southampton. Rupert Lowe has to take a large percentage of the blame for bringing in a manager in Harry Redknapp and not supporting him financially.'

A week after Redknapp's appointment, Southampton were beaten 5-1 at Tottenham. Redknapp later took a call from Dave Bassett. 'Are you sure you know what you are doing?' enquired the Rotherham boss, alarmed by the lack of depth in Southampton's squad. It was a pertinent question. Later in the campaign Bassett would gain a first-hand insight into the Saints' dearth of talent by taking Leandre Griffith, the young French midfielder, on loan. In a season which Rotherham ended at the bottom of the Championship, Griffith failed to make the first team.

Away defeats to Liverpool and Manchester City further underlined the need to strengthen, not least defensively. Yet Redknapp's transfer dealings remained subject to severe financial constraints. The midfielder Nigel Quashie, who at £2.1m became Redknapp's most expensive acquisition, followed Jim Smith and Kevin Bond from Portsmouth. But the signings of Olivier Bernard, the former Newcastle full-back, and the peripatetic Tottenham centre-half Calum Davenport, who was brought in on loan, were an inadequate response to Southampton's defensive malaise.

More influential was Jamie Redknapp, who arrived on

a free from Spurs determined to help dad beat the drop. At thirty-one the former Liverpool captain's injury-plagued career was nearing an end, but his determination to play through the pain of a knee injury that would force him to retire five months later impressed even Lowe. 'Jamie played with a very, very bad knee,' says Lowe. 'They used to have to take a pint of fluid off his knee after every game he played, and he couldn't train during the week because of that. He was entirely committed and, I think, a very decent chap.'

The first victory of the Redknapp era, a 3-1 FA Cup third-round win at Northampton, ought to have provided some respite. Instead, the draw for the next round realised Redknapp's worst fears: Southampton would host Portsmouth. 'I had a feeling that this was going to happen when I was watching the draw,' said Redknapp. 'When there were only eight teams left, I said, "It's a certainty, this." Amazing. I would have preferred to avoid them, for sure. Maybe there'll be a backlash. But I took them from next to the bottom of the First Division to where they are today. Maybe if I'd never gone there they wouldn't be in the Premier League now.'

Redknapp's sentiments were echoed by Peter Crouch, who suggested in the build-up to the game that the revenue generated by his sale had been central to Pompey's resurgence. 'I don't think I owe them anything because I scored goals there,' said Crouch. 'They paid £1.2m for me and sold me for £5.5m. Harry built the team that they are now with the money they got for me. I'd like to think I did good business for them, so I'm hoping I don't get a bad reception. That said, I'm not fussed about stick.'

The Hampshire constabulary, on the other hand, were fussed. Very fussed indeed. As rival fans hurled virtual vituperation at each other on the message boards, sparking a war of words in which even the respective club chairmen became involved, all police leave was cancelled. A four-hundred-strong contingent of officers was assembled. Extra horses were brought in from the Avon and Somerset police force. It was like the prelude to a war rather than the build-up to a football match.

Of greater concern to Redknapp, however, was the need to locate reinforcements for the league battles that lay ahead. His quest took him to Rome, where he tried to sign Vincent Candela, the Roma and France left-back. Candela agreed a loan move to Southampton but later reneged on the deal, opting for Sam Allardyce's Bolton instead. 'He must have got lost,' quipped Redknapp. Yet the trademark humour was beginning to wear thin. Glum, anxious and drained, Redknapp was far from his normal self. On his return from Rome, Sandra ushered her weary husband into an armchair before unpacking the contents of a small box. 'Lovely,' thought Redknapp, 'she's bought me a present – a nice bottle of wine or something.' The red occupying Sandra's thoughts was of a different kind: her 'gift' was a blood pressure monitor. 'I rolled up my sleeve and hoped for the best,' said Redknapp. 'Luckily, Sandra said it was OK.'

Had she been on hand when Redknapp arrived in the Southampton dugout that Saturday lunchtime, it might have been a different story. As a banner bearing the legend 'Redknapp: forgotten but never forgiven' fluttered in the Solent breeze, invective rained down from the visitors' section. Redknapp drew the lightning like a golf club in a thunderstorm. Fans who only weeks earlier had nothing but praise for the architect of Portsmouth's renaissance were now united in their loathing. As their vitriol-soaked chants rang out, Redknapp remained subdued, impassive, his forays into the technical area infrequent, his hands tucked deep inside his black leather jacket.

Events on the pitch did nothing to dampen the rancorous atmosphere. A debatable penalty award which enabled Yakubu to cancel out Matthew Oakley's opener for Southampton earned the referee, Steve Bennett, the derision of the home support. The official then fell foul of the visiting fans too by harshly dismissing the Pompey striker Diomansy Kamara for a second bookable offence. That, though, was as nothing compared to their fury when Bennett – on the advice of his linesman, Mike Tingey – awarded Southampton a penalty deep into injury time. 'There's going to be a riot!' yelled Jim Smith as Bennett gestured to the spot after a vigorously-contested handball decision against Matthew Taylor.

Seconds earlier, Redknapp had been resigned to the nightmare prospect of a Fratton Park replay. Now, as Crouch planted the ball on the penalty spot, he hardly knew whether to laugh or cry. 'Oh my gawd,' said Redknapp, 'not Crouchy! Not him. He'll fucking head it!' He looked over again at Jim Smith, who was by now shaking his head incredulously. 'Crouchy can't score,' muttered Smith. The object of their anxiety had other ideas. As the Portsmouth players vented their frustration at Bennett, Crouch waited patiently, hands on hips, for the pandemonium to abate. He then calmly sent Kosta Chalkias, Pompey's debutant keeper, the wrong way.

When Bennett blew the final whistle a few moments later, Redknapp turned to the away section, shrugged and broke into applause. A lengthy round of hugs and handshakes with the Portsmouth players followed. 'I'm glad it's out of the way,' he later reflected. 'But I'd much rather have three points. Survival has to be our priority. I don't have hard feelings against anyone at Pompey. Everyone came into my office beforehand, the players, officials, the kit man and even the coach driver. I signed all of them.'

It would be late April before Redknapp's hooded eyes next looked upon his former charges. In the interim, things did not go well. Beating Portsmouth should have been the catalyst for an upturn in Southampton's fortunes. Instead, Redknapp's side won just three of their next thirteen games. Various factors contributed to the slump, from injuries and indiscipline to the familiar rumblings of internal discord. But at the heart of the Saints' difficulties was a defensive vulnerability that would have a defining influence on their season.

The late capitulation against Middlesbrough with which the Redknapp era commenced set the tone for the remainder of the campaign. To Redknapp's mounting dismay, Southampton developed a chronic inability to hold a lead. The problem was highlighted when Everton visited St Mary's a week after the Portsmouth win. Deep in injury time, with Southampton leading 2-1, Crouch received the ball on the half-way line. Instead of heading for the corner flag to run the clock down, the lanky striker unleashed a miscued shot which allowed the goalkeeper Nigel Martyn to release Marcus Bent for a late equaliser. The theme became a recurring one. A fortnight later, Brentford retrieved a two-goal deficit to earn an unlikely Cup replay. When Southampton repeated the trick with five games remaining, losing 3-2 to Aston Villa despite early goals from Crouch and Phillips, Redknapp's frustration finally boiled over.

'All the negatives were at the back,' he snapped after watching his side concede three goals for the third consecutive match. 'The back four could not defend. There were no other problems for us, apart from our defending. We are short of pace at the back, we have no quick defenders. I don't know what I was watching in the second half. When you go in at half-time two up and then not win there has to be something wrong. If you cannot hold on to a two-goal lead when you have played like that then you have to be fearful.'

'We were forever messing things up in the last minute,' recalls Crouch in his autobiography. 'It became our thing. We were haunted by the constant fear that we were going to chuck it all away with some stupid mistake.'

Few positives were unalloyed. A goal-less draw at the Hawthorns in late February ended a run of seven consecutive away defeats, but a dominant performance was marred by an inability to convert what Redknapp described as 'gilt-edged chances.' A 1-1 home draw with Arsenal was overshadowed by the brutal challenges on Mathieu Flamini and Robert Pires that earned David Prutton a red card and a ten-match ban. An unbeaten home record dating back to the previous September was maintained with a 1-0 win over Martin Jol's Tottenham, but a weakened side fell to a crushing FA Cup quarter-final defeat against Manchester United in the next outing at St Mary's.

Even when Southampton beat Middlesbrough to move out of the bottom three for the first time since Redknapp's arrival, the focus was elsewhere. Lowe, it emerged, had lined up Sir Clive Woodward, the mastermind behind England's 2003 Rugby World Cup triumph, to join the Southampton coaching staff. Was Woodward set to become another Velimir Zajec? Redknapp said that rugby's wandering knight 'wouldn't be coming in as a director of football' and simply wanted to 'learn the game.' Yet his actions encouraged an alternative reading. Ducking the post-match media briefing at the Riverside, Redknapp boarded a plane for Dubai, finally taking the holiday he had postponed four months earlier in order to join Southampton. Had he been trying to make the point that life could go on as before, he could not have done so more clearly.

Lowe dismisses the suggestion that his courting of Woodward had a destabilising effect on Redknapp's tenure. 'Absolute poppycock,' he says, 'and Redknapp knows that. He was consulted. He met with Clive on several occasions [and] he supported Clive's appointment privately. He and Clive met down at his house [and] Harry was very polite to him. Harry doesn't confront anybody; he tells everybody what they want to hear.

To anyone with even a passing acquaintance with Redknapp's career, the non-confrontational figure described by Lowe is surely unrecognisable. Redknapp's directness has ruffled feathers everywhere from the Bournemouth vice-president's lounge, where he once seized Ken Gardiner by the throat, to the Marchwood training ground, where he lambasted the likes of Darren

Kenton and Calum Davenport for their defensive shortcomings. That said, it is not difficult to see why he trod a more diplomatic line where Woodward's appointment was concerned. Fresh from one verbal feud at Portsmouth, the last thing he needed was another at Southampton. In any case, the facts spoke for themselves. Nobody needed to be briefed to appreciate that the revelation of Woodward's arrival might be an unwelcome distraction. Neither was there any serious doubt – least of all among supporters – that the money invested in the appointment would have been better spent on new recruits. 'The majority of the fans would agree with that,' says Leon Crouch. 'The decision to bring in Clive Woodward definitely undermined Harry's position and, I think, ultimately played a major role [in the relegation struggle]. I don't think Harry Redknapp would take kindly to having to work under or alongside someone like Clive Woodward. I don't think that was a good move by Rupert Lowe.'

One factor for which nobody could be blamed was the fixture list, which had dealt Southampton a daunting run-in. An onerous trip to Portsmouth would be followed by tussles against Norwich City and Crystal Palace, both fellow relegation candidates, before the season finale at home to Manchester United. 'It's going to be a strange day and I am not looking forward to it,' said Redknapp ahead of his much-anticipated return to Fratton Park. 'I'm sure I'll come in for plenty of stick – that goes with the territory because I've left Portsmouth and joined Southampton. It seems to be some kind of crime to do that. But it's only a game of football as far as I can see.' What of rumours that he had received threats? 'The only threats I've had this week have been from the wife for not doing the washing up.'

Nevertheless, advice from the local constabulary to enlist personal protection did not go unheeded. With the police once again out in force, Redknapp entered the Fratton Park bear pit flanked by two former-SAS men. A third minder lurked nearby. Nothing, though, could defend him from the venomous reception that greeted his emergence from the tunnel. No chisel-jawed chaperon could protect him from the blow of losing Crouch to a lingering hamstring injury before kick-off. And a whole battalion of bodyguards could not alter the reality that results had gone against him the previous afternoon, leaving Southampton rooted to the foot of the table. Steve Dunn's whistle had the cheerless timbre of a call to the gallows.

The match was effectively over inside twenty-seven minutes. Yakubu stroked home an early penalty before Arjan de Zeeuw and Lomana LuaLua, who helped himself to a brace, sealed a 4-1 win. Southampton were within a miscued clearance of the Championship. Redknapp was magnanimous in defeat. At the final whistle, he turned to the directors' box and gave Mandaric the thumbs up. No post-match enquiry was shirked. Yes, his side had defended abysmally; no, the loss of Crouch was not to blame for the defeat; naturally, he understood the fans' barracking. 'It's very hard to play when you keep giving goals away,' he muttered ruefully. 'I've never seen Harry so low,' said Jim Smith.

The emotional turmoil continued at Norwich the following weekend. Southampton fell behind to an early goal, equalised within four minutes, took the lead, relinquished it twice – once after a Higginbotham own goal – and finally recovered to win 4-3 with two minutes remaining. The combination of three points and a favourable goal difference was enough to drag the club from the bottom of the table to the safety of seventeenth place, but for Redknapp the afternoon had been a white-knuckle ride of virtually unrelieved trauma. His Norwich counterpart Nigel Worthington thought otherwise, talking enthusiastically of 'a terrific game.' 'He said that?' stammered an incredulous Redknapp. 'What is he, a psychopath?' He meant masochist. It hardly seemed to matter.

Seven days later, Higginbotham's dramatic injury-time equaliser against Crystal Palace set the scene for the most fraught finale to a relegation battle in years. Redknapp likened it to musical chairs: when the music stopped, one of the four clubs involved would lose its seat at English football's top table. 'Anything is possible,' mused Redknapp, 'so I won't be listening to a radio. The situation will change so many times between three o'clock and four forty-five. All of us have our pride at stake. Sunday will be the best day of our football life if we pull it off, but three of the four are going to have an all-time low in their football life.'

Dragging Southampton towards that nadir was the weight of a professional and personal history that seemed ripe for revision. Almost three decades earlier, Lawrie McMenemy's Southampton had pulled off one of the great FA Cup shocks by beating Manchester United 1-0 at Wembley. 'United gave us the greatest day in our history,' said McMenemy. 'Now they could provide us with our worst.' The noises emanating from the United dressing room did little to dampen those fears. On the final day of the 1994/95 campaign, Redknapp had thwarted Sir Alex Ferguson's bid for a third successive Premier League title by holding United to a draw at Upton Park. Now, so the rumour went, Fergie wanted to get even.

Elsewhere, the talk was of lucky charms. Redknapp had worn a talismanic bulldog tie throughout Southampton's best run of the campaign, but dispensed with it after his side were drubbed 4-0 by United in the Cup quarter-finals. Now he was pinning his hopes on the toy angel given to him by his wife. Would his faith in superstition serve him any better this time round? By ten past three on the day of reckoning, it looked as though it just might. A sudden attack of the Higginbothams saw John O'Shea put through his own net at precisely the same moment as Norwich – for whom a win at Craven Cottage would ensure survival – shipped the first of half a dozen goals. As things stood, Southampton were safe.

Yet Ferguson's men were playing for their places in the Cup final against Arsenal the following weekend and a backlash was inevitable. Sure enough, Darren Fletcher equalised and, shortly after the interval, Ruud van Nistelrooy put United ahead. A few minutes later, over in the Black Country, another United man found the net, Kieran Richardson completing his five-month loan spell at West Brom in style by scoring the second goal in a 2-0 win against Portsmouth. The game was up. Southampton were consigned to the drop for the first time in over a quarter of a century, Redknapp to only the

CHAPTER SEVEN

second relegation of a management career spanning a similar period.

In retrospect, Redknapp believes – unsurprisingly – that joining Southampton was a mistake. 'It was very difficult, but you do what you do,' he says. 'I had a right to go to work. I had fallen out with the owner at Portsmouth, and I'm a football person so I went to work. If I could turn the clock back I wouldn't have gone there, looking back on it. Sometimes you jump into things and we all make mistakes in life. Show me a man who doesn't make mistakes and I'll show you a liar.'

'It's all very well for Redknapp to say it was a mistake,' counters Lowe. 'You could say he made a mistake by taking Southampton down – but nobody seems to say that. He had described us as a proper club. At the end of the day he made the decision to come here and he was keen to come. He got extremely well paid, in terms of both his salary in the Premier League and a bonus when he kept us up. But we didn't stay up. I got some of the blame from some of the numbskulls who supported the club, but I certainly didn't pick the team. I think you make your own luck, and I'm not sure he made his luck with us. We lost some crucial games by giving goals away in the last minute, and indeed all we had to do was maintain one of those leads and we wouldn't have gone down.'

Whichever way you look at it, taking over at Southampton was the worst decision of Redknapp's career. It was a knee-jerk reaction to his falling out with Mandaric that did neither him nor the club any favours. Yet he had taken on a bigger challenge at Portsmouth and succeeded, and he has since done the same at

Tottenham. Moreover, for all the obstacles he encountered, he came within two points of keeping the club in the Premier League. You wonder who could have done more.

Chapter Eight

It was, surely, unthinkable. 'Dad,' implored Jamie, 'you can't go back. You're mad.' Mad? If Redknapp's proposed return to Portsmouth, a club where he had required personal protection only eight months earlier, could be described as such, then yes. If it was crazy to look beyond the 'Dirty Harry' t-shirts sported by Pompey fans, to forget the abusive phone calls and online invective, then Harry Redknapp was barking. There are certain things you don't do, even in the anything-goes world of football. Leaving Portsmouth for arch-rivals Southampton was one of them; making the return trip was off the scale. But there is a tide in the affairs of men which, taken at the flood, leads on to fortune – and Redknapp has an oceanographer's knack for spotting it. In time, his decision to jump ship and head back down the Solent would lead to the most significant victory of his career. In late 2005, however, the priority for anyone taking over at Fratton Park was to avoid relegation.

Second from bottom of the Premier League, Portsmouth were a shadow of the team that Redknapp had left behind twelve months earlier. Gone were the experienced campaigners who had kept Pompey up before, the likes of Sheringham, Berger and Stone. Gone too was Yakubu, the chief goal threat, shipped off to Middlesbrough at substantial profit. In their stead, dragging Pompey ever closer to the Championship, came a succession of unheralded imports, most more extravagant of name than ability. Even for a manger without Redknapp's baggage, Fratton Park held little obvious allure.

In a strange way, though, Redknapp's emotionally turbulent relationship with Portsmouth was the very thing drawing him back along the M27. Despite the brusque manner of his departure – and for all the pressures associated with the club's see-saw introduction to Premier League life – Fratton Park was replete with good memories. It was there that Redknapp had resurrected his career, there that he had conjured a First Division struggler into a top-flight stayer. Milan Mandaric may at times have been as much sparring partner as cornerman, but better the fire of a tumultuous friendship than the ice of a workplace culture where the chairman addressed him by his surname.

Redknapp might have raised eyebrows when he referred to Portsmouth as his spiritual home but, had he spoken of Southampton in such terms, it would have stretched credulity beyond breaking point. If Sir Clive Woodward's appointment at St Mary's achieved nothing else, it demonstrated that Redknapp had been right to leave Portsmouth before Velimir Zajec arrived. On a personal level, Redknapp had no problem with

Woodward, whose role as performance director stopped short of any influence over first-team affairs. But if Harry wasn't in charge of performance, what was he even doing at Southampton? His growing disenchantment was compounded by Woodward's recruitment of Simon Clifford, the self-advertising skills guru, as his number two. Predictably, Clifford's grandiose assessment of his own prowess – 'I will own the England team', he declared – cut no ice with Redknapp. An inevitable falling-out culminated in Clifford's departure after only four months. He did not go quietly. 'Just because you played thirty or forty years ago doesn't mean you have the best coaching brain or talent and ability,' said Clifford. 'Bizarre,' sniffed Redknapp, who not long afterwards declared himself 'sick and tired' of the 'stuff that goes on off the field' at Southampton.

Meanwhile, Mandaric had problems of his own. Alain Perrin, Portsmouth's seventh manager under his ownership, had overseen just four victories in twenty-one games – one less than Zajec, his predecessor. When supporters chanted 'You don't know what you're doing' during a late November defeat at Liverpool, the writing was on the wall for the Frenchman. Less than a week later – a year to the day after Redknapp's resignation – Mandaric wielded the axe, immediately sparking fevered speculation about Perrin's successor. Various managers were linked with the job, including Neil Warnock, Alex McLeish and Lawrie Sanchez, but none had Redknapp's credentials. He knew the club inside out, had the sureness of touch to make the most of the January transfer window, and was a past master at fighting a relegation battle. Crucially, he also had the chutzpah to complete the transition from Judas to Messiah – as was evident when he informed Lowe of his desire to hear what Mandaric had to say. 'It would make history,' said the Pompey midfielder Gary O'Neil. 'Not many people leave here and go to Southampton, let alone come back. But if anybody can do it, Harry can.' News of Redknapp's possible interest in a return to Portsmouth had barely registered in the St Mary's boardroom before he quit. 'Once I told Rupert Lowe I wanted to speak to Portsmouth, I felt I had burned my bridges at Southampton,' Redknapp explained. 'Once I'd said that, it was impossible to go back.'

Lowe described Redknapp's defection as 'the most extraordinary story in an extraordinary industry.' The passage of time has done nothing to alter his view. Apocryphal tales of graffiti on an M27 bridge reading 'Welcome back, Agent Redknapp, mission accomplished' may have been a source of mirth elsewhere, but Lowe wasn't laughing. 'We had a fantastic squad, we'd become very well established in the League and Harry failed,' says Lowe. 'He left Mandaric, [we went] down and then he went back to Mandaric. I still haven't squared that circle in my own mind.'

The explanation is relatively prosaic. Disenchanted with the chaotic nature of life at St Mary's, Redknapp needed a change. Faced with the prospect of a return to the Championship, Mandaric needed a manger. Within five days of Redknapp's departure from St Mary's, both had their wish. Lowe's demand for compensation led to a temporary impasse, briefly threatening to leave Redknapp unemployed. But a deal was thrashed out and, on the afternoon of Wednesday December 7, Redknapp was reinstated as Portsmouth manager. 'It took about one minute to sign a contract,' he revealed. 'I signed a contract without figures in it. I just said: "Let's do it until the end of the season." Milan said: "Don't worry, I will look after you".'

Many saw the pair as unlikely bedfellows. After the caustic fallout from Redknapp's resignation, how could they have come full circle so soon? Neither was giving much away. The sole point of consensus concerned the involvement of Frank Lampard Snr, who accepted an invitation to have a drink in the Fratton Park boardroom after watching his son Frank play for Chelsea in a late November league game. According to Redknapp, Lampard came away with the impression that Mandaric would welcome the chance to renew old acquaintances. Mandaric suggested it was the other way round, with Lampard intimating that Redknapp would be keen on a return. Whatever the reality, the groundwork for what Mandaric describes as 'a brave decision by both of us' was laid not on the south coast, but in South Kensington.

'I had dinner with my daughter and her family at Scalini in London, and somebody told me that Harry was sitting in the other room with Frank Lampard Snr,' recalls Mandaric. 'They were there with their families. Harry was there with Sandra. A few minutes after that, I saw Harry coming towards my table with a bottle of wine that he had bought for me. It was a moment that really made me feel that I missed Harry. He was still at Southampton, but then the time came [subsequently] when we both realised how much better we work together – we said, let's be bigger than one of us individually. The guts of it was that we both had to be brave – but that's how we both realised that we were better together, that together we had a better chance than not of pulling things together.' Many supporters thought otherwise, and were not afraid to tell Mandaric so. 'I'd been criticised left and right with the media and with the supporters, who were [normally] so loyal to me,' he says. 'They were coming into my office and giving their [season] tickets back, saying they would buy them back when Harry went away. I took their tickets and after several games they came back to get them and said they'd made a mistake. I said "Well, sorry, I've sold your tickets now." The rest is history.'

So too were Portsmouth, if Redknapp's first training session was anything to go by. 'Gaffer,' said Dejan Stefanovic, the Pompey captain, 'you've got no chance here. This is the worst team I have ever seen. You must be mad.' It was becoming a disconcertingly familiar refrain. But with a morning's training came the realisation that Stefanovic was right, if not about Redknapp's sanity then certainly about Portsmouth's survival prospects. 'What am I going to do with this lot?' Redknapp mused to himself as he surveyed the rag-tag assembly of foreign imports. 'Where they found some of them, God knows.' The answer took in various ports, few of them near Portsmouth. Denmark, France, Colombia, Greece, Zambia, Norway, Uruguay – barely a nation, it seemed, had eluded Pompey's global quest for reinforcements. Fewer still had yielded players of the right mettle for the Premier League. To Redknapp's dismay, three members of the squad he inherited could not even speak English. 'I think they are called Dario, Mario and Lucio,' he quipped of the trio more familiarly known as Dario Silva, John Viafara and Zvonimir Vukic. 'From what I've heard, they will all be on the X-Factor next week.'

'I was over the moon when Harry came back,' says Stefanovic. 'I knew that he was the only person who could keep Portsmouth in the Premiership, and I knew if he signed before the transfer window he would sign some good players to help us get out of relegation. Don't get me wrong, Alain Perrin is a good coach but, at that time, in English football, he was not good enough – simple as that. He bought ball players, European players – they were good players for other leagues, like the Spanish league, or the Portuguese or German leagues – but not for the Premiership. We got fifteen or twenty new players and it was difficult. Maybe if we had played together for two or three years it would have been a different story, but as soon as I saw all these European players, no one from England who had played in the Premiership before, I knew it was going to be a very difficult time. I said to Harry, "With the players that we've got at the moment, we have no chance to stay up". I told him that, to stay up, we needed seven or nine good players who knew the Premiership.'

With the January transfer window still over three weeks away, Redknapp put his immediate faith in what remained of the old guard, restoring Linvoy Primus to the starting line-up and promising to pick 'the ones I know'. The first match after the interregnum was away to Tottenham, where a game but limited Portsmouth side came within five minutes of a precious point before losing 3-1. 'We were fantastic, they gave everything,' said Redknapp after watching a debatable penalty award trigger a late collapse. 'But it will need a miracle to stay up, won't it? I knew that when I walked in. I can only do my best here. I inherited the situation of just ten points in sixteen games, but if we play and work hard like we did against Spurs then we can turn it around.' The remainder of the Christmas programme suggested his confidence was not misplaced. A first win of the campaign at Fratton Park, 1-0 against West Brom, was closely followed by a 1-1 draw at West Ham and another home victory, 1-0 against Fulham. Portsmouth ended the year on a high that would have seemed barely credible a month earlier. 'It's a different atmosphere now Harry is back,' enthused Svetoslav Todorov, whose return to fitness after two injury-plagued seasons coincided with Redknapp's second coming. 'We are doing better and defending well. He has got everybody going again and it's great to work with him again. He knows the Premiership very well, he knows the players – he knows everything. He can find the way to win games.'

Redknapp was more circumspect. 'A couple of victories or defeats early in the month could change things at the bottom,' he warned. Successive losses against Ipswich, Everton and, most damagingly, fellow relegation candidates Birmingham – a 5-0 mauling that left Redknapp bemoaning defensive frailties – did indeed change things, dragging Portsmouth back down a place from eighteenth to nineteenth. But a potentially more significant alteration in Pompey's circumstances was the arrival of Alexandre Gaydamak, a French businessman of Russian descent who acquired a fifty per cent stake in the club. Overnight, Portsmouth were cast as the new Chelsea. 'It was ideal for Harry,' says Stefanovic, 'because he likes to bring good players to his clubs and good players cost money. And at that time, Portsmouth needed quality players.'

Gaydamak insisted that he was no Roman Abramovich, but neither the fans nor Redknapp were complaining. Not when the largesse of Pompey's new co-owner led within days to the arrival of the Zimbabwe striker Benjani Mwaruwari, signed from Auxerre for a club record fee of £4.1m. Not when Redknapp was able to splash £7m on the recruitment of Pedro Mendes, Sean Davis and Noe Pamarot from Tottenham's reserves. Not when the quartet were subsequently joined on the south coast by Emmanuel Olisadebe, Dean Kiely, Wayne Routledge, Ognjen Koroman and Andres D'Alessandro, the Argentina playmaker. 'It's every football club's dream,' said Redknapp, 'a rich guy coming in who wants to take the club on. What an opportunity he gives this club. He can take us on to a completely different level.'

Redknapp's upbeat assessment of Portsmouth's future under Gaydamak concealed a deep grief. Even as he strove to gain maximum benefit from the January transfer window, he was privately coming to terms with the death of his father. It was the same business-as-usual stoicism that he had shown in April 2001 when his mother, Violet, passed away during the final weeks of his West Ham tenure. 'He died on the Thursday, then we lost to Birmingham on the Saturday,' said Redknapp. 'He was eighty-one, and fit as a fiddle. But he had a fantastic send-off, there were hundreds there. Trevor Brooking came, young Frank Lampard, Patsy Holland, a load of the old boys. Lots of ex-boxing champions, too. I remember Ron Greenwood saying to me "I wish they were all like your dad Harry, he was there every week but he never interferes". I loved my dad to bits, I absolutely loved him. A big part of my life has changed forever.'

Against a personal backdrop that put football in perspective, circumstances were conspiring against Redknapp's side. Prominent among them was the African Nations' Cup, which claimed the services of the strikers Lomana LuaLua and Benjani. Depleted at one end of the field, Portsmouth were subsequently shorn of vital experience at the other, first when Stefanovic was forced to have surgery on a long-standing ankle injury, then when Pamarot succumbed to a hamstring problem. A draw against Bolton at the beginning of February promised a change of fortune, breaking a run of four successive defeats and raising hopes that a visit to Newcastle, who were struggling under Graeme Souness, might yield a much-needed win. But Portsmouth again failed to get the rub of the green. Two days before the game, Souness was sacked. Glenn Roeder was appointed caretaker manager and – as is often the way in these circumstances – a resurgent Newcastle romped to victory, carried away on a tide of emotion as Alan Shearer broke Jackie Milburn's goal-scoring record. Dressing-room morale suffered a further blow when LuaLua's return from Egypt was overshadowed by news of the tragic death of his baby son. Even the fixture list seemed to be against Portsmouth, whose desperate quest to pick up points was not helped by successive games against Manchester United and Chelsea, lost 3-1 and 2-0 respectively.

When the unmarked Milan Baros nodded home the winner in a 1-0 victory for Aston Villa at the beginning of March, making it nine away defeats on the trot for

Portsmouth, the Rubicon appeared to have been crossed. Mathematics might have suggested otherwise, but footballing reality had a superior claim. Anchored in the relegation zone after just five wins all season, Portsmouth were eight points away from safety with no discernible cause for optimism. The January newcomers had failed to make the predicted impact. Benjani had been unable to translate endeavour into goals. Davis looked lightweight in the middle of the park. So too did Mendes, despite showing occasional glimpses of the class that had made him a European Cup winner at Porto under Jose Mourinho. They were not the only underperformers. With eight points from thirteen matches, Portsmouth's return under Redknapp was now two points worse than it had been under Perrin after the same number of games. It was time to start penning the obituaries. 'It is with sadness that we report that Portsmouth Football Club passed away as a Premiership force on Saturday after much suffering,' wrote the man from the *Times*, catching the prevailing mood admirably. 'There will be a weekly memorial service until May.'

'It was a difficult time for Harry,' says Stefanovic. 'Every manager has pressure when money is spent. Expectations were high, but it's different if you can start from pre-season in July with your own players. Harry signed in December and he didn't have plenty of time to sort things out. He had to keep the players that he had and add some more. He signed some very good players like Sean Davis, Pedro Mendes and Benjani, but some of these guys were not playing regular football at their old clubs. Pedro and Sean weren't playing at Tottenham before they came, and Benjani was coming to England to

221

play in the Premiership for the first time after playing in the French league, which is totally different. We all knew they were going to be excellent signings for us, but it was going to take a little bit of time.'

With only ten games left, however, there was no time. Relegation would have repercussions felt far beyond the club's coffers. The impact of a fall from Premier League grace would shatter a dream that united chairmen and fans alike. For Gaydamak and – especially – Mandaric, no less than those in the stands, the shards of splintered ambition would provide a piercing reminder of the club's failure to become, once more, an established top-flight force. Promotion two seasons earlier had wiped away fifty years of almost unrelenting hurt; how much sharper the pain of relegation would feel for having briefly tasted the high life. Portsmouth's wealthy benefactors would, surely, walk away, consigning the club to another interminable spell treading the lower-league backwaters. As for Redknapp, relegation for the second time in two seasons would leave his reputation in tatters, the Pompey chimes sounding the death knell on a job that – albeit not for the first time – he had insisted would be his last in football.

But then came Manchester City; then came Pedro Mendes, and the two stunning goals from distance that would radically alter the trajectory of Portsmouth's season. Short of form and sharpness after toiling in Tottenham's reserves for six months, Mendes had struggled since his arrival eight weeks earlier. But Redknapp had believed all along that the midfielder's class would eventually out, and now Mendes rewarded that faith twice over, ferociously bending in the opener from a half-cleared corner before performing an explosive stoppage-time encore. Portsmouth's 2-1 win was their first of the year. The emotional and psychological value of Mendes' decisive contribution – and of an impressive performance from D'Alessandro at the apex of a midfield diamond – was incalculable. 'We were seconds away from being dead and buried, but Mendes came up with two fantastic goals,' said Redknapp after a victory that ensured Portsmouth reaped maximum benefit from a lunchtime draw between relegation rivals Birmingham City and West Brom. 'We were on our way to the Championship before Pedro scored that goal. You could not have written it any better. He is a quality player and could play in any team in the Premier League. We've got to go and pick up a result or two, win away from home somewhere. But all we could ask is that we're still in there.'

'It was definitely the turning point of the season when Pedro scored twice against Manchester City,' says Stefanovic. 'We showed desire and there was togetherness – between the players, and with the supporters as well. Portsmouth supporters are excellent, they're the best in England for me, especially at home. Because of them and Harry and the togetherness of the players, once we had one or two wins in a row, we kept going and believed we could stay up.'

Hindsight suggests another layer of significance to Mendes' goals and the extraordinary run that they sparked, for they were in a sense vindication – not simply of Redknapp's management methods, but of his footballing philosophy *per se*. Vindication of his belief in playing the game properly, with the emphasis on expression rather than attrition. Vindication of his lifelong commitment to signing players with the necessary skills to implement that vision. Vindication, above all, of his refusal to let Portsmouth's plight divert him from his natural instincts at a time when the ambition of many managers would have stretched no further than defending from the front and hoping to nick something on the counter. 'Just because you are in trouble, you still need to play,' said Redknapp after his side had consolidated the City result with wins – their first away from home for five months – at West Ham and Fulham. 'I play with D'Alessandro and I've got two up front. When we haven't got the ball, we are open because a lot of teams play with one up front and five across midfield. But we're scoring goals, so we're going for it. You've got to play. You can't just put in players who are there to run around. It's all about having good players.'

If Portsmouth's freedom of expression bucked the trend of a relegation battle in which the other contenders were looking increasingly edgy, so too did Redknapp's unorthodox motivational methods. The visit to Craven Cottage – where Gary O'Neil scored twice in a 3-1 win, either side of a typically flamboyant individual effort from Lomana LuaLua – was preceded by a Friday night trip to the Billy Joel musical *Movin' Out*. 'I think a few of them weren't that impressed with the idea,' chuckled Redknapp. 'But it was either that or Abba. I said to them "Which one do you want?" and they went "Are you having a laugh, or what?" Half the foreign lads weren't quite sure who Billy Joel was. But I enjoyed it, anyway. Our next away game is at Charlton, so I'll really punish them. I'll take them to see *Mamma Mia*.'

Beneath the camaraderie lay a resolve, hardened by Redknapp's memories of the successful battle against relegation two seasons earlier, to harness his squad's flourishing *esprit de corps*. 'Harry did a marvellous job,' says Stefanovic. 'We went a couple of times to see musical performances when we were playing against London clubs and we were staying there. Every day, he tried to do everything he could to persuade us to believe that we could stay up in the Premiership – every single day, [both] at the training ground and when we were commuting [to games], when he would show us ProZone videos.'

Diligence is the mother of good fortune, and Redknapp's hard work behind the scenes coincided with a welcome change of luck. Imminent cup engagements persuaded opposing managers to field weakened teams, first at West Ham, where Portsmouth won 4-2, and later when Middlesbrough were beaten 1-0 at Fratton Park. Pompey twice recovered from a goal down to salvage a point against Blackburn, while Arsenal's visit left Redknapp hailing another 'massive point' as Portsmouth rode their luck to clinch a 1-1 draw. If providence was at work, Redknapp was, as ever, actively courting it. He wore the same 'lucky' ensemble – blazer, sweatshirt, shirt and tie – throughout the six-game unbeaten run that hauled Portsmouth out of the relegation zone on goal difference. 'If we stay up,' he quipped, 'I'm having the damn thing framed.' Meanwhile, suggestions that Redknapp's escapology was rooted in a different kind of fortune were given predictably short shrift. 'I've heard people complaining that we spent £11m in January and moaning that we are buying our way out of trouble,' said Redknapp. 'But other teams did their shopping in the summer. That money needed to be spent. We couldn't have played like that before January, but we have improved.'

While acknowledging that chance played a part, Stefanovic identifies Redknapp's ability to rally the troops as the key to Pompey's recovery. 'Every good manager has a little bit of luck,' he says, 'but the main reason was Harry himself. He is the perfect man-manager. So many players don't like to play for their manager, for whatever reason, but Harry is different. Maybe from twenty-five players you can find twenty-four who, even if they don't play, say "OK, it's no big deal, I'm going to be on the bench – or I'm not even going to be on the bench – but still, when I do play, I'm going to give my best for him." I've had maybe eight or ten managers in my career, and I've never seen this happen in my life. Harry is excellent like that.'

For Redknapp, the emotional highlight of a run from which Portsmouth garnered fourteen of a possible eighteen points was the trip to West Ham. Because the Hammers' relegation at the end of the 2002/03 season had coincided with Portsmouth's promotion, it was the first time he had returned to Upton Park since his abrupt departure nearly five years earlier. He revelled in it. After a rousing welcome, he made an almost stately progress to the uncharted territory of the away dugout. Autographs were signed, pictures posed for, well-wishers warmly acknowledged. 'Blimey,' said Redknapp, later reflecting on an afternoon that brought precious points and cherished memories in equal measure. 'I can remember when Bobby Moore would sing "I'm forever drinking doubles" instead of "I'm forever blowing bubbles."

What memories. I look around and see all the pictures of Bob and the boys. We all grew up together. It's in your blood, this place. It's where I come from. If you can't get a great reception here, where can you?'

With Sunderland already relegated, survival would hinge on outperforming Birmingham and West Brom for another four games. Redknapp calculated that seven of the available twelve points would do the trick, but a late implosion at Charlton, where goals from Bryan Hughes and Darren Bent cancelled out D'Alessandro's opener in a 2-1 defeat, cast renewed doubt on Pompey's future. 'At the end I was just so sick,' said Redknapp. 'With fifteen minutes to go I thought to myself, "This is the day we get out of trouble. This is the day we survive." But it wasn't to be.' Instead, Birmingham won their game in hand four days later to move clear of the bottom three at Portsmouth's expense. They followed up by holding Everton to a draw at Goodison Park. If Pompey failed to respond by beating Sunderland, Birmingham's fate would be in their own hands.

'Odd', said Redknapp of the Kevin Kyle handball that gave Portsmouth a penalty two minutes from time against Sunderland. And odd it was. Inexplicable that Kyle should handle. Extraordinary that Pompey should be awarded their first league spot kick for twelve months at the very moment their need was greatest. Outlandish that, two games from the season's end, uncertainty surrounded the identity of Pompey's nominated penalty taker. 'Matt held his nerve well,' Redknapp later reflected, having watched Taylor wrestle the ball from Todorov before sending his former Luton team-mate Kelvin Davis the wrong way to clinch a 2-1 win. 'You always get put through it, but we ain't going out with a whimper.'

Two points clear of danger with two games to go, there was every chance they weren't going out at all. But with Liverpool set to visit Fratton Park for the season's denouement, there was an air of finality about the ensuing trip to Wigan. If Birmingham failed to beat Newcastle at St Andrew's, victory would secure survival. Reverse the scenario, and Portsmouth would be left needing a final-day win against the European champions to reach safety. No wonder Redknapp was in Kevin Keegan mode. 'I would love it to be settled [at Wigan], because it takes over your whole life,' he said. 'I'm only looking forward to the end of the season if we can pull it off, because it would be a fantastic escape. It would be a good trip home from Wigan.' It would also maintain a Portsmouth tradition of clinching late-season survival in north England. A decade earlier, at Huddersfield's McAlpine Stadium, Deon Burton had preserved the club's second-tier status on the last day of the campaign. Two seasons later it went down to the wire again, Paul Durnin and Sammy Igoe scoring the goals in a 3-1 win at Bradford. But while the portents were good, the reality of the opening half at the JJB Stadium could hardly have been worse. Henri Camara was on fire. By half-time, he had given Wigan the lead, had a legitimate goal chalked off and spurned a glut of further chances. That he was a former Southampton man – worse still, one of Redknapp's – merely rubbed salt into southern wounds.

Half of Hampshire seemed to be crammed into the North Stand but, as the players trudged off for the interval, the mood among the Pompey support was unusually subdued. Fortunately, the stunned silence did not extend to Redknapp, who was soon dishing out fresh orders. The task as he saw it was clear: stifle Wigan's raids down the left, tighten the defence, seize control in midfield and score two goals without reply. And to think Brian Clough used to call it a simple game. Redknapp set about the puzzle in typically forthright style. Taylor was shifted forward from left-back, while the defensively lightweight D'Alessandro was switched to the right. Noe Pamarot, who replaced Sean Davis, filled the resulting gap in the back four, while Gary O'Neil moved into central midfield. A wholesale tactical reshuffle had been achieved with just one substitution. 'Harry knows his football,' says Stefanovic, 'he's a good tactician. So many times over the four years I was there, at the turning point, when we were losing the game, he would make changes that helped us to win, and it was the same at Wigan.'

The benefits of Redknapp's tactical acuity were soon plain to see. Wigan's influence waned, Portsmouth's waxed. The stage was set for a fresh chapter to be written in Pompey folklore. Even Redknapp, however, could not have guessed that Benjani would share co-authorship. The indefatigable Zimbabwe striker had toiled for over nineteen hours in search of his first goal. His ceaseless endeavour had earned him a place in supporters' hearts, but he was desperate for more tangible reward. So too was Redknapp, who joked about the barn-door-with-a-banjo tendencies of his star signing – 'After shooting practice I have to drive up the M27 to collect the balls' – but must in truth have grown weary of the need to reassert, week in, week out, that Benjani was 'a quality player'. 'I would love him to be the one who keeps us up,' he said on the eve of the game. Yet if Redknapp was relieved when Benjani nodded home the equaliser from a Matt Taylor rebound, he did not show it. Hands on hips, locked in touchline conversation with Kevin Bond, he remained a study in concentration. Portsmouth were level, but less than half an hour remained to find another goal.

The relationship between Redknapp and Portsmouth should never have worked. It defied the basic law of physics which says that opposites attract and likes repel. Redknapp and Pompey were cut from the same cloth: perennial defiers of the odds who were routinely portrayed as throwbacks, charming anachronisms; one the salt of the earth, the other the salt of the Solent. Above all, they were united by a strange susceptibility to fortune's buffets and rewards at their most extreme. Survival against the odds, promotion as 33-1 outsiders – if it could happen, it did. So when Todorov clipped a far-post cross onto the forehead of Benjani with the goalkeeper stranded after racing in vain from his line, it all felt too easy. Anticlimactic, almost. Surely it couldn't end in such uncomplicated fashion, with Benjani scoring to clinch survival just as Redknapp had hoped? Narrative consistency, no less than the emotional logic of a nerve-wracking season, demanded a more extravagant finale. It was Wigan's Gary Teale who rescued the script from the shredder. Teale's raised arm diverted Benjani's goal-bound header, the referee Mike Riley brandished a red card, and in an instant the cliff-hanger that the situation demanded was supplied: Portsmouth's season would hinge on a penalty.

The scenes that followed play before the mind's eye like

a slide show. Benjani raised two clenched fists. Gary O'Neil locked him in a bear hug. One end of the stadium erupted in a paroxysm of joy. Everywhere else, groans of exasperation resounded. Through it all, Redknapp remained imperturbable. While his backroom staff shifted nervously, he stood motionless, elbow cupped in hand, gazing intently across the pitch. If there were nerves, they were betrayed only by the contemplative manner in which his fingers gently traced an invisible line across his mouth. Not for Harry the wild celebrations that followed Taylor's second successful spot kick in as many weeks. Not for him the raucous scenes that accompanied the final whistle twenty minutes later. Even when news belatedly filtered through from St Andrew's that Birmingham had only drawn – that Portsmouth were safe, the great escape finally a matter of incontrovertible fact rather than fanciful conjecture – Redknapp barely mustered a smile. The relegation dogfight had been won, but five months of unrelenting pressure had drained him of his trademark animation.

'I've been through the mill these past two years,' said Redknapp. 'It does take its toll, without a doubt. On your family as well. If we had gone down, I think I would have thought maybe it was time to call it a day. This one is better than the first time I kept them up because this wasn't my team. I had to throw a team together. I took over a poor squad. There were players who were nowhere near good enough and players who didn't want to play for this club. I had to take some gambles and they've been great. They've all played their part. We've taken twenty points from nine games. I'm happy for everybody but I don't mind saying I'm happy for myself. I don't want to sit here and thank everybody else.'

He didn't need to – they were thanking him. 'Harry is the main reason why we survived,' says Stefanovic. 'It was an amazing season. If we had had any other manager at that time, we would have gone down, believe me. Some of the players and I had meetings with Milan Mandaric when Harry was not there. We told him that he was the only manager who could keep us in the Premiership and that he had to get him back in. After one or two months, we sorted things out and we [started] to play well. Harry was totally the reason.' Mandaric, for his part, was glad that he had listened. 'It was unbelievable,' he recalls, 'a tremendous reward for all that Harry had done. He put back smiles on everyone's faces. No other manager could have got us out of it. Harry doesn't panic. It was a nervy time, with a lot of pressure, but he kept his head.'

Survival marked a watershed for both Portsmouth and Redknapp. Two months later Alexandre Gaydamak completed his takeover of the club, purchasing the remaining fifty per cent from Mandaric. By then, Redknapp had committed to a new three-year contract. Backed by Gaydamak's millions, and with the prospect of a global recession no more than a twinkle in the banking fraternity's eye, decades of struggle seemed finally to be at an end. The accent would at last be on consolidation rather than survival. No longer would Redknapp be obliged to work wonders on limited funds; the Harry Houdini persona could be discarded. Gaydamak's willingness to play Croesus to Redknapp's Midas – Pompey's transfer kitty was rumoured to be around

£30m – promised an unprecedented freedom. Freedom for Redknapp to show his team-building skills to their best advantage. Scope to secure the kind of A-list players who might have been tempted to play for him before had he been able to afford them. Licence, above all, to prove beyond doubt that he was more than just a firefighter, a man for poor seasons. 'I think the future at Portsmouth is very good,' said Redknapp, who could not have known that it would be another year before Gaydamak wielded the chequebook in earnest. 'They're not here to scrap around the bottom of the league every year, they want to be successful.'

The first evidence of that ambition arrived in the form of Glen Johnson, who was brought in from Chelsea on a year-long loan deal. Hailed by Redknapp as 'the kind of player most Premier League sides would give their right arm for', Johnson – who made no secret of his determination to win an England recall – would soon find himself surveying a dressing room awash with players of top-four pedigree. None were without baggage – some had acquired veteran status, others had simply been discarded – but, like Johnson, all had a point to prove. Andrew Cole, the former Manchester United front man, moved south from Manchester City. The arrival of David Thompson, the ex-Liverpool midfielder, was followed in January by that of another Anfield alumnus, Djimi Traore. Strongest of all was the Arsenal connection, the initial link in which was established when Tony Adams replaced the Newcastle-bound Kevin Bond as Redknapp's number two. 'I'd love Tony to become manager here one day,' said Redknapp, with greater prescience than he could have imagined. Nor did he shirk from adding further North London spice to a recipe in which the former Tottenham players Mendes, Davis and Pamarot had been early ingredients. The striker Nwankwo Kanu, once of Highbury, was recruited on a free from West Brom. Five months later came Lauren, the tenacious Cameroon international who had formerly been a mainstay on the right side of Arsène Wenger's defence. Most notably, Sol Campbell resurfaced at Fratton Park after leaving Highbury a few weeks earlier amid talk of a possible move abroad. Though only a month away from his thirty-second birthday, Campbell, a seasoned England international with Premier League and FA Cup medals to his name, was a totemic figure. He had just returned from the World Cup and the memory of his outstanding, goal-scoring performance against Barcelona in the Champions League final was still fresh. Unsurprisingly, Redknapp saw the defender's signing as a 'statement of where we want to go,' casting him as a natural successor to Paul Merson and Teddy Sheringham.

Time would tell how much Campbell had left in the tank, but his mere presence lent substance to Redknapp's claim that Portsmouth were going places. If Sol Campbell could be lured to Fratton Park, players of comparable stature would surely follow. Confirmation of that theory arrived in the imposing form of David James, the goalkeeper on the brink of an England recall that would lead, in due course, to his longer-term restoration as the nation's chief custodian. 'Sol was the thing that steered me here,' said James. The following May, Redknapp added further defensive steel, signing James' former Manchester City team-mate, Sylvain Distin, on a free. 'Staying up was a turning point,' says Stefanovic.

'Afterwards, so many good players were brought to the club, so many internationals, and Portsmouth went on to play European football – all because of Harry.'

Significantly, however, Portsmouth's initial makeover was achieved at minimal expense. Only the signing of Niko Kranjcar – the Croatia playmaker recruited from Hajduk Split for £3.5m on transfer deadline day – involved a sizeable fee. In the absence of the predicted war chest, moves fell through for accomplished performers such as Nicolas Anelka, Stilian Petrov and Gareth Barry. As questions were raised about the true extent of Gaydamak's resources, Redknapp's remodelling adhered to a familiar template: a core of experienced players, a few old favourites, a splash of youthful potential here, a loan signing there. The end product was arguably the most impressive feat of team-building of his career: from what was effectively an illusion of wealth, Redknapp conjured a team of genuine substance. Moreover, he did so against the backdrop of an uncertainty that ranged beyond finance. Speculation was rife that Arkady Gaydamak – Alexandre's ebullient, controversial father, who was the subject of an international arrest warrant issued in France for his alleged involvement in arms trafficking – was the real driving force behind the new regime. Matters were not helped by the appointment of Avram Grant, the former Israel head coach, as Portsmouth's technical director – a decision which, an unimpressed Redknapp later suggested, was taken without his knowledge. It was impossible to escape the feeling that all was not as it seemed at Fratton Park.

Rising above the swirling political intrigue, Redknapp

galvanised his remodelled side to impressive effect. By mid-September, with five games played, Portsmouth sat proudly at the league summit, a point clear of Manchester United. They had scored nine goals, conceded none and Kanu was the division's top scorer. After the nightmare of the previous season, it was the stuff of fantasy. But while Portsmouth were asking all the questions on the pitch, the off-field focus was elsewhere. On the afternoon that Pompey went top with a 1-0 victory at Charlton, the post-match spotlight fell on Redknapp's implication in a BBC Panorama investigation into alleged transfer irregularities, due to be aired three days later. 'Watch it, lads, watch it,' Redknapp invited a packed press room. 'You'll find it very interesting. I know the missus will be watching and she might even tape it for me. But it doesn't worry me because I'm one million per cent the innocent party. I think the BBC are trying to say they've caught me tapping up a player, but it's pathetic.' The case against Redknapp amounted to nothing more substantial than a secretly-filmed conversation in which he discussed a possible move for Blackburn's Andy Todd with Peter Harrison, a football agent. 'I like him,' Redknapp is heard to say, 'I think he's a tough bastard.' What Panorama regarded as tapping up, Todd is likelier to have taken as a compliment.

Redknapp has long had to put up with this kind of thing. Groundless gossip and unsubstantiated rumour have been regular companions. It stems from his characterisation as a cross between Del Boy and Arthur Daley, an image that is both undeserved and unflattering. Perhaps the most extreme expression of this tendency comes from the writer Tom Bower, who – crossing the boundary between fact and fiction – describes Redknapp in his book *Broken Dreams* as a 'former barrow boy' and 'aspiring second-hand car dealer' before questioning his 'financial ethics'. Bower's case against Redknapp is of the most rudimentary nature, full of sound and fury, signifying nothing. In essence, Bower's case is as follows: Harry Redknapp is a cockney from a working-class background who makes a few bob, loves a gamble and is noted for his work in the transfer market, *ergo* he is self-interested and potentially venal. The social and cultural stereotyping is crude, the corroborative evidence non-existent. More pertinent than any point raised by Bower is the question of why a bloke as streetwise and wealthy as Redknapp would risk losing so much for so little. As he said at the time of the Panorama investigation: 'You tell me you are a manager, you are earning plenty of money – and you have got to go to sleep at night knowing that any idiot can pick up the phone, ring a newspaper and finish your career. It's bullshit. You walk into a dressing room, every player, they've got agents who might say to them, "I've given your manager a few quid". You're going to get respect from those players? They can stand up and say: "I know all about you".'

By Christmas, when league commitments took Portsmouth to Arsenal, the focus had reverted to Gaydamak. Did the club's enigmatic, interview-shy owner have the resources to justify Pompey's billing as the poor man's Chelsea? The scrutiny intensified when Manuel Fernandes, a Portugal international brought in on loan from Benfica, failed to take the field. Portsmouth had scored either side of the break to take a 2-0 lead against Arsenal at the Emirates Stadium, and the introduction of Fernandes – a defensive midfielder likened by Redknapp to 'a young Paul Ince' – would have added a welcome layer of additional protection to Pompey's back line. However, Fernandes had featured in the two previous games and a third successive appearance would have committed Portsmouth to a £12m permanent transfer. With the Portuguese enforcer warming the bench, Arsenal fought back to secure a draw. 'The owner did a deal that if he started three consecutive games we would buy him. He's a good player, but I wouldn't put my name to a £12m fee,' said Redknapp, diplomatically.

A month later, after the resignation of the Portsmouth vice-chairman David Chissick had raised further questions about the new ownership, Gaydamak finally popped his head above the parapet. Portsmouth were ensconced in sixth place and European qualification was beckoning for the first time in the club's history. 'Now is the time to strengthen, surely,' said Redknapp. Gaydamak was thinking along different lines. 'Would I like to go into Europe next season?' he mused in an interview with the *Sunday Times*. 'Is that realistic? Is it realistic we are sixth in the league? Is it realistic we have Sol Campbell playing for us? How can I answer those questions? It's football. It's not a problem of funding, it's a problem of reality.' Not one for trawlers and seagulls, Redknapp offered a plainer assessment. 'No one is going to be walking in here tomorrow,' he said. 'We're not close to doing anything.'

The modest outlay that subsequently brought Traore and Lauren to Fratton Park did little to quell doubts about the extent of Portsmouth's financial leverage.

Similarly unpersuasive, in the wake of a new Premier League television deal worth £1.7bn, was Peter Storrie's suggestion that the doubling of the club's wage bill was to blame. The impact of Portsmouth's failure to strengthen was felt in a miserable new-year run that yielded one win in three months. But while a combination of injuries, suspensions and the ageing sinews of an overstretched squad might have slowed Portsmouth's early-season momentum, Redknapp quietly refused to give up on the dream of Europe. His defiance was epitomised by a 2-1 home win against Manchester United, achieved in the absence of both Sol Campbell and Pedro Mendes. A notable double was achieved when Liverpool were beaten by the same score three weeks later, and by the time Arsenal arrived at Fratton Park on the final day of the season, Portsmouth were one win away from clinching a Uefa Cup place. It was a tricky assignment – Pompey had not beaten Arsenal since 1958 – but not one beyond a side beaten at home only three times all season. However, Graham Poll marked his refereeing swansong by chalking off a legitimate Niko Kranjcar effort, and Redknapp was left contemplating a goal-less stalemate. 'I spoke to Graham,' he sighed. 'But what can he say – "Sorry about that?" He has robbed us. The only time Portsmouth have been in Europe was when Nelson invaded somewhere or other.'

There was nonetheless much to celebrate. Redknapp had transformed his side from relegation strugglers the previous season to ninth in the Premier League, the club's highest finish in over half a century. Only the top four could point to a superior home record, and only two teams outside that elite quartet had conceded fewer goals. There was a significant personal milestone, too, in the form of a mid-January league game at Bramall Lane that was supposedly Redknapp's one thousandth as a manager. If doubt surrounded the precise point at which the landmark had been reached – it was subsequently suggested that Redknapp had passed it thirty-nine games earlier – it did not stop Gaydamak from presenting him with a commemorative decanter the following week. 'I don't feel any different to how I did thirty years ago,' he said. 'It is a great achievement.' And his secret? 'Some people, and they might have played for twenty years, they couldn't pick a player if he hit them in the face. Some people are judges, some people are not.'

Gaydamak had seen enough to realise that Redknapp belonged in the first category. There would be no more philosophising about the relationship between football and reality. Three of the new arrivals that summer – Sulley Muntari, David Nugent and John Utaka – broke Portsmouth's previous transfer record. It would be shattered twice more the following year, first by the £7.5m January acquisition of Jermain Defoe from Tottenham, then by the £9m addition of Peter Crouch from Liverpool. Gaydamak was not alone in his faith in Redknapp's judgement; further support arrived in the form of England recalls for Campbell and James. Injury forced Campbell's withdrawal from the squad to face Germany in an autumn friendly at Wembley, but James made a second-half appearance to become the first Portsmouth player since Jimmy Dickinson in 1956 to feature for the national side. (Strictly speaking, the former Pompey striker Mark Hateley had left for Milan by the time he won his first cap against the USSR in the summer of 1984). At sixty, Redknapp's stock was on the rise again.

The twelve months that followed were the most eventful of Redknapp's career. By early January he had presided over the highest-scoring game in Premier League history, been strongly linked with the England job, arrested, and come within a hair's breadth of joining Newcastle. By May he had guided Portsmouth to a second consecutive top-ten finish, an unforgettable FA Cup victory and European qualification. Not bad for a campaign that began in ominous fashion, with four of Pompey's first six league engagements against the big four. Redknapp's men emerged from that early-season phase with a haul of eight points, two of them earned against United and Liverpool. By late September, they were fifth. Curiously, however, in a season that would culminate with Redknapp being hailed for his defensive pragmatism, the result that got them there – which came in the wake of three successive clean sheets – was a 7-4 win against Reading. Redknapp drew breathless comparisons with Real Madrid's 7-3 European Cup final victory against Eintracht Frankfurt in 1960, but, with Benjani deployed as a lone striker, the goal-fest owed as much to defensive ineptitude as free-spirited attacking. 'It is not easy to play with one striker at home, and it is not really in my nature to do it,' said Redknapp. 'But I don't like square pegs in round holes. I ended up with people playing where they like to play in a four-five-one. I thought "I can't see them scoring", but we ended up with eleven goals. It shows you what a load of crap it is talking about systems when you play one up and go and score seven.'

If the Reading game was among the season's highs, there was no doubt about the nadir. In late November Redknapp travelled to Stuttgart on a scouting mission. He arrived back at Heathrow the following morning to learn that police investigating alleged transfer irregularities had carried out an early-morning raid on his home. Redknapp went directly to Chichester Police Station, where he became one of five men – the others were Peter Storrie, Milan Mandaric, Amdy Faye and the agent Willie McKay – arrested on suspicion of conspiracy to defraud and false accounting. He strongly denied any knowledge of alleged payments to Faye arising from the player's £1.5m transfer from Auxerre to Portsmouth four years earlier, and was released on bail the same day. Redknapp, who suggested that his involvement stemmed purely from a desire to add profile to the case, was infuriated by the distress caused to his wife and by the inexplicable presence during the raid of photographers, whose handiwork subsequently appeared in a national newspaper. He successfully sued the City of London police, whom, the High Court later ruled, had not satisfactorily explained to a magistrate why a search warrant was necessary. Flaws in the warrant were described by the judges as 'wholly unacceptable.' Redknapp recovered a quarter of his legal costs and was awarded £1000 damages, which he donated to charity. Both McKay and Faye have since been cleared of any wrongdoing in relation to the Faye transfer. So too, it is understood, have Redknapp and Mandaric. As this book went to press, however, the official focus had reportedly switched to an alleged payment of £100,000 made to Redknapp following the transfer of Peter Crouch from

Portsmouth to Aston Villa in 2002. The enquiry provoked an exasperated response from Redknapp, who told the *Sun*: "This is about a discrepancy of around £10,000 in income tax. I've paid £10m in income tax over the past ten years and this is what it's come down to. It's in dispute whether the money is owed anyway and I've been totally up front with everyone about this. I'm sick of it. If it had been anyone else, a normal member of the public, they would have dropped it or told them to pay up with a bit of interest and that would have been the end of the matter."

Redknapp's frustration is understandable, for such episodes have done nothing to enhance his career prospects. The England job was vacant at the time of his arrest and the odds on him succeeding Steve McClaren as manager had been contracting sharply. Once the police had knocked on his door, the FA were never likely to follow suit. Barely a fortnight later, Fabio Capello was appointed England manager and Redknapp was left to reflect on an opportunity lost in the most dispiriting circumstances. Those most familiar with his methods believe that the FA threw away a pearl richer than all its tribe. It is hard to disagree. Vastly experienced, adept at dealing with the media and respected by players and fans alike, Redknapp's credentials are obvious. Throw in the fact that he has successfully managed many England regulars already, nurtured the likes of Rio Ferdinand and Frank Lampard through the youth ranks and has a gift for getting the best out of his players, and the case becomes compelling.

'I believe Harry would have made a great England manager,' says Tony Carr, West Ham's Director of Youth

Development, 'because one of his major strengths is that he knows what makes a team tick. He knows how to put a team together and he can handle top players with no problem at all. I don't think you last in the game at the very top level as long as Harry has done without knowing everything about management – tactics, players, psychology, how to get the best out of players. I think Harry is good at all those things. His game is uncomplicated. He gives players the confidence to go out and do the job, he's tactically aware and he knows what the game's about – that's why he's a Premiership long 'un. Harry would have been a good choice [for England]. I know he could do the job.'

Carr's thoughts are echoed by Bobby Howe, who remains confident that the toxic tracksuit would sit well on Redknapp's shoulders. 'Does Harry have the confidence and the credentials? Absolutely,' says Howe. 'He's managed some of the best players in the world. He was really unlucky that when his name was brought up, there was that controversy at Portsmouth with respect to payments. The timing for Harry was not good. But I think that if the opportunity presents itself again, he'd be in a great position.'

John Williams believes that it is more a question of when rather than if. 'Harry is an exceptional man in so many ways, and I'm sure one day he'll manage England,' says the former Bournemouth defender. 'He missed out last time, but I'm sure he'll go on to that at some stage. He's the best Englishman around, he's good at picking the right team and with the players at his disposal I'm sure he could do it. There's not many around who could – there aren't many brave enough to get the ball down and play football against the Man Uniteds and the Chelseas – but he's certainly one of them.'

Rodney Marsh goes further, arguing that the man he first met as a harum-scarum winger for West Ham four decades ago should have been preferred to Capello. 'I think Harry Redknapp should be the England manager now,' says Marsh. 'I don't like the fact that we've had to go to an Italian to be the manager of our national team. I never wanted to see that – not because he's not a fantastic manager, not because he's not one of the best coaches in the world. It's just that he's an Italian. I've got nothing against Italy or Italians, but can you imagine Italy appointing an Englishman? There's a wedge between the cultures of the two countries. Harry Redknapp has all the skills it takes. He has the respect of players, a simple view of the game, and he does recognition and correction – the ability, during a game, to see a tactic that isn't working, a player who is having an off day, or an opposing player who is causing problems – as well as anyone in the game.'

As Marsh acknowledges, the contrast between Redknapp and Sven-Göran Eriksson, England's first foreign manager, is pointed. 'I saw every game under Eriksson's management, and sometimes I looked at him on the bench and thought "You haven't got a clue what's going on here." I was at Windsor Park when we had that nightmare evening against Northern Ireland. I looked at Eriksson on the bench and his eyes looked like they belonged to another person. But Harry Redknapp always looks to me as though he knows what he's doing. You can see him thinking "We'll get him off, we'll get him on," and you know that he's thinking ahead of it all.

Harry instils confidence in me – I look at him and think "You know what you're doing, buddy".'

The Newcastle United owner Mike Ashley thought likewise. In early January, with Newcastle treading water in mid-table, Ashley called time on Sam Allardyce's brief reign as manager. Mindful of a 4-1 thrashing recently administered by Portsmouth, his thoughts turned immediately to Redknapp. Within forty-eight hours, a formal approach had been made. Sir Alex Ferguson immediately perceived the dilemma facing Redknapp. 'Harry would have been disappointed with what happened with the England job, because he was in the frame for that and there was a lot of support for him,' said Ferguson. 'So with the Newcastle job coming up so soon after that, maybe he's thinking the time is right to take this one. This is the dilemma that will face him. Harry certainly has the charisma to deal with a job of that size. He's intelligent enough to know what he's doing, but it will be a difficult choice for him in a way. He has a wonderful set-up at Portsmouth, a lovely house, his wife is settled there, so there's a big decision to make.'

When Redknapp cancelled his scheduled press conference ahead of a league visit to Sunderland, leaving Portsmouth's Eastleigh training ground in his Mercedes with Peter Storrie alongside him, most onlookers felt the decision had been made. 'Joe Jordan took training and by the time we'd got back Harry had left the training ground,' wrote David James in his *Observer* column. 'It was a strange one and instinct told me he wouldn't be coming back. Harry's never been one to just disappear. He's a real training-ground manager: you always know you can find him.'

CHAPTER EIGHT

The following morning, however, Redknapp was back. 'My heart is with Portsmouth,' he declared, having slept on an offer from the Newcastle chairman Chris Mort and considered the exhortations of friends who believed that it might be his last chance to manage a big club. 'The players I have bought here, I sold the club to them and persuaded them to come here. To walk away would not be right. I had a great offer, and to be given the chance to manage a club like Newcastle was a fantastic opportunity, but at the end of it I had no intention of going. This is where I enjoy being and the fans have been great to me. I have never been afraid to take a chance. The supporters are enjoying their football, and to kick that into touch would not be the right thing to do.'

'I felt the buzz when Harry turned up to take training,' wrote James. 'I saw him as I arrived at the training ground and it was as if nothing had ever happened, business as usual. But with an extra smile. Harry obviously decided that he couldn't leave. A massive opportunity was presented to him, but he decided to stay. It's not often that you witness that kind of loyalty or feeling.'

The decision proved to be among the best of Redknapp's career, although it might not have seemed that way when Portsmouth, still going well in the league, were drawn away to Manchester United in the FA Cup quarter-finals. Harry was playing golf with his son Jamie when the draw was made. They tuned in live on Jamie's mobile and when news of Pompey's fate came through, Redknapp's eight-iron felt the brunt of his displeasure, flying down the fairway. Despite the famous wins against United with Bournemouth and West Ham, Redknapp, in a quarter of a century of trying, had never been beyond the last eight of the game's most venerable knockout competition. Now, for all Jamie's efforts to persuade his father otherwise, the prolongation of that dismal record seemed inevitable.

Remarkably, however, Redknapp was to pull off a third shock win against Manchester's finest. Few scented an upset when Sir Alex Ferguson submitted a team sheet on which all the big guns were named. But Redknapp, just as he had done at Dean Court nearly a quarter of a century earlier, sent his players out brimming with belief. 'I keep telling the newspapers how good you are,' he told them. 'I keep saying I've got the best goalkeeper [James] in the country, two centre-halves [Campbell and Distin] I wouldn't swap for anybody, a right-back [Johnson] who should be playing for England, that there's no better midfield player anywhere than Diarra and that Kanu's a magician. Well, get out there and prove it, will you?' He didn't need to ask twice. A combination of relentless industry and outstanding defensive work enabled Portsmouth to weather the inevitable United storm until fourteen minutes from time, when the goalkeeper Tomasz Kuszczak – a half-time replacement for the injured Edwin Van der Sar – was dismissed for a foul on Milan Baros. Sulley Muntari beat Rio Ferdinand from the resulting penalty. There was, inevitably, an element of fortune, most notably when Cristiano Ronaldo was denied a strong penalty claim, but Portsmouth's luck was earned, not gifted.

The same day, Chelsea lost 1-0 to Barnsley, who had previously accounted for Liverpool. With Arsenal also out, the winner would come from outside the top four for the first time in twelve years. More auspiciously still, Portsmouth – whose only top-flight opponents had been United – were the last Premier League side left in the competition. In the semi-finals, Cardiff defeated Barnsley 1-0 while Pompey duly saw off West Brom by the same scoreline. Redknapp was one win away from lifting the first major trophy of his career.

Portsmouth versus Cardiff: it might have lacked the glamour that the presence of a Liverpool or a United would have conferred, but it was – undeniably – a proper Cup final, a throwback to the days when the competition genuinely meant something. Redknapp, mind you, would have afforded the occasion due reverence whether the opponents had been Chelsea or Chelmsford. The previous season, on learning that Arsenal and Liverpool had fielded weakened sides, he lamented the gradual erosion of the traditions once associated with the old silver pot. 'It breaks my heart the way people are devaluing the Cup,' said Redknapp, who – like Cardiff counterpart Dave Jones – now stood to become the first Englishman to lift the trophy since Joe Royle thirteen years earlier. 'Cup Final day used to be the biggest of the year and the whole country used to come to a standstill. Maybe foreign managers don't understand how much the Cup means to us because in their own countries the cup does not count for anything.'

For Redknapp, it could hardly have meant more. The previous month, Sandra's twin sister Pat Lampard had died suddenly of pneumonia. Redknapp talked in the prelude to the game of lifting the trophy for his wife. He spoke too of his father, who would have bristled with pride at the sight of his son leading a team out for the

Wembley showpiece. With all the family present – Jamie and Louise, Mark and Lucy, six grandchildren, Frank Lampards young and old – it was a poignant occasion. 'At the final whistle I just felt an overwhelming sense of relief,' said Redknapp after Kanu had capitalised on a handling error by the Cardiff goalkeeper Peter Enckelman to give Portsmouth a 1-0 win. 'Today was difficult because everyone thought we were going to win, but it has been a funny year for the FA Cup. So many upsets. It was difficult because Sandra has been so low, and when it's hard for her, it's hard for me. I so badly wanted to win to put a smile on her face. She knew how much it meant, so she'll be happy today. That is the most important thing for me.'

Watching Redknapp hoist the trophy aloft, a blue and white scarf draped around his neck as he inched his way past the assembled dignitaries in the Royal Box, the mind incongruously drifted back to more troubled times. To the early days at Bournemouth, when his side leaked goals for fun; to his initial struggles to keep West Ham in the Premier League; to the defensive shortcomings of his Southampton team, forever found wanting at the death. The contrast drove home how important adaptability has been to Redknapp's longevity. The manner of Portsmouth's triumph – it was their fifth 1-0 victory in six games – confirmed as much. Rarely recognised for his emphasis on the defensive side of the game, Redknapp had surprised even seasoned observers by reinventing himself as the arch pragmatist. As his reaction at the final whistle demonstrated – eschewing triumphalism, he went immediately to commiserate Dave Jones – it was the same old Harry. But the subtle shift of emphasis in his approach was reflected in his post-match comments: Kanu aside, he reserved his most fulsome praise for James and Campbell.

'With Kanu, I knew he still had something to offer,' said Redknapp. 'He was on a free, his wages were small, I wanted to give him a go. How old is he? About forty-seven. He was in the dressing-room after the game saying, "Gaffer, gaffer, you give me a three-year contract." I said we'd talk about it on Monday. David James, I couldn't tell you the amount of people who rang me when I took David James. I wouldn't want to embarrass them. I had a few phone calls, all saying: "Are you mad?" But he is a fantastic keeper and I had no doubts he was the best around. I knew what I could get from him. I knew who I wanted.

'Sol Campbell was the same. All the phone calls: "He's finished. What are you doing taking him? You must be off your head." After I met him, I knew that he still wanted to play and still had a point to prove. He walked away from Arsenal. How do you walk away from Arsenal? He had three years of his contract left, worth something like £15m, and he walked away to join Portsmouth. I'll admit it wasn't the cleverest thing I've seen anyone do. Looking back, I don't know why I did take him, behaving like that. Particularly to come here on half the money. But I was up and down to London every day for about a week meeting him because I knew how much I wanted him to come. That was the key. He felt he wasn't wanted at Arsenal, but I said I'd make him captain and told him how good he was and what he could do for us.

'Once I got Sol and David James I knew we'd have no more relegation battles. With those two at the back, I could enjoy the next year because there was no way we'd be going down. There is no secret to it. I get the best out of them because I treat them well, with a bit of respect. If they have a problem and need a day off, they get it. As long as they respond in the right way, that's fine. I'm not a schoolteacher. I talk to a player and straight away I know whether he is up for it and whether he still wants to do something.'

'It was amazing for a club like Portsmouth to win the FA Cup and get European football,' says Dejan Stefanovic. 'Harry's got something special in him – like a magic – to persuade players to play for him.' Having taken Portsmouth as far as they could realistically go, many wondered if Redknapp would ever get the chance to cast his spell on a grander stage.

Chapter Nine

When it comes to animals, Harry Redknapp's preference is for dogs. Just as well. You wouldn't have fancied being a cat in the Redknapp household, not in the early weeks of 2005. Even the family bulldogs, Buster and Rosie, were probably steering well clear. The wounds from Redknapp's Portsmouth departure were still raw, Southampton remained deep in the relegation mire and his new club had been drawn against his old in the Cup. Definitely time to kick the proverbial cat, you would have thought, rather than kick back and think of North London. Redknapp saw it differently. 'Tottenham was the only big job where I got lots of mentions,' he said, recalling speculation eighteen months earlier that he was a contender to replace David Pleat. 'I thought that was a real possibility last season. That would've been good for me, but it's gone now.' At the time, there seemed little reason to doubt that gloomy prognosis. Though Redknapp had cried wolf before, there was a genuine feeling within the game that the Southampton job would be his last. That theory again proved wide of the mark, but subsequent events – the traumatic relegation, the return to Portsmouth, the rejection of Newcastle – merely hardened the impression that the chance to manage one of the so-called glamour clubs had permanently eluded him. By the time the FA Cup had been restored to the Fratton Park trophy cabinet for the first time since the Second World War, his bond with Pompey appeared unbreakable. Redknapp, it seemed, would see out the remainder of his professional life at the dilapidated old ground where the most memorable phase of his career had been played out. Big clubs don't come calling for managers specialising in escapology and the performance of miracles on a shoestring budget, however strong their other merits. They don't have to. Yet Redknapp has rarely kept company with convention, and it was in appropriately unusual circumstances that the path to preferment opened up. Too unusual for the liking of most Tottenham fans.

By early October of the 2008/09 season, a campaign that had started with talk of Spurs qualifying for the Champions League looked likelier to end in relegation. When a 1-0 home loss against Hull stretched a miserable league run to seven games without victory, leaving Tottenham bottom of the Premier League with just two points, it became the club's worst start to a season since 1912, the year the Titanic went down. When Spurs were subsequently beaten 2-1 at Stoke, it was rebranded the club's worst start to a season since before the First World War. By the time they had crashed to a third successive defeat, this time at Udinese in the Uefa Cup, it was open season. All at the club were fair game, but the bullet-dodger-in-chief was Juande Ramos, the Spanish head coach. Ramos had arrived a year earlier from Sevilla with a reputation for expansive football and a haul of five trophies in fifteen months, including consecutive Uefa Cups, that had established him as one of the hottest properties in world football. High expectations were matched by substantial investment – £77m in the previous summer alone – but, despite an impressive League Cup final win over Chelsea, Ramos had struggled to get the measure of the English league. Daniel Levy, the club chairman, was keen to give him more time – unsurprisingly, given that he had angered supporters by installing Ramos at the expense of Martin Jol, Tottenham's most successful manager for a quarter of a century. But time had run out; the situation demanded an explanation.

It is understood that the morning after the Udinese defeat, a group of senior players including Ledley King and Jonathan Woodgate was summoned before the club hierarchy. Had Ramos been a fly on the wall as the players confirmed that he had lost the faith of the dressing room, there is every chance he would have remained none the wiser. Almost a year after his arrival in N17, Ramos spoke barely a word of English. Already nonplussed by the language of Premier League football, his inability to communicate with his labouring, demoralised squad compounded the tactical uncertainty and inconsistency of selection undermining Tottenham's fortunes. Ramos had become a shadow of the man once praised by the Sevilla goalkeeper Andres Palop for his meticulous preparation and incisive team-talks. As tongue-tied of Tottenham stood silently brooding –

arms folded, impassive, a grey man in a grey coat – it fell to his assistant, Gus Poyet, to coax and cajole from the sidelines. The appearance was one of management by proxy.

In mitigation, Ramos was in part undermined from within. Damien Comolli, the sporting director at the heart of the ill-conceived continental-style system imposed by Levy, was a culpably ineffective custodian of Tottenham's transfer fortunes. Comolli failed to fill the attacking void created by the departures of Robbie Keane and Dimitar Berbatov, for Liverpool and Manchester United respectively, and ignored Ramos' requests for a central defender and a midfield anchorman. The Frenchman instead recruited a raft of attackers including David Bentley and Luka Modric – lampshades to the requested sofas, to borrow from the managerial idiom of Rafael Benitez. Like Ramos and his first-team assistants Poyet and Marcos Alvarez, Comolli would soon be clearing his desk.

While the holders of one domestic cup were labouring on the pitch, the champions of the other were struggling away from it. For most Portsmouth fans not drawing a pension, May's trip to Wembley had been the most rewarding day of their lives as disciples of the Fratton faith. Amid the euphoria of reaching the final, Alexandre Gaydamak talked eagerly of improving the club's infrastructure by building a new stadium and proper training facilities. Peter Storrie, who suggested afterwards that a statue of Redknapp should be erected at Fratton Park in honour of his achievements at Portsmouth, shared his enthusiasm. 'We're going to bring in more players, strengthen the team and get better and better,' he said. 'We'll be looking to bring more quality players in and widen the squad as well. It's our job to go on and win more. We're not going to stand still now. We need to build on this.' Financial factors would dictate otherwise, however. Gaydamak had funded the construction of Portsmouth's Cup-winning side with hefty loans; as the global economy lurched from credit crunch to recession, and a debt that had stood at £44m by the end of May spiralled closer to £60m, it became clear that the club was living beyond its means. Departures were inevitable. By the start of the next campaign, half the Cup-winning midfield had been sold, Sulley Muntari leaving for Internazionale and Pedro Mendes for Rangers. By December, Gaydamak had put the club up for sale. Redknapp did not need to wait until that moment – or for the next transfer window, and the inevitable sale of more big names – to realise that his zenith as Portsmouth manager was already behind him.

Even with this confluence of circumstances – and for all his receptiveness when Levy called him to broach the subject of replacing Ramos – Redknapp had a decision to make. Successive top-ten finishes and the acquisition of a major trophy had cemented Pompey's status as a solid Premier League club. At sixty-one, with money in the bank, a house of dreams in one of Europe's most sought-after locations, and a negligible daily commute, why opt for upheaval?

'I think it's like everything else in life,' says Milan Mandaric, 'at certain times, there are certain things that need to be done. The timing was right for Harry. He's always had admiration for [Tottenham], and it's a big club. Harry had been at Portsmouth a long time and he had proved how capable he is – it was time for him to make one more big move in his life. It was a tremendous opportunity. Once I knew that he had a chance there, I knew Harry would take it. He had to take it, there was no way in a million years that he would have missed out on that one.'

Alan Hudson chalks up the decision to experience, suggesting that the two-club man of a decade earlier would not have seized the moment with such alacrity. 'He couldn't go any further at Portsmouth and he could see what was going on at Tottenham,' says Hudson. 'Ten years ago, Harry probably wouldn't have seen it that way. But he can spot things like that now, it's part of his make-up. That comes down to experience.'

'Harry had never had the chance to manage a top club,' says Jimmy Gabriel, who watched the latest improbable twist in Redknapp's career with rapt fascination. 'All the clubs he's been at before, he's wheeled and dealed. He's gone and got the players that he wanted and brought them to the level that he knew he could bring them to, and his clubs would not have survived if Harry hadn't done that. But now it's his turn to be at the top. I'm looking forward to Tottenham, in the next few years, rising back up to where they were in the sixties, when Dave Mackay was there and they won the league and Cup. They were a fantastic team then, with a great coach. And I think that's what Harry can do for them. Not to put any burden on him, but having worked with him, and seen how good he is at managing, I think it's something he can do.'

Gabriel's assessment might raise a few eyebrows along the Tottenham High Road, but Trevor Hartley – who briefly took up the reins at Spurs himself following David Pleat's departure in 1987 – likewise believes that Redknapp can roll back the years. Perhaps not to the glory, glory days of the early sixties, but certainly as far as that memorable 1986/87 campaign when Spurs finished third, reached the FA Cup final and made the semi-finals of the League Cup. 'When I was at Tottenham as David Pleat's number two, we had a very good team,' recalls Hartley, Redknapp's former West Ham and Bournemouth team-mate. 'They've had a lot of foreign managers since, but I think Harry could become the best manager they've had since David left. It's a long overdue opportunity for Harry, because he's always had to fight for recognition, fight for money [to buy players], and cope with players who are coming to the end of their careers – the Sol Campbells, the David Jameses. He's always done well with getting teams away from the relegation zone, taken them into mid-table, and people have said "Good old Harry". But I think he wants to work at the other end of it now, the top end. Winning the FA Cup gave him a huge lift because he'd won something big, and I think he wants to take that on. The chances of doing that look better at Tottenham than at Portsmouth, where the chairman wanted to leave. Although that came out a bit later, Harry would have known that. So he's stepping up the ladder at the biggest club he's managed so far, and I'm sure he'll have designs on challenging at the upper end of the table.'

The evidence that Redknapp can get the once-proud cockerel crowing again has so far been encouraging. The first seven months of his Tottenham career fell into three distinct phases. First came a dramatic nine-game run during which he could do no wrong, inspiring a 2-1 win over Liverpool, draws against Arsenal and Manchester United, and an impressive return of seventeen points that lifted Spurs clear of the relegation zone. A month-long lull during which the Midas touch briefly deserted him brought three defeats – including losses against Newcastle and West Brom, sides that would later be relegated – and two draws, leaving Tottenham above the bottom three only on goal difference. But then came the third phase, a powerful resurgence from late January onwards which carried the club to an eighth-place finish. Given the situation Redknapp inherited, it was a remarkable turnaround. Repeated over the course of the entire season, his average return of 1.63 points per game would have taken Spurs into the Europa League ahead of Fulham. Throw in a run to the League Cup final, where the trophy won under Ramos was prised from Tottenham's grasp by Manchester United only after extra-time and penalties, and the potential for progress is clear.

'Harry had to put in a hell of a lot of effort to try and lift people when he arrived,' says Alvin Martin, who has experienced Redknapp's ability to lift a demoralised dressing room at first hand. 'There was a lot of pressure on the players because of their position. It's very hard to come into that situation and follow it through. But he's now had a proper pre-season with the players, he's had a chance to see what he needs to work on, and – with all that taken into consideration – I think Spurs will improve impressively.' The early months of the 2009/10 campaign have offered ample support for Martin's optimistic forecast, an impressive opening-day win over Liverpool providing the platform for Tottenham's best start to a season in fifty years.

Redknapp's appointment at Tottenham heralded the dismantling of an ethos. Shifting away from sporting directors and the other paraphernalia associated with the continental style of football management, Spurs have embraced a more traditional model, one based on managerial autocracy. It could not have been otherwise. Even without the markers laid down by the Velimir Zajec and Clive Woodward episodes, Levy must have known that Redknapp would not tolerate having players foisted upon him by a middle man. The opening of the January 2009 transfer window emphasised that point. It is unimaginable that Comolli would have countenanced Redknapp's re-signing of Jermain Defoe, Pascal Chimbonda and Robbie Keane, all of whom had been allowed to leave the club during his tenure as sporting director. That Redknapp felt it necessary to bring back the trio was a glaring indictment of the maladroit manner in which club's resources had been handled. 'I don't know of a squad in world football assembled in as poor a way as the one that was assembled by Tottenham,' says Martin. 'It was so disjointed and ramshackle, without any real intelligence. I think it reflects the poor judgement of the people who were at Tottenham before. Harry knows a player, and the fact that they'd been selling players who he would have kept casts a great shadow over the people who were there before.'

More mischievous observers might be tempted to suggest that, in recruiting former Tottenham players, Redknapp was merely indulging a familiar habit. He has spent so much of his recent career poaching personnel from White Hart Lane that you began to wonder why the Tottenham board didn't just appoint him manager and be done with it. Those who come over all misty-eyed at the mere mention of the Double-winning 1960/61 season will no doubt put this trend down to a natural harmony between Redknapp's preference for flair players and the attacking tradition founded by Bill Nicholson. Martin, however, cautions against such a reading. 'Harry only brings players in who he knows are going to do a job for him,' he says. 'He will take risks on players, but whether or not they've played for Tottenham before won't matter a jot to Harry. All that matters is whether they're the right player. So he looks at that – forget the other bits and pieces, he looks for a player. He'll ask "What can he do, and does my team need that?" That's the be all and end all for Harry.' Richard Cooke, who grew up on Redknapp's new manor, is not so sure. 'Harry likes ball players,' says Cooke, 'and Tottenham were brought up on that style – players who can play. So it doesn't surprise me that he's always gone to Tottenham to get players.'

As the Ramos era demonstrated, however, there is a profound difference between buying talented players and bringing their ability to the surface. A case in point is Luka Modric, the Croatia playmaker whose £16.5m acquisition from Dinamo Zagreb equalled the club transfer record established by the signing of Darren Bent. The addition of a player whose intelligent prompting in the final third twice embarrassed England in qualifying for the European Championships – and later won him a place in Uefa's team of the tournament – seemed certain to give Spurs a new dimension. Slaven Bilic, Modric's manager at international level, was not alone in the belief that his countryman would become 'the star of [Tottenham's] team.' But Ramos deployed Modric in a central midfield role that rendered him a peripheral figure, denying him the space and time to bring the full range of his substantial repertoire to bear. Before long, many onlookers were of the view that Modric lacked the physical presence to make an impact in the Premier League.

Redknapp demolished that myth within hours of his arrival, simply by shunting Modric into a more advanced role behind Roman Pavlyuchenko. 'That is his position,' he said after the win against Bolton that marked the turning point in Tottenham's season, 'he needs to be free. I've never seen him as part of a four-four-two, because that withdrawn role is where he can do most damage. I had Eyal Berkovic at West Ham United and Portsmouth, and he was very similar. Give him the ball and give him space and he can win the game for you.' Another influential performance in the 4-4 draw with Arsenal three days later – including a vital contribution in the build-up to Tottenham's dramatic late equaliser – confirmed Redknapp's initial instincts. 'I've seen Modric play for Croatia and he's undoubtedly a special player,' he said. 'It's difficult for him to play as one of two central midfielders. He's got to play further forward. He's got that amazing football brain.'

Tottenham's Uefa Cup meeting with Spartak Moscow offered further evidence of Redknapp's tactical acumen and ability to get the best from his players. Spartak's hopes of progressing to the knock-out stages hinged on beating Spurs by two clear goals while hoping that NEC Nijmegen could do the same against Udinese. With injuries rife and league points the priority, Redknapp was forced to field a weakened side. The Russians took full advantage, their technical virtuosity overwhelming Tottenham as they established a 2-0 half-time lead. Redknapp was visibly unimpressed. Gilberto, the left-back whose inexplicable failure to complete a routine clearance led to the opening goal, no doubt felt the brunt of his manager's wrath. The Brazilian was substituted, Gareth Bale filled the resulting gap in defence and Aaron Lennon came on to inject greater dynamism down the right. It was the kind of clear-headed, incisive decision-making that so frequently seemed to elude Ramos – and it reaped dividends. Lennon's pace and trickery set up Modric before Bale, uncharacteristically more effective as an overlapping full-back than he had been on the left of midfield, centred for Tom Huddlestone to equalise. Tottenham were through to the knockout phase.

One newspaper described the turnaround as 'near miraculous', but to Jimmy Gabriel the greater surprise lay in Spurs' early sluggishness. 'It was unusual for a Tottenham team under Harry – or any team under Harry – to go out and play like they did in the first half,' says Gabriel. 'There were no attacking moves, no finishing moves. It was like they were playing the game just to enjoy it. Then, in the second half, they came out and they were going for the jugular. They scored two goals, got back in the game, made it 2-2, and almost won it. There were two different teams, one in the first half and one in the second. Who brought that out? Harry. He finds the spot that will get the players out there ready to do better, ready to work harder. It's that extra something that all the great managers have. They can press a button inside their players' heads somewhere that gets them to play like Tottenham did in the second half of that game; they know how to get them motivated. That comes from the understanding of the individual players you've got in there, and from the understanding of the players as a group as well. Having been there with Harry in dressing rooms before, I thought "Look out, Spartak, a storm is coming your way." You just knew it. And that's talent. You've got to have the talent and [command] the respect to be able to do that. All players have that bit extra for when they need it, and I think Harry's great at getting a line on that and bringing it to the surface. The great managers do that.'

'I treat all players the same,' says Redknapp, whose real work at Tottenham is just beginning. 'It takes time to build a team, it's a bit like a jigsaw if you like. But in the end all the players have got to where they are because as kids they really, really loved playing the game.'

Half a century ago, Redknapp himself was one of those kids, loving every second as he chased a ball up and down Barchester Street with his mates. That passion, and the pin-sharp footballing intelligence that underlies it, remains undiminished. Something for the FA to bear in mind when Fabio Capello eventually steps down as England manager.